CHINESE AMERICA
HISTORY AND PERSPECTIVES
The Journal of the Chinese Historical Society of America
2009

SPECIAL ISSUE
Seizing the Moment:
Twentieth-Century
Chinese American Activism

CHINESE HISTORICAL SOCIETY OF AMERICA
with UCLA Asian American Studies Center

Chinese America: History & Perspectives – The Journal of the Chinese Historical Society of America
"Seizing the Moment: Twentieth-Century Chinese American Activism"
A special volume on the fortieth anniversary of a wealth of activism in the San Francisco Bay Area and beyond
(San Francisco: Chinese Historical Society of America with UCLA Asian American Studies Center, 2009)

Chinese Historical Society of America
Museum & Learning Center
965 Clay Street
San Francisco, California 94108
chsa.org

ISBN 13: 978-1-885864-40-6

Design by Side By Side Studios, San Francisco.
Printed in the USA by Thomson-Shore, Inc.

To order additional copies or inquire about large-order discounts, see order form at back or email *bookstore@chsa.org*.

Articles appearing in this journal are indexed in *Historical Abstracts* and *America: History and Life*.

About the cover image:

Students at San Francisco's Galileo High School march in 1970 to make the family-oriented Chinese New Year's Day a school holiday. *East/West* reported 250 students marching on Van Ness Avenue. (Leland Wong photograph, reproduced courtesy of the photographer; *East/West* March 11, 1970, Philip P. Choy Collection, CHSA)

Contents

List of Images

TAKING TO THE STREETS
Scenes from 1968–72

ART AND LIVING REVOLUTION
Gary Woo and AION Magazine

A BOOKSTORE FOR EVERYBODY

SCENES FROM THE *BAODIAO* MOVEMENT IN THE UNITED STATES

MAURICE H. CHUCK AND *THE SAN FRANCISCO JOURNAL*
Promoting U.S.-China Friendship and Relevant Asian American Issues

THE MAKING OF THE *CHINESE AMERICAN SYMPHONY*

Introduction

Seizing the Moment: Twentieth-Century Chinese American Activism

*A special volume on the fortieth anniversary of a wealth of activism
in the San Francisco Bay Area and beyond*

The 2009 issue of *Chinese America: History & Perspectives* is subtitled "Seizing the Moment: Twentieth-Century Chinese American Activism" and includes articles highlighting political activism in certain causes among the Chinese in America from the late 1920s to the present.

During the 1920s and 1930s China was victimized by Western imperialism, while in America racial discrimination was common. Thus it is not surprising that some Chinese in America chose to support the revolution in China to cast off the yoke of imperialism as a step to rebuild the nation and restore China as a respected member of the international community. They believed this development would also upgrade the status of Chinese in America. Zhang Bao, author of "Chinese Communists in the United States during the 1920s and 1930s," was a student from China who joined the American Communist Party (CPUSA). He describes activities supporting the Chinese revolution led by the Kuomintang (KMT), supported by the Chinese Communist Party and allied with the Soviet Union. His experiences in the American Communist movement up to the early 1930s reflected those of other early Chinese CPUSA members, many of whom were students who intended eventually to return to China to participate in the revolution.

Him Mark Lai presents a somewhat different perspective in "The Life and Times of Benjamin Fee." He describes the career of a Chinese American who joined the Young Communist League and then CPUSA during approximately the same period as Zhang Bao. However, by the early 1930s the Chinese revolution was at a low point, and during the Great Depression in the United States the Communists not only participated in activities supporting the Communist revolution in China but also turned to labor organizing and other activities to build a base of support in the Chinese American community. The essay on Ben Fee includes excerpts from letters Fee wrote to Him Mark Lai during the early 1970s discussing his career as a party activist. One of these comments on an article by Him Mark Lai on the Chinese Left in America. Fee apparently left the party during the 1940s and his reflections on pre–World War II CPUSA activities, written three decades afterward, are interesting commentaries by a former party insider. The essay also presents Fee's views on the literary movement that arose among the Chinese Left in

America during the 1940s, an important goal of which was to give expression to the Chinese American identity in literary writings originating from the Chinese American community. Elsewhere in this issue are translations of six poems from Fee's *Collected Poems of Mu-yün*, most of which touch on contemporary political and social issues. Except for "On the Shore of the Black Sea," which was written in the USSR in 1931, these poems were written after he had left CPUSA.

After World War II the Communist victory in China resulted in the founding of the People's Republic of China (PRC), which became involved in the Cold War between the Western and Communist blocs, resulting in two decades of tension and hostility with the United States. The founding of China Books and Periodicals as an initial small step toward bridging the gulf between these two great powers is described in an excerpt from founder Henry Noyes's autobiographic *China Born*, while Him Mark Lai's "The Changing Roles Played by China Books and Periodicals" discusses the roles of this company and Chinese international corporations as the United States and the PRC took successive steps toward normalization of diplomatic relations and the PRC became an increasingly important player in international commerce and exchanges.

A Chinese American identity that had been evolving ever since the first Chinese American was born and raised in this country became firmly established after World War II as relaxation of discriminatory legislation and practices fostered the growth of a Chinese American middle class during the postwar expansion of the American economy. Along with other U.S. ethnic minority communities, Chinese Americans continually sought equal rights in American society. By the 1960s, in an environment influenced by the ongoing Civil Rights movement, members of the Chinese American community moved to critically examine community issues and problems and to bring the community in as an equal part of American society. William Wong's "*East/West*: The Chinese American Journal" narrates the history of a weekly that for more than twenty-two years recorded and reported on issues and changes in the San Francisco Chinese American community. The paper also helped educate readers on the Chinese historical role and contributions in the building of America. These efforts helped enable the Chinese Historical Society of

America to convene the first seminar on Chinese American history in 1969, targeting educators. This volume reprints a critique of this event by L. Ling-chi Wang, "California Chinese seminar a landmark."

The social ferment in America sparked by the Civil Rights and anti–Vietnam War movements of the late 1960s also gave birth to activist groups in a number of ethnic minority communities, including the Chinese. These groups often were part of Asian American coalitions that challenged the existing conservative leadership dominating the Chinese communities. This issue includes three articles by members of one such group, Wei Min She, which operated out of the Asian Community Center (ACC) in San Francisco Chinatown. Jeanie Dere's "A Wei Min Sister Remembers" is an autobiographic essay by a San Franciscan from a progressive family that also paradoxically held traditional Chinese attitudes toward females. The article traces her transformation into a political activist, from participation in the SFSU student strike to active roles in Wei Min She, the Revolutionary Communist Party, and other activist groups. Harvey Dong's "Third World Liberation Comes to San Francisco State and UC Berkeley" analyzes the student strikes at SFSU and UC Berkeley during the late 1960s that resulted in the founding of ethnic studies programs in these institutions, and his "A Bookstore for Everybody" narrates the history and struggles of the first bookstore established in San Francisco Chinatown since the 1950s, selling publications from the PRC.

The Protecting Diaoyutai movement, which Chih-ming Wang describes and analyzes in "Tracking Baodiao: Diaspora, Sovereignty, and Chinese American Resistance," was inspired by the example of the Asian American movement but initiated by a territorial dispute between China and Japan. This movement was of short duration, but a number of the activists also became participants in Asian American movement groups in the San Francisco Bay Area.

The *San Francisco Journal* can be considered the voice resulting from the confluence of efforts to improve U.S.-China relations and advocacy on relevant Asian American issues. A number of Baodiao and Asian American activists became actively engaged with the paper. Its story is related in "Maurice H. Chuck and the *San Francisco Journal*: Promoting U.S.-China Friendship and Asian American Issues," which consists of selected sections translated from a chapter in Xiong Guohua, *An American Dream: The Life and Times of Huang Yunji (Maurice H. Chuck), Chinese American*.

During the last half of the twentieth century the Chinese American identity also began to be expressed in the arts and literature. An example is presented in Jon Jang's "The Making of the *Chinese American Symphony*."

In this volume the editors strove for consistency in transliteration of Chinese terms and names within each essay but not throughout the publication. Spellings used in the United States are given preference.

Chinese Communists in the United States during the 1920s and 1930s
A Memoir
二三十年代美国的中国共产党人

Zhang Bao 张报

TRANSLATION AND ANNOTATIONS BY HIM MARK LAI 麦礼谦

Translator's Note: These are the memoirs of Communist Party member Zhang Bao published in *Guoji Gongyun shi ziliao* 国际共运史资料 (Historical Materials on the International Communist Movement), seventh collection, ed. CPC Bureau for Editing and Translation of Works of Marx, Engels, Lenin, and Stalin 中共马恩列斯著作编译局 (Beijing: Remin Chubanshe 人民出版社, 1982).

Zhang Bao (1903–96) was a native of Guangxi province. Originally named Mo Guoshi or Mo Zhengdan, and also known as James Mo in the United States, he graduated from Beijing Normal University in 1926 and became a graduate student at George Peabody College for Teachers in Tennessee and the University of Chicago. He joined the American Communist Party (CPUSA) in 1928 and became active in the All-America Alliance of Chinese Anti-Imperialists (AACAI) and editor of the AACAI organ *Chinese Vanguard*. He also was secretary and lecturer at CPUSA's Workers School in New York. Mo succeeded Li Tao Hsuan as secretary of the Chinese Bureau around 1931 after the latter was arrested and deported. He in turn became the target of harassment by U.S. authorities in August 1932. He was forced to resign his position at the Chinese Bureau and Chee Fun Ho was summoned from Philadelphia to succeed him. With the help of the CPUSA organization Mo secretly fled to the Soviet Union, where he studied at the Lenin School in Moscow. In 1935 he changed his name to Zhang Bao and transferred his CPUSA membership to membership in the Communist Party of China (CPC). That year *Giu Guo Sh Bao/Au Secours de la Patrie*, the organ of the CPC delegation to the Comintern, began publication, and Zhang became its deputy editor under chief editor Li Lisan. This newspaper was at first a semimonthly, then a weekly, and then a five-day publication. It was edited in Moscow and published in Paris.

In February 1938 Zhang was caught in the anti-Trotskyite purges in the Soviet Union and was sent to a labor camp in the Komi Autonomous Republic near the Arctic Circle. He was not released until September 1955. Returning to China in early 1956 after an absence of three decades, he was in charge of broadcasting programs in Russian. In 1964 he joined the CPC Central Committee's Editing and Translation Bureau and was involved in translating selected works of Mao Zedong and Zhou Enlai, as well as numerous documents issued by the Central Committee. During the Cultural Revolution he was sent to the 7 May Cadre School in Jiangxi.[1] In 1972 he returned to Beijing's Editing and Translation Bureau, from which he retired in 1983.[2]

The memoirs cover the initial period of Chinese Communist activities in the United States from the mid-1920s to the early 1930s from the perspective of a participating Communist revolutionary. At the beginning of this period the Chinese Communist Left in America was allied with the Kuomintang in its move to unify China. Through the early 1930s the movement developed as the opposition to the Kuomintang, which had broken with and purged the Communists in 1927. During this period the principal objective of the Chinese Marxist Left in the United States was to support the Chinese revolution and many, especially the students, eventually returned to China, often playing important roles in political developments. It was only later that the Chinese left successfully established workers' and youth organizations and a daily newspaper, *China Daily News*, to reach out to the Chinese community in America.

The author wrote these memoirs half a century after the events. Annotations by the translator/editor point out some discrepancies with other accounts and provide biographical information, where available, on these early Communists to give the reader a more complete overall picture of the personalities and events of the period.

Variations in spelling due to different transliteration schemes at different periods pose a challenge to consistency in this translation. The translator/editor has chosen to use the transliteration scheme of the period in which the person being discussed was active wherever such transliterations are known. If only the Chinese characters were available, however, then the transliteration is in Hanyu pinyin. —HML

At the end of the 1920s, Chinese students in the United States and progressive elements of the Chinese community began to join the Communist Party, thus establishing a Chinese Communist Fraction and a Chinese Bureau in the party.[3] The hardships and struggles of Chinese Communist Party members in America in uniting as one to strive for communism and for the Chinese revolution are worth recalling.

EARLY CHINESE COMMUNIST PARTY MEMBERS AND THE CHINESE BUREAU

The actions of progressives among Chinese students and in the Chinese community in joining the Communist Party at that time could be said to be natural and logical results of developments in the Chinese revolution. Soon after the failure of the Great Revolution of 1927, students from China Shi Huang 施滉 (Shih Huang),[4] Ji Chaoding 冀朝鼎 (C. T. Chi),[5] Xu Yongying 徐永煐 (Y. Y. Hsu),[6] Luo Jingyi 罗静宜 (S. S. Lo),[7] Zhang Youjiang 章友江 (Y. C. Chang),[8] Shi Zuo 石佐 (Shih Tso),[9] and Mei Ru'ao 梅汝璈 (Ju-Ao Mei)[10] in San Francisco and Chicago (all except S. S. Lo were students from Qinghua [Tsinghua] School)[11] saw through the reactionary nature of Chiang Kai-shek and the Kuomintang regime and firmly believed that only the Communist Party could carry the revolution to a successful conclusion, and that only socialism could save China. Therefore in 1927 they were determined to join CPUSA and became the first group of Chinese students abroad to become Communist Party members. Other students in San Francisco, Chicago, Philadelphia, Boston, and Madison who later became CPUSA members included:

Xie Qitai 谢启泰 (aka Zhang Hanfu 章汉夫)[12]

Li Daoxuan 李道煊 (Li Tao Hsuan)[13]

Huang Gongshou 黄恭寿

Li Fahuan 李法寰

Wu Zhaofa 武兆发

Hu Dunyuan (Thomas T. Y. Hu) 胡敦元[14]

Zhang Bao (aka Mo Guoshi 莫国史, Mo Zhendan 莫震旦, James Mo)

He Zhifen 何植芬 (Chee Fun Ho, Henry Hahn)[15]

Su Kaiming (Frank K. M. Su) 苏开明[16]

Yu Zhipei 虞芝佩

Wei Minghua 魏明华[17]

Chen Kemei 陈科美[18]

Yu Guangsheng 余光生 (aka Yu Rixin 余日辛)[19]

Zhang Hongmei 张鸿眉

Workers in the Chinese community who joined the party at that time included:

Liu Kemian 刘克勉[20]

Zhao Yue 赵跃[21]

Lin Tang (Thomas Lem Tong) 林棠[22]

Ouyang Ji 欧阳基[23]

Xie Chuang 谢创 (Xavier Dea)[24]

Chen Huijian 陈慧剑 (Cen Huijian 岑慧剑, Alice Sum)[25]

Zhang Hentang 张恨棠 (Benjamin Fee)[26]

Zeng Dingyuan 曾丁垣

Chen Houfu 陈厚父[27]

He Huiliang 何惠良

Feng Hanping 冯汉平

Zhou Binghun 周冰魂

Xu Jiyun 许纪云

By the beginning of the 1930s, Chinese Communist Party members in the United States totaled approximately fifty, with San Francisco, Philadelphia, and New York being the cities with the greatest numbers of party members.

Because the Communist parties in every country were all under the leadership of the Communist International (Comintern), Chinese who became Communist Party members in the United States all joined the grassroots organizations led by CPUSA and participated in their activities. To facilitate activities among Chinese students and the Chinese community, Chinese party members became a Chinese Fraction 中国党团 with a Central Chinese Bureau 中央中国局 that provided leadership for such activities. Chinese Bureaus 中国局 were established in areas where there were more party members, such as San Francisco, New York, Philadelphia, Chicago, Boston, and Madison. If an area had fewer than three Communist Party members, then they were led by the nearest Chinese Bureau and the Central Chinese Bureau. The Central Chinese Bureau was located in the same locale as the CPUSA Central Committee. For example, when the CPUSA Central Committee moved from Chicago to New York City in January 1927, the Central Chinese Bureau also moved to New York City. The first leader (secretary) of the Central Chinese Bureau was Shih Huang, followed by Li Tao Hsuan, Zhang Bao, and Henry Hahn. From what I could find out, Y. Y. Hsu, Yu Guangsheng, and Tang Mingzhao 唐明照 (Chu Tong) succeeded them.[28]

At that time CPUSA was public, but for obvious reasons the Chinese Fraction was clandestine. Each Chinese party member had a name he or she used within the party. For example, Shih Huang was known as Dongsheng, C. T. Chi as Dongping 动平, Y. Y. Hsu as Huafa 化发, Zhang Bao as Xuehan 学涵, etc. Chinese party members usually did not openly reveal their party membership. The principal reason was to avoid attracting the attention of U.S. authorities, Kuomintang reactionaries, and their special agents, and also to facilitate their activities among students and in the Chinese community, and their participation in underground activities after they returned to China.

THE PRINCIPAL TASK WAS TO ADVANCE THE CAUSE OF THE CHINESE REVOLUTION

Chinese Communist Party members in the United States all had to participate in CPUSA activities, including the party's internal struggles. It is worthy of mention that members of the Chinese Fraction all firmly supported the correct line during the internal party struggles of the 1920s, such as the struggle against the Trotskyists as represented by James Cannon.[29] When William Z. Foster led the CPUSA "minority" to struggle against Jay Lovestone's "majority,"[30] members of the Chinese Fraction stood on the side of the "minority's" relatively more correct line. Beside these activities, members of the Chinese Fraction also participated in daily tasks and political activities planned and led by CPUSA.

But on the whole the central task of the Chinese Fraction was to advance the cause of the Chinese revolution. First, under the leadership of the Central Chinese Bureau, Chinese Communist Party members all actively coordinated with and participated in all activities organized by CPUSA to support the Chinese revolution. For example, in April 1927, when CPUSA organized a large-scale "hands off China" movement opposing American imperialistic interference in the internal affairs of China through support of Chiang Kai-shek against the Communists, the Chinese comrades played useful roles in various U.S. cities to enable the movement to be better organized and have a greater publicity impact. The Chinese comrades also often provided the CPUSA news organ *Daily Worker* with documents on the Chinese revolution received from the CPC and had them published in party organs of ethnic minorities such as *Advance*.

C. T. Chi, Zhang Bao, and others also used pseudonyms to submit essays on the Chinese revolution, such as "Progress in the Chinese Revolution and Its Future," "The High Tide of the Chinese Revolution and the Trotskyite Liquidationists," and "The Chinese Bourgeoisie and the Democratic Revolution," for publication in the *Communist*, CPUSA's publication on Communist theory. In 1931 Chi and Zhang, using the pseudonyms Dongping and James, respectively, collaborated to publish the pamphlet *Soviet China*, introducing the background of the Chinese revolution, the current situation, and the successful growth of the Chinese Soviet Red Army under CPC leadership. It was a work welcomed by the American people. Later the Chinese delegation to the Comintern gave it to the Foreign Workers Publishing House in Moscow to reprint and distribute.

The Chinese comrades, beside actively participating in mass meetings and demonstrations in support of the Chinese revolution and opposing attempts by Chinese warlords to provoke trouble (such as in September 1929, when the Communists opposed attempts by warlord Zhang Zuolin 张作霖 [Chang Tso-lin] to provoke the Soviet Union),[31] also actively participated in other public activities, such as celebration of May 1 and commemoration of the October Revolution, sending representatives to speak and call upon the audience to support the Chinese revolution. Through the Workers School of the CPUSA Central Committee (Zhang Bao was at the time secretary and lecturer at the school), the Chinese Communists also organized Sunday lectures where the principal speakers, besides C. T. Chi and other Chinese comrades, included

CPUSA leaders such as William Z. Foster. After the speeches, many in the audience enthusiastically made comments showing their support for the Chinese revolution.

To strengthen publicity among students, the Central Chinese Bureau in the summer of 1931 sent C. T. Chi and Zhang Bao to Columbia University to participate in a debate in the English language with students in the Kuomintang right-wing faction on the topic "The Current Situation and the Future in China." Chi and Zhang presented the facts logically in their speeches and rebuttals, pointing out that Chiang Kai-shek, in toadying to foreign nations to seek glory, was bringing calamity to the nation and the Chinese people and in the end would certainly be defeated. The Communist Party and the Soviet Red Army (the Chinese Soviets fighting valiantly to liberate the Chinese people) would surely win in the end. After the meeting many American students expressed their agreement with Chi and Zhang.

The Chinese comrades also were active in some mass organizations of the American people; for example, they actively worked with the leadership of the Seamen's Union of New York, calling upon seamen and longshoremen to refuse to load scrap iron and other military materials destined for Chiang Kai-shek and his reactionary regime, and attained some tangible results. This led Mao Zedong, Zhou Enlai, and Zhu De to send a cablegram to the CPUSA Central Committee in 1937 expressing their gratitude.

THE ALLIANCE OF CHINESE ANTI-IMPERIALISTS AND OTHER ORGANIZATIONS

At that time there were about 300,000 to 400,000 Chinese in the communities and several thousand Chinese students. They were doubtless the principal targets of the activities of the Chinese Communist Party members. However, in this sector the Chinese Bureau encountered difficulties and obstacles that were not insignificant. The majority of Chinese in the community, in addition to being influenced by the Kuomintang's reactionary propaganda, were also fettered by the feudalistic thinking of the traditionalist fraternal, native-place, clan, and guild organizations, such as Chee Kung Tong, Chinese Consolidated Benevolent Association, Chiu Yat Association, etc., which made it difficult for them to understand or to be interested in communist ideals and the true picture of the Chinese revolution. Another part of the population, such as the Kuomintang right-wing faction, the Nationalist groups, and the promonarchy party,[32] however, furiously carried on anti-Communist activities. In spite of this, Chinese Communist Party members under the leadership of the Central Chinese Bureau patiently continued their difficult task, overcoming difficulties step by step, and attained the results sought by their propaganda and organized activities.

The great majority of Chinese in America made their living in Chinese restaurants and laundries; therefore the Chinese Bureau organized restaurant and laundry unions to target this situation. But because they did not go deeply among the masses and were inflexible in the application of organizing methods, and also because these Chinese workers were scattered all over the city, not many joined the unions. At that time most who responded positively were members of the AACAI 美洲华侨反帝大同盟. Just as its name implies, this was a united-front organization based on the principles of anti-imperialism and support for the Chinese revolution. Chinese in any trade or profession as well as students belonging to any party or clique could join. Shih Huang established AACAI in San Francisco in 1927. Later branches were established in some U.S. cities, as well as Cuba and Canada. AACAI moved its headquarters to New York City in 1928. Following the political divisions in China, which were becoming more obvious day by day, one after another of the more politically conscious students and community Chinese joined AACAI and caused it to become one of the peripheral organizations led by the Central Chinese Bureau that had a relatively large membership. The Chinese Bureau also frequently organized public activities among students and community Chinese using AACAI as the sponsoring group.

In addition, AACAI often participated in meetings and marches led by CPUSA or other revolutionary organizations with pretty good results. For example, on May 1, 1931, AACAI's bright red horizontal banner with Chinese characters was displayed prominently in a large-scale parade in New York City. AACAI members who participated in the parade marched in a square formation, holding signs with slogans in English, such as "Hands off China," "Support the Chinese revolution," "Protect world peace!" and "We oppose unemployment and demand relief." Everyone also sang revolutionary songs such as the "Internationale" and "Workers, peasants, soldiers work together" in unison. Onlookers on both sides of the street responded with friendly smiles and enthusiastic applause. At the end of the parade the participants held a mass rally at Union Square, and AACAI's representatives were among those who spoke on the platform, calling upon everyone to oppose U.S. interference in China and to support the Chinese revolution. There were similar events in other cities and venues.

In the minds of community Chinese and students, AACAI was a peripheral organization close to the Communist Party; therefore AACAI members were all suspected of being Communist Party members, and most of those who considered joining the Communist Party joined AACAI first to receive the party's training and testing. At that time AACAI was quite influential and had rather high prestige. Those leading AACAI activities in various years included Shih Huang, Y. Y. Hsu, Li Tao Hsuan, Zhang Bao, Henry Hahn, Liu Kemian, Zhao Yue, and Yu Guangsheng.

To increase activities among Chinese students in America, Shih Huang and other comrades established the Zhongshan Xuehui 中山学会 [Sun Yat-sen Learned Society] in San Francisco in the summer of 1927. Its program was the study and publicizing of the revolutionary Three Principles of the People.[33] Soon afterward, branches were formed in Chicago, Philadelphia, New York, and Madison. Though the Zhongshan Xuehui did not have a large membership, it had a positive influence and some positive achievements in the struggles opposing Chiang Kai-shek, the Kuomintang right wing (including the West Hills Conference Clique 西山会议派),[34] and the Nationalist groups (such as the Dajiang Xueshe 大江学社 [Great River Learned Society] led by Luo Longji 罗隆基 and others). C. T. Chi and Yu Zhipei were successively elected president of the Chinese Students Alliance. After formation of the Chinese Fraction in CPUSA, some Zhongshan Xuehui chapters were dissolved and everyone joined the AACAI. Other chapters (such as the one in Madison) changed their name to the Marxism Study Society. From then on, the Chinese Communist Party members propagated Marxism-Leninism and the guiding principles and policies of the Communist Party more openly.

In addition, Chinese Communist Party members encouraged students and community Chinese to join CPUSA-led mass organizations, such as International Labor Defense, the National Unemployed Alliance, the American Committee for the Protection of the Foreign-Born, Friends of the Soviet Union, etc., and also established Chinese branches of these organizations in various localities.

CHINESE VANGUARD AND CHINESE STUDENTS' MONTHLY

In the publicity sector, Chinese Communists in the United States, in addition to holding meetings and speaking, as well as issuing official statements and passing out handbills to students and community Chinese, used as their principal medium *Chinese Vanguard* 先锋报.

Chinese Vanguard published its first issue in San Francisco at the end of 1927 as the official organ of AACAI. At the time there were quite a number of daily newspapers connected with the Kuomintang and the associations. For example, in San Francisco there were *Kuo Min Yat Po* 国民日报, the *Chinese Times* 金山时报, *Young China* 少年中国, and *Chinese World* 世界日报. In New York there were *Mun Hey Yat Po* 民气日报 and *Chinese Commercial News* 商报. All of them were printed from lead type and were rather widely circulated. *Chinese Vanguard* was only a mimeographed weekly newspaper with limited space for text and a limited number of printed copies. Therefore it was at a disadvantage in both circulation and frequency of publication. But because its arguments were new and original, it became a special category among Chinese newspapers and had quite a few readers.

In 1928, Chinese Communist Party members Y. Y. Hsu, C. T. Chi, and others received a donation from a sympathizer named Montgomery and used the funds to acquire a set of Chinese lead type from Commercial Press in Shanghai, thus enabling the establishment of a printing facility. *Chinese Vanguard* changed to typeset printing and expanded to be an octavo-size weekly with four pages. The new format made *Chinese Vanguard* better able to compete with other Chinese newspapers, and its circulation grew. Even though *Chinese Vanguard* was the organ of the AACAI, its perspective and attitude were explicitly those of the Communist Party. In addition to publishing political news items and editorial commentaries, it also often carried special reports on the Chinese Soviet Red Army that arrived through the party organization. These items were highly welcomed and valued, and their influence could not be limited simply by the number of copies printed. *Chinese Vanguard* was distributed far more widely than any of the other Chinese newspapers. In addition to the United States and China, there were readers in Canada, Latin America, European countries, Southeast Asia, Australia, and even Africa, and because readers passed copies on to others, it could be said that circulation of one copy was equivalent to distribution of several copies.

These results stemmed not only from the efforts and cooperation of Chinese Communist Party members in every country but also from the active help of Chinese seamen (some of them Communist Party members) who went ashore in New York. They not only disseminated *Chinese Vanguard* everywhere they went but also passed along the names and addresses of Chinese in various countries to the paper's editorial department, thus enabling the latter to maintain contacts with a number of readers. When conditions were suitable, the seamen induced readers to approach and join revolutionary organizations where they resided. A few readers on their own initiative also approached and joined these organizations through contacting *Chinese Vanguard*. Thus one can say that *Chinese Vanguard* not only publicized and exhorted, it also organized. Successive editors of *Chinese Vanguard* included Shih Huang, Y. Y. Hsu, Li Tao Hsuan, Zhang Bao, Henry Hahn, and Yu Guangsheng.

From the end of the 1920s to the beginning of the 1930s, Communist Party members among students in the United States, after intense struggles with the Nationalist group, seized the leadership of the Chinese Students Alliance and therefore were able to use the alliance's official publication, *Chinese Students Monthly* 中国留美学生月刊, for propaganda purposes. (The publication was in English; the editors were Thomas T. Y. Hu and others.) In addition to articles on politics, economics, society, science, technology, and literature, it published other articles, such as "Wages and Working Conditions in China" (November 1927), "The Agrarian Problem in China" (April 1929), and "Land Tenure" (May 1929), all written by Earl Browder, a leader in CPUSA, who at that time was writing as a member of the

international workers' delegation visiting China. Besides these, there were articles such as "Three Days of Terror in Guangzhou" (February 1928), written by "an Eyewitness"; "China's Labor Unions," written by Deng Zhongxia; and "The Communist International's Evaluation of the Nanjing Regime" (May 1929). These articles and materials could be said to have had a positive effect at that time on left-wing students, who, however, were in the minority in the alliance. But their potential for leading to a contrary reaction among the majority, whose political consciousness was not high, should have been considered. In 1930, right-wing forces seized the opportunity to counterattack and opposed Yu Zhipei to become president of the alliance, and *Chinese Students Monthly* had to announce cessation of publication. This was the lesson from this experience.

EXTERNAL RELATIONS AND ACTIVITIES OF THE CENTRAL CHINESE BUREAU

The Central Chinese Bureau of CPUSA once had rather numerous external contacts and activities. First, it used to contact the CPC delegation at the Comintern through the CPUSA Central Committee and from there receive directives on tasks and other matters (I remember that Deng Zhongxia of the CPC delegation once transmitted such directives). To develop cadres that could return to China to participate in party tasks, the Comintern Chinese delegation at one time through CPUSA sent Chinese Communists in America to Moscow for training. For example, in 1927–28 Zhang Hanfu, Y. C. Chang, Huang Gongshou, Li Fahuan, and S. S. Lo were sent to Moscow's Chinese Labor University to study. In 1929 Shih Huang and several others (names not known) were sent. The Chinese Bureau of CPUSA did not have frequent official contacts with the CPC, but because individual comrades who returned to China from America knew the secret contact address in New York, the party organization in China could use it when necessary to contact Chinese comrades in America directly. For example, once during the early 1930s, the Central Chinese Bureau received through the party organization in China a letter from Hong Kong requesting remittance of funds to a certain person in Hong Kong to rescue a comrade who had been arrested and jailed. On that occasion we all donated some number of U.S. dollars. We heard later that our help had achieved the expected results.

The Central Chinese Bureau also often received through comrades in China and seamen publications from inside China, such as *Red Flag* 赤旗报 and *Chinese Seamen* 中国海员. These were very helpful to CPUSE members in their study of [policies and Marxist theory] and in their activities. The Central Chinese Bureau also had close contacts with Chinese Communists in Canada and Latin America. In 1929 the CPUSA Central Committee sent Shih Huang to Cuba and Canada to help these Chinese comrades expand their activities. The Central Chinese Bureau and the European branch of CPC also frequently helped and supported each other. For example Communist Party member Xie Weijin 谢唯进 in Berlin frequently mailed Marxist-Leninist literature in Chinese published by the USSR Foreign Language Books Publishing Bureau (led by the Comintern) to Chinese comrades in New York to sell. And Chinese comrades in Germany, Great Britain, France, Belgium, and other countries also actively offered for sale copies of the U.S.-published *Chinese Vanguard*.

In September 1932, when Zhang Bao was going to the USSR from the United States, one of the tasks given him by the Central Chinese Bureau was to meet and talk with Chinese comrades in London, Paris, Berlin, and other cities to exchange experiences and to strengthen cooperation and mutual aid. The Central Chinese Bureau also maintained close ties with Chinese comrades in Southeast Asia and other regions.

STRUGGLE AGAINST PERSECUTION BY U.S. AUTHORITIES

As everybody is aware, U.S. authorities had always discriminated against and oppressed the Chinese. It was to be expected that they would ruthlessly persecute Chinese Communists who participated in revolutionary activities in the United States. This was especially so during the end of the 1920s and the beginning of the 1930s, when the U.S. economic crisis was worsening day by day. At the same time the American authorities were ruthlessly suppressing the revolutionary movement of the American masses among workers and farmers, they were intensifying their persecution of Chinese Communists in the United States. Under ordinary circumstances, each "suspected" Chinese comrade was followed and a target of surveillance. Regardless of whether he was American-born or not, and whether he had legal residency or not, such a "suspect" ran the risk of being arrested and jailed by police and immigration authorities at any time. At the end of demonstrations, marches, and rallies, the police often seized the opportunity to provoke incidents so they could beat up and arrest participants. Chinese Communist Party members, especially those who went up on the platform to speak or actively shouted slogans, bore the brunt of the assaults.

If U.S. authorities found out that a Chinese was a Communist Party member and also had lost his "legal" right to live in the United States (e.g., was a student who had not registered to attend school), they immediately would arrest him and jail him on Ellis Island at the foot of the bronze statue of the goddess of liberty in New York Harbor (it was a mockery that this island was also named Liberty Island) to facilitate deporting him to China. (For example, this happened to Xavier Dea and Li Tao Hsuan during the 1930s.[35]) If an arrest

could not be made at the time, the authorities would send out a nationwide arrest warrant and would search everywhere for the person (for example, for Zhang Bao during the summer and fall of 1932), and could even wrongly identify a person and mistakenly arrest him. (For example, Chinese student Zhong Zhaohu 钟兆琥 was once mistakenly identified as Zhang Bao and suffered accordingly.) There were quite a few incidents of this type.

Faced with the relentless persecution of the U.S. authorities, the Chinese Communist Party members developed certain procedures for defense and resistance. For example, they tried to avoid public exposure (although sometimes this could not be done), used pseudonyms in contacts with the public, and sought means to retain legal residency in America (for example, registering in school even though they did not attend classes). But the most positive method was to unite and work together with CPUSA members and the masses to resist the persecution by the U.S. authorities. Here it should be pointed out especially that acts expressing the internationalist spirit of CPUSA members and revolutionary masses gave the Chinese comrades great help and encouragement. For example, when the police tried to provoke a mass meeting or marchers in formation, American comrades would disregard police beatings and courageously protect the Chinese comrades to prevent their being arrested, at times even rescuing those who had been arrested. If a Chinese comrade was brought to detention quarters, International Labor Defense would send an attorney to defend him in court.

At the beginning of the 1930s, when Xavier Dea and Li Tao Hsuan were successively jailed on Ellis Island in preparation for deportation to China, the CPUSA Central Committee organized a large protest movement and *Daily Worker* and different party newspapers of various minority groups printed banner headlines with news items and articles protesting the action, demanding that Li and Dea be released. As a result, Dea and Li were allowed to leave the country for the USSR. In the summer of 1932, when the American authorities sent police to the Labor School in New York to arrest Zhang Bao, the female secretary of the school astutely delayed these uninvited guests, thus enabling Zhang Bao to escape from a side exit to the home of a CPUSA member in a New York suburb. Tight protective measures adopted by the CPUSA Central Committee as well as assistance given by the CPUSA member's family enabled Zhang Bao to eventually escape from the tiger's mouth and safely reach Lenin's home town.

During the 1930s the branches of Friends of the Chinese People in different parts of the United States and its organ *China Today* also waged a determined campaign strenuously objecting to the persecution of Chinese Communist Party members. The internationalist spirit exhibited by CPUSA members and revolutionary masses not only strengthened the confidence and determination of the Chinese Communist Party members but also reinforced the unity of the Chinese and American parties and masses in the struggle.

WORKING STYLE OF UNITING AND WORKING HARD

It is only natural that the actions of Chinese Communists in America were not without shortcomings. Principally these lay in their strategy and methods being too rigid and not flexible enough in application. They were guilty of a bit of left-wing infantilism[36] and therefore could not attain the expected and greater results. But on the whole their spirit and style of uniting to fight hard for the cause of the Chinese revolution and communism should be commended and continued. They were separated from China by the ocean that extended beyond the horizon, yet they were still concerned with developments in the ancestral land and resolved to save it from annihilation and to liberate it. They also connected patriotism with communism and recognized that only the Communist Party, only socialism, could save China. Hence they disregarded the ruthless White Terror[37] in China that saw the slaughtering of numerous Communists and were still determined to join the Communist Party. The firmness of their resolution deserves praise.

And among them the Chinese students abroad not only did not have the slavish air of fawning on America and worshipping the West, but on the contrary voluntarily relinquished the degrees that could have been their stepping-stones to wealth and honor and instead attached their fates tightly to the future of the ancestral land and all its people. These were also difficult and praiseworthy decisions. Their sincerity in supporting the ancestral land, the Chinese people, the party, and the revolution led them to be tightly united in the ideological, political, and organizational sectors. In their activities and their lives they continued to exhibit a spirit of unity and mutual support as they worked hard at difficult tasks. The following few examples are illustrations of these points.

When Chinese Vanguard purchased a set of lead type from Commercial Press, it was the Chinese comrades themselves who built the partitioned shelves to store the type. They themselves set the type so that no typesetters needed to be hired. There were no editors, as they themselves did the editing. There were no newsboys to sell the newspapers, as they themselves performed that function. Other than the printing, which was done in the printing plant of the Daily Worker, the remaining tasks of production, such as writing articles, editing, proofreading, makeup, and distribution, were all done by the Chinese comrades. With insufficient personnel and numerous tasks to perform, everyone was kept very busy. On many Sundays during hot weather, when others went swimming in the ocean for recreation, Chinese comrades were perspiring and working hard, chatting and joking with high morale in the ten-to-twenty-square-meter "newsroom."

In another instance, the New York comrades once rented an apartment at East Twelfth Street with thirty or so square meters of floor area divided into one large and two smaller rooms. This was the main headquarters of the AACAI (and also the headquarters of the New York branch). More than a dozen tenants lived here. Y. Y. Hsu and his wife lived in one of the small rooms, and the remaining tenants (all male) occupied the remaining two rooms. There were only two single beds, and the rest of the people all slept on the floor. Early in the morning, each person would fold his bedding and place it under the bed or in some unobtrusive corner. Each night each person would spread out his bedding at his designated spot, forming tidy ranks like a school of black carp. Rent and board were the responsibility of AACAI and the individuals did not have to pay. These expenses actually were voluntary donations from those tenants who were still employed. At the time, the United States was caught in the vortex of an economic crisis and there were many unemployed, including most of the Chinese comrades. Only a small minority continued to work in restaurants, laundries, or stores, and any of them could have been discharged any morning. That is why the unemployed, other than those working at Chinese Vanguard, would look for work whenever they had some free time, even going on the streets to shine shoes. Some comrades who made a living in small shops in Chinatown, such as comrade Zeng Dingyuan, would buy and bring some Cantonese-style foods (cooked food, cakes, etc.) as gifts for everybody at AACAI.

This suite was the site for AACAI meetings to set policies, and it was a place for comrades to live and relax. It was also where comrades in arms got together happily during weekends. Life was difficult, but everybody generously helped and was concerned with one another, treating one another with brotherly love. Their spirits were upbeat because everyone believed in the lofty ideals of fighting valiantly for the Chinese revolution and communism.

NOTES

1. The 7 May cadre schools were set up in late 1968 in accordance with Mao Zedong's 7 May Directive of 1966. Farms, later called cadre schools, were established where cadres and intellectuals "sent down" from the cities would perform manual labor and undergo ideological reeducation.
2. Josephine Fowler, *Japanese and Chinese Immigrant Activists: Organizing in American and International Communist Movements, 1919–1933* (New Brunswick, N.J.: Rutgers University Press, 2007), 163–64; *Huaqiao Huaren baikequanshu, renwu juan* [Encyclopedia of Chinese overseas, volume of who's who] (Beijing: Chinese Overseas Publishing House, 2001), s.v. "Zhang Bao"; "Fang zhuming guoji Gongchanzhuyi zhanshi, shiren Zhang Bao de guju" [A visit to the former home of Zhang Bao, famous international Communist warrior and poet], *http://hi.baidu.com/shan3520/blog/item/33dda8dd8912c0355882dd32.html* (accessed July 6, 2008); *Wu Yuzhang huiyilu* [Memoirs of Wu Yuzhang] (Beijing: Zhongguo Qingnian Chubanshe, 1978), 176–85.
3. The Chinese Fraction was the CPUSA term for the ethnic Chinese fraction of the total party members in a district or the

nation. The Chinese Bureau provided leadership for the Chinese Fraction from district to national levels.

4. Shi Huang (1900–1933) was known as Shih Huang in the United States. He was a member of the Bai nationality of Yunnan province. While attending Tsinghua School in 1920 he led students to form Weizhen Xuehui (Truth-only Learned Society), which had three main objectives: to seek truth to improve society, to value physical labor and understand the living conditions of the impoverished masses, and to stress moral behavior and match words with actions. Weizhen Xuehui members became active among Beijing workers, attempting to raise their political consciousness. In spring 1923 Shi Huang formed and led Chaotao (Surpassing the Peach [Garden]), a secret policy-making core group within Weizhen Xuehui that sought to effect national salvation through political action and advocated learning from the revolutionary spirit of Sun Yat-sen and V. I. Lenin. Chaotao members were Shi Huang, C. T. Chi, Y. Y. Hsu, S. S. Lo, Y. C. Chang, Ju-Ao Mei, Thomas T. Y. Hu, and Luo Zongtang (who did not come to America for college). "Qinghuayuan zhong de juhuoren—Shi Huang" [Shih Huang—the one who lit a fire on the Tsinghua campus], ed. Zhonggong Dali zuzhibu [Dali Organization Department of the CPC], June 30, 2003, at *http://dldj.ccp.org.cn/second/read.aspx?n_id=111*.

5. C. T. Chi (1903–63) was from Shanxi province. After graduating from Tsinghua School he enrolled at the University of Chicago in 1924, majoring in history. Chi became active in the anti-imperialist patriotic movement among the Chinese in America and joined CPUSA in 1927. The same year the party's Central Chinese Bureau sent Chi and Y. C. Chang back to China (via Moscow) to participate in the Communist revolution. When they reached Moscow the Chinese delegation attending the tenth-anniversary celebration of the October Revolution passed along the message that Chi and Chang should not return to China at that time. In 1928 Chi returned to the United States and joined the editorial staff of the *Daily Worker*. He was a founder of *China Today* and *Amerasia*. Chi returned to China in 1941 and worked for the Nationalist government in the financial sector. After the founding of the PRC, Chi was involved in the international commerce sector. "Ji Chaoding tongzhi fangwenlu" [Record of interview of Comrade C. T. Chi], *http://kui-shi.blog.hexun.com/9251626_d.html* (accessed July 26, 2007).

6. Jiangxi was the ancestral province of Y. Y. Hsu (1902–68). After graduating from Tsinghua, Hsu came to the United States in 1925 and attended the University of Chicago (1925), the University of Wisconsin (1926), and Stanford University (1927). He joined the Kuomintang in 1926. When the Kuomintang began purging Communists in China in 1927, Hsu joined CPUSA and was one of the founders of the Chinese Bureau. He remained a member of the bureau during most of his time in the United States. He also participated in the founding of Meizhou Yonghu Zhongguo Gong-Nong Geming Datongmeng (Grand Alliance Supporting the Chinese Workers and Peasants Revolution, ACWP), which later became AACAI. He was one of the founders and editors of AACAI organ *Chinese Vanguard*. From 1941 to 1946 he was a researcher at the Institute of Pacific Relations. Hsu returned to China in 1946. In the PRC, Hsu headed a group translating *Selected Works of Mao Zedong* into English. Yao Xiaoping, "Xian wei en zhi de hongse gemingjia—Mei-Gong Zhongguoju chuangbanren he 'Maoxuan' yingyi zhuchiren Xu Yongying" [A red revolutionary that few people knew: Y. Y. Hsu, founder of the American Communist Party's Chinese Bureau and the head of the team translating selected works of Mao Zedong into English].

7. S. S. Lo (1905–98) was born in Shanghai. She was the lone female and Cantonese in the Chaotao group. At the time she was attending the middle school attached to the Beijing Women's Normal College. She arrived in California in 1925 to study at the University of California and then Stanford University. In 1927 she joined CPUSA and in 1928 was sent to attend Moscow's Chinese Labor University, after which she returned to China to become a translator for the CPC Central Committee. In 1931 she became secretary for the CPC branch in Hong Kong. From 1936 to 1949 she did underground work in various parts of China. "Luo Jingyi tongzhi shishi" [The passing away of Comrade S. S. Lo], *People's Daily*, August 11, 1998.

8. Y. C. Chang was a member of the Chaotao group. After graduating from Tsinghua School he came to the United States in 1926 and joined CPUSA in 1927. The same year the party's Central Chinese Bureau directed him and C. T. Chi to return to China; however, acting on the advice of the Chinese delegation attending the tenth-anniversary celebration of the October Revolution, they remained in Moscow. Some time after Chi returned to the United States in 1928, Wang Ming dismissed Chang from the Communist Party. Later he became a university professor and also joined the Revolutionary Committee of the Kuomintang. "Ji Chaoding tongzhi fangwenlu" [Record of interview of Comrade C. T. Chi], *http://kui-shi.blog.hexun.com/9251626_d.html* (accessed July 26, 2007).

9. Shih Tso was active in the San Francisco Bay Area. Shi Huang, Y. Y. Hsu, and he were on the Kuomintang General Branch's five-member Committee on the Abolition of Unequal Treaties. Fowler, *Japanese and Chinese Immigrant Activists*, 120–22, 124, 130, 137–38; *Zhongguo Guomindang zhu-Sanfanshi zong-zhibu di-erci daibiao dahui shimoji* [Proceedings of the second convention of the San Francisco branch of the Kuomintang of China] (San Francisco: Young China, 1928), 163.

10. In fact, Mei Ru'ao (1904–73) was the lone member of the Chaotao group who did not join the Communist Party. In 1924 Mei entered Stanford University after graduating from Tsinghua School. He received a BA in 1926 and then entered the University of Chicago, where he received his LLD in 1929. Meanwhile he helped C. T. Chi organize the Zhongshan Xuehui 中山学会 (Sun Yat-sen Learned Society). Mei returned to China in 1929 and entered academia, teaching law. In 1946–48 he was China's representative to the Far East International Military Court trying Japanese war criminals. "Mei Ru'ao," *http://baike.baidu.com/view/176402.htm* (accessed July 8, 2008).

11. Tsinghua School began operations in Beijing in 1911 to prepare Chinese students to study in America. It was funded by the portion of the Boxer indemnity returned by the United States. It officially became National Tsinghua University in 1928. "Qinghua University," in *Zhongguo gaodeng xuexiao bianqian* [Changes in institutions of higher education in China], ed. Ji Xiaofeng and Wang Xianming (Shanghai: Huadong Shifan Daxue Chubanshe, 1992), 18–28.

12. Zhang Hanfu (1905–72) was from Jiangsu province. After graduating from Tsinghua School, he came to study in the United States, where he joined CPUSA in 1927. The following year the party sent him to study in the Soviet Union. He returned to China in 1931 and was assigned to underground work in Hong Kong but was caught and deported. In 1933, he was caught again in Shanghai and was bailed out by his father. During the War of Resistance against Japan he was with the CPC's *New China Daily* in Chongqing. In 1945 he joined the staff of Dong Biwu and came to San Francisco with him as part of China's delegation participating in the founding of the United Nations. After the founding of the PRC he was with the Ministry of Foreign Affairs. During the Cultural Revolu-

tion he was accused of being a turncoat and was jailed in 1968. He died in jail in 1972. Li Da'nan, "Yidai waijiaojia Zhang Hanfu" [Zhang Hanfu, the diplomat of this generation], *Renwu* 6 (2002), *http://www.renwu.com.cn/UserFiles/magazine/article/ RW0160_200207101640008* (accessed September 1, 2007).

13. Li Tao Hsuan (aliases "H. Linson" and "Toddy") joined the Communist Party in San Francisco but apparently soon left for New York to enroll in Columbia University and became active among the Marxists left there. By December 1929 he had become acting secretary of the Chinese Bureau of the Chinese Fraction of CPUSA and was working closely with the party's Anti-Imperialist Committee in New York. Fowler, "To Be Red and 'Oriental': The Experience of Japanese and Chinese Immigrant Communists in the American and International Communist Movements, 1919–1933" (PhD diss., University of Minnesota, 2003), 407–8 (hereafter cited as "Japanese and Chinese Immigrant Communists").

14. Thomas T. Y. Hu (1902–75), one of the Chaotao eight, arrived in the United States in 1925 and enrolled in Columbia University. He became active in the All-American Anti-Imperialist League (AAAIL) and in 1927 joined CPUSA. Due to his opposition to the Chiang Kai-shek regime, the Nanjing government stopped funding his education in the United States and issued orders for his arrest. Hu subsequently left the Communist Party and during World War II was active in the District of Columbia organizing support for China's war effort, working closely with the China Aid Council. In 1951 he returned to China, where he later became a professor at the Institute of Foreign Commerce. Wang Guangze, "Jixi Longchuan liu-Mei boshi Hu Dunyuan" [Thomas D. Y. Hu from Jixi Longchuan, who received his doctorate after studying in America], April 16, 2006, *http://www.jixinet.com/jxwenyi/ArticleID=107* (accessed August 19, 2007).

15. Chee Fun Ho (1902?–55?) was from Dongguan, Guangdong. In the United States he was a standing committee member of the Chicago branch of the Kuomintang before joining CPUSA during the late 1920s. He was a member of the Central Chinese Bureau and an editor at *China Daily News*. After he returned to China he was chief editor of the China News Service during the early years of the PRC. Xu Suizhi, "Xu Yongying shengping nianbiao [Chronology of the life of Y. Y. Hsu], pt. 3, n. 21, *http://blog.voc.com.cn/sp1/xusuizhi/001607233581. shtml* (accessed July 11, 2007); Fowler, *Japanese and Chinese Immigrant Activists*, 154.

16. Frank K. M. Su (1904–88) was from Henan province. After graduating from Tsinghua, Su came to the United States to attend the University of Wisconsin and Harvard University, from which he received a BA and an MA, respectively, in history. Su joined CPUSA in 1929. He also joined Zhongshan Xuehui and the AACAI and became an editor at *Chinese Vanguard*. During World War II Su was active in Philadelphia doing publicity for American Friends of the Chinese People (AFCP) and the China Aid Council. He returned to China in 1953 with his American wife and daughter, going by way of Sweden and the Soviet Union. Later he became an editor of the periodical *China Reconstructs*. "Su Kaiming 1904–1988," *http://shtong. gov.cn/node2/node2245/node69322/node69341/ node69492/ node69496/userobject1ai67656.html* (accessed September 4, 2007); Language Centre, Australia book sale announcement, *http://www.languagecentre.iinet.com.au/catalogues/asiasale.pdf* (accessed August 12, 2007).

17. Wei Minghua joined CPC in 1927 as a student at Tsinghua School. He arrived in the United States in 1928. In June 1930 he moved to Los Angeles, where he became a student at the University of Southern California and became active organizing branches of the AACAI and the Unemployed Alliance as well as giving speeches on the Chinese revolution and the Chinese Soviets. In November 1932 he was arrested by the Los Angeles Police Department's "Red Squad" and turned over to immigration authorities, who deported him to the Soviet Union. "Qinghua di-yi ge dangzhibu de jianli [The founding of the first party branch at Tsinghua], *http://news.tsinghua.edu. cn/new/news.php?id=13390* (accessed August 22, 2006); Fowler, *Japanese and Chinese Immigrant Activists*, 163; *Chinese Vanguard*, February 1, 15, 1933.

18. Chen Kemei (1898–1997) was from Hunan province. He graduated as an education major from the University of Illinois in 1923. In 1924 he obtained an MA from the University of Chicago, and he entered Columbia University in 1926 for his doctorate. After his return to China he was in academia, specializing in education.

19. The ancestral province of Yu Guangsheng (1906–78) was Zhejiang, but he was born in Japan. He graduated from Shanghai's Jiaotong University in 1927 and in 1928 entered the University of Michigan, where he joined the AACAI. Yu joined CPUSA in New York in 1932. He was editor at *Chinese Vanguard* and *China National Salvation Times*. Yu returned to China in December 1939 and the next year went to Yan'an, where he became editor of *Liberation Daily*. In the PRC he was connected with the Railroad Ministry. "Yu Guangzhong," *http://zjtz.zjol.com. cn/05zjtz/system/2005/12/14/006403096.shtml* (accessed June 19, 2006).

20. Liu Kemian was a member of the standing committee of the Philadelphia branch of the Kuomintang. Xu Suizhi, "Bainian Xu Yongying zhi Xu Yongying zhuanlue" [A short biography of Y. Y. Hsu at his centennial], pt. 3, May 24, 2007, *http://xusuizhi. blshe.com/post/3238/55621* (accessed July 11, 2007).

21. Zhao Yue was a member of the executive committee of the Philadelphia branch of the Kuomintang. Ibid.

22. Thomas Lem Tong (1905–97) was an immigrant from Taishan, Guangdong. He joined CPUSA during the 1930s. He was editor at *China Daily News* during World War II and was a member of CPUSA's Central Chinese Bureau. During the early years of the PRC after his return to China he was a member of the Overseas Chinese Affairs Commission under the Ministry of Political Affairs. Xu Suizhi, "Xu Yongying shengping nianbiao [Chronology of the life of Y. Y. Hsu], pt. 3, n. 22, *http://blog. voc.com.cn/sp1/xusuizhi/001607233581.shtml* (accessed July 11, 2007).

23. Ouyang Ji was a member of the left-wing faction of the Kuomintang branch in Philadelphia. *Second Convention of San Francisco Branch of Kuomintang*, 187.

24. Xie Chuang (Xavier Dea), *Chongyang nan zu baoguoxin* [Seas and oceans cannot block an intention to serve the nation] (Guangzhou: Hua'nan Shifan Daxue Yinshuachang, 1993).

25. Alice Sum was an activist in the syndicalist Unionist Guild in the 1920s. She later became active in the Women's Section of the Kuomintang and also joined CPUSA. After the successful San Francisco laundry workers' strike, Chan and she were asked to give a report to the San Francisco Labor Council. This was the first time leaders of the American labor movement showed interest in Chinatown labor issues. Chan and Sum, who were husband and wife, were later sent to the Soviet Union to study in the 1930s. Fowler, *Japanese and Chinese Immigrant Activists*, 54, 124; *Chung Sai Yat Po*, February 1, 4, 1929; *Labor Clarion*, February 15, 1929; Xavier Dea, interview by author in Guangzhou, November 3, 1979.

26. China-born Benjamin Fee (1909–78) emigrated to California in 1922. He became a leader in the left-wing San Francisco Students Association in the late 1920s and joined CPUSA in

1928. He went to the Soviet Union for training in 1930. After his return he became a labor organizer on the West Coast and was one of the founders of San Francisco's Chinese Workers Mutual-Aid Association in 1937. Due to his marital problems the party put Fee on probation, and in 1938 he moved to New York, where he left the Communist Party. After World War II he became business agent for an International Ladies' Garment Workers' Union local having many Chinese members. Benjamin Fee, interview by author, March 28, 1975; Virginia Fee, sister of Ben Fee, interview by author, June 24, 1990; Roger Wong, brother-in-law of Ben Fee, interview by author, August 1, 1991; Virginia Fee, note to author, June 10, 2005. Benjamin Fee was also an active member of the Chinese American literary left. A selection of his poems as well as his comments on that movement are included in "Selections from *Collected Poems of Mu-yün*," this volume, page 19.

27. Chen Houfu was an immigrant from Taishan, Guangdong. He joined CPUSA in 1931 in Philadelphia and was active in AACAI, International Labor Defense, and the Seamen's Union. In 1943 he became Chinese secretary at the Chinese Hand Laundry Alliance of New York and was active at *China Daily News*. He returned to China in 1951 and served as a deputy mayor of Taishan. *Guangzhou Shi zhi, Huaqiao zhi* [Gazetteer of Chinese overseas, gazetteer of Guangzhou] (Guangzhou: Guangzhou Chubanshe, 1996), 101.

28. Tang Mingzhao or Chu Tong (1910–98) was a native of Enping, Guangdong, who emigrated with his parents in the early 1920s. In 1927 he returned to China for schooling. After graduating from Tianjin's Nankai Middle School, he entered Tsinghua University, where he joined the CPC in 1931 after Japan attacked northeast China (Manchuria). Tang returned to the United States to enroll at the University of California, Berkeley, in 1933 and became active in the CPUSA branch at the university. After graduation in 1938 he became English secretary at the Chinese Hand Laundry Alliance. He played a leading role in the founding of *China Daily News* in 1940 and became its first publisher and chief editor. After the Korean conflict broke out, he and his family returned to China. The PRC resumed China's seat at the United Nations in 1971, and Tang was elected a United Nations undersecretary in 1972. Wu Dongping, "Tang Mingzhao qiren" [Tang Mingzhao the person], March 6, 2006, *http://book.sina.com.cn/nzt/his/xiandaimingren/86.shtml* (accessed July 10, 2008).

29. When the Communist Party of the Soviet Union (CPSU) was riven by a succession struggle after Lenin's death, James Cannon supported Leon Trotsky's critique of Josef Stalin's bureaucratic policies. He and other Trotskyists were expelled from CPUSA in 1928 and formed the Communist League of America, which in 1938 became the Socialist Workers Party that participated in the formation of the Fourth International. "Communist League of America," *http://en.wikipedia.org/wiki/Communist_League_of_America* (accessed July 14, 2008).

30. William Foster joined CPUSA in 1923. In the succession struggle following Lenin's death he led a faction supportive of Stalin. A large faction led by Jay Lovestone was sympathetic to Bukharin. In 1929, after Bukharin was expelled from the CPSU, Lovestone was expelled from CPUSA and Foster replaced him as general secretary. Lovestone and a few followers formed the Communist Party (Opposition), which became the Independent Communist Labor League and in 1938 the Independent Labor League of America before dissolving in 1941. Meanwhile, a heart ailment forced Foster to step down as CPUSA general secretary in 1932, with Earl Browder replacing him. Foster reoccupied the position when Browder was removed

in 1945 after attempting to dissolve CPUSA as a party. Foster retired in 1956. "William Z. Foster," *http://en.wikipedia.org/wiki/William_Z._Foster* (accessed July 14, 2008); Jay Lovestone," *http://en.wikipedia.org/wiki/Jay_Lovestone* (accessed July 14, 2008).

31. In 1896 czarist Russia wrested a concession from China to build a Chinese Eastern Railway across northern Manchuria by way of Harbin as an extension of the Trans-Siberian Railway to Vladivostok. The Russians completed the railroad in 1901, as well as a line from Harbin to Lüshun (Port Arthur) in 1903, thus extending Russian power to an ice-free deepwater port on the Pacific. This set up Russia's collision with a Japan that was expanding from Korea into southern Manchuria. The resulting Russo-Japanese War of 1905 was fought on Chinese soil. After the war Japan gained control of the line from Harbin to Lüshun, which became part of the South Manchurian Railway. After the October Revolution in Russia, operation of the Chinese Eastern Railway remained in the hands of the Soviet Union.

After the Kuomintang established the Nanjing government in 1927, the latter looked for a pretext to gain control over the railway. In May 1929, Chinese authorities in the Northeast Provinces (Manchuria) accused the Soviet Union and the railway of spreading Communism in the region, arrested the Soviet consul and his staff in Harbin, and confiscated documents from the consulate. In July the Chinese ordered seizure of the railway. After the USSR protested and issued an ultimatum, its army attacked and defeated the Northeast Army and captured Manzhouli. The Chinese were forced to negotiate and signed an agreement on December 22 reestablishing the conditions that had existed prior to July. The Chinese Eastern Railway was finally returned to Chinese control on December 31, 1952, under the PRC. "Zhong-Dong lu shijian" [The Chinese Eastern Railway affair], in Wang Weili, ed., "Zhongguo xiandaishi dashi jishi benmo" [The events from beginning to end of important events in modern Chinese history] (Harbin: Heilongjiang Renmin Chubanshe, 1987) 1:572–74; Wang Weiyuan, "Zhong-Dong lu shijian: 1929 nian Zhong-Su zhi zhan" [The Chinese Eastern Railway affair: The Chinese-Soviet conflict of 1929], *http://washeng.net/HuaShan/BBS/junshi/b5current/143180.shtml* (accessed July 15, 2008); "Chinese Eastern Railroad," *http://en.wikipedia.org/wiki/Chinese_Eastern_Railway* (accessed August 11, 2008).

Zhang Bao's memory of this event was faulty. Zhang Zuolin (1873–1928) was the warlord ruling over the Northeast Provinces (Manchuria), but he was killed in June 1928 by a bomb planted by Japanese agents and was succeeded by his son Zhang Xueliang, who supported the Nanjing government. It was the latter who was responsible for instigating the conflict over the Chinese Eastern Railway.

32. The Nationalist groups were such groups as the Dajiang Xueshe (Great River Learned Society). The promonarchy party was the Baohuanghui (Protect the Emperor Association). By the time of the Republic, the latter had already changed its name to the Constitutionalist Party of China; however, some Chinese, especially those hostile to the monarchists, persisted in referring to the organization by its earlier name.

33. The three cardinal policies were alliance with the Soviet Union, cooperation with the Communists, and assistance to the peasants and workers.

34. In November 1925, a section of the right wing of the Kuomintang met in the Western Hills near Sun Yat-sen's tomb to express opposition to the three cardinal principles set forth by Sun Yat-sen.

35. Zhang Bao's memory was inaccurate in the case of Xavier Dea. In May 1931 Dea was arrested and confined in the Angel Island Immigration Station in San Francisco Bay. He was deported from there in mid-1932 on a German vessel that took him to Hamburg, whence he took a train to the Soviet Union. Li Tao Hsuan was arrested in late 1930 and threatened with instant deportation to China. After negotiations he was allowed to be deported to the Soviet Union. Xie, *Seas and Oceans*, 22–31; Fowler, *Japanese and Chinese Immigrant Activists*, 163.

36. This phrase was derived from Lenin's essay "Left-Wing Communism: An Infantile Disorder," in which the author criticized the ultraleftism that advocated against compromises with the capitalist class, against working within reactionary trade unions, and generally in favor of boycotting elections. Lenin considered such ultraleft actions disruptive at the time in the movement toward socialism.

37. The term White Terror refers to acts of violence carried out by conservative groups as part of a counterrevolution. In the context of this essay, the term refers to actions by conservative groups and authorities in China against Communists and other members of the left.

The Life and Times of Benjamin Fee

Him Mark Lai

The original Chinese text of several of Benjamin Fee's published poems with translations by Ellen Yeung and Him Mark Lai appears in "Selections from Collected Poems of Mu-yün," this volume, pages 19–35. The 2008 special issue of Chinese America: History & Perspectives, *"Labor and San Francisco's Garment Industry," published the first English translation, by Ellen Yeung, of Ben Fee's 1935 report, "The Chinese American Garment Industry."*

Author's note: The following biographic sketch of Benjamin Fee (Zhang Hentang) 張恨棠 (1908–78) is based on items in newspapers and his writings. Other sources include letters from Benjamin Fee to Him Mark Lai and an interview of Fee by Gilbert Woo and Him Mark Lai, all in the 1970s, which provide glimpses of Fee's personal insights and interpretations regarding his activities. Due to lack of documentation for many periods of Fee's life, the coverage in this sketch is uneven and inadequate in certain areas. It is hoped that some scholar will pick up where this essay leaves off, fill in the gaps, and correct the inadequacies. —HML

Benjamin Fee was the oldest son of Jay B. Fee 張伯飛, American-born interpreter at the Fook On Lung 福安隆 general merchandise store in San Francisco Chinatown. Fee senior was of Shafu, Xinhui 新會沙扶, ancestry and had gone to China to get married. Benjamin Fee was born in Guangzhou,[1] and his grandfather wanted him to remain in China. It was not until June 1923 that young Fee arrived in San Francisco, accompanied by his father.[2]

During that period China had a weak central government, while different regions of the country were dominated by foreign powers or ruled by warlords. A revolutionary regime in Guangdong led by Sun Yat-sen and the Kuomintang was trying to build its military forces to drive north to rid the country of warlordism and cast off imperialist domination. In 1923, shortly after Fee arrived in America, Sun Yat-sen made an alliance with the Soviet Union, admitted Chinese Communists into the Kuomintang, and actively supported China's working and peasant classes. A feeling of impending change inspired hope and expectation among Chinese concerned with the future of their nation, young Fee among them.

FEE'S EARLY YEARS IN AMERICA

When Fee began attending school in San Francisco to learn English he met schoolmates with similar political convictions, such as Xavier Dea 謝創.[3] He also became more proficient in written Chinese through study and practice. When he was sixteen or seventeen, he collaborated with Miss S. S. Lo, a progressive university student from China, to translate the second stanza of the "Internationale" from English into Chinese. This experience served to spark his lifelong interest in Chinese poetry.[4]

In the mid-1920s the cooperation between the Kuomintang right and left to achieve the Chinese revolution was exhibiting signs of severe strain. In 1926 there was an open split in the party in America, with the right-wing and left-wing factions struggling for control. The left-wing faction convened a national party convention on January 1, 1927, to elect a new party executive committee and to found a new party organ, *Chinese Nationalist Daily of America (Kuo Min Yat Po* 美洲國民日報). The case of H. T. Tsiang 蔣希曾 (1899–1971) was typical of events in this rapidly changing political scene, replete with shifting alliances and changing allegiances.

Tsiang arrived in the United States in 1926 as a student and became an editor of *Young China,* the organ of the KMT right wing. For some reason he soon became critical of Chiang Kai-shek and was bodily expelled from *Young China.* However, the left wing denounced him, claiming that in spring 1926 he had attended a Shanghai meeting of the executive committee of the KMT right-wing faction that opposed Sun Yat-sen's policies.[5] The Communists also tried to use Tsiang to further their political objectives, but they remained distrustful of him and rejected him as a party member. Although Benjamin Fee was just a neophyte political activist at the time, he was well aware of the relations of the Marxist left and H. T. Tsiang. According to Fee:

> During this great confusion and void, Tsiang came to the scene and published the *Chinese Guide in America* 美洲評論. It was divided in English section and Chinese section. Tsiang edited the Chinese section, an American, Owens, edited the English section, and I managed the organization behind the weekly. While his weekly enjoyed popularity, particularly among the progressive sector of the Americans, he was personally erratic, financially irresponsible and politically dubious. When the Chinese

revolution crystallized into fixed positions, he lost hold of the situation and disappeared. Years later, he reappeared again in New York City as an English poet and actor. He published a small volume of his poetry in English, and secured a role in the movie "Good Earth." Still later, he seemed to decide to seek his fortune in Hollywood and was seen a couple times in small bit parts.[6]

In April 1927, a few months after Tsiang's defection, Chiang Kai-shek led the right-wing faction of the Kuomintang in China to terminate the alliance with the Soviet Union and launched a bloody purge of Communists and their supporters from the party. It was a period of turmoil and high tension in China, which spread to the Chinese communities overseas. At first the Kuomintang left wing in the United States, supported by the Communists, published the *Chinese Nationalist Daily* in opposition to the right wing. However, the right-wing faction in America, backed by the Chiang regime in China and emboldened by the anti-Communist atmosphere in America, was ready to use all means, including violence, to gain control.

Fee participated in this struggle but did not play a leading role, probably due to his age and inexperience. He recalled that tense period:

> When the Wuhan Government under Wang Ching Wei 汪精衛 collapsed and turned on the Communists, the Chinese left in the U.S. were in great disarray and the American sympathizers were left in great shock. On the heel of that, a wave of KMT terror arose in America. In Vancouver, B.C. the editor Lei Mingxia 雷鳴夏 and the manager Huang Youmei 黃友梅, of the 加拿大晨報 were shot down in their office, and the Chinese Nationalist Daily 國民日報 in S.F. was an armed camp. Rifles were laid close by in the newspaper's office. We seldom dared to venture into the street without arming ourselves.
>
> As far as I can recall, Sanminding 三民鼎 was the goon-squad of the right wing K.M.T., the West Hills group 西山派 adhered to Hu Hanmin 胡漢民 and the C. C. clique 二陳派, and functioned through the San Min Club 三民俱樂部. It was composed of some KMT toughies and some of the newshawkers of the KMT paper, the *Young China* 少年報. . . . Not long afterward, the so-called left leaders like Chen Boxing 陳伯興, Zhu Guanri 朱貫日, Zhou Huisan 周恢三 went back to the reactionary fold of the KMT one by one.[7]

By the beginning of 1928 the Wuhan regime had negotiated a settlement to join the Nanjing regime. In the United States the Communists were expelled from the Kuomintang and the *Chinese Nationalist Daily*.[8] In opposition, the Communists organized the Grand Alliance Supporting the Chinese Workers and Peasants Revolution (ACWP) 中國工農革命大同盟, which was reorganized as the All-America Alliance of Chinese Anti-Imperialists (AACAI) 美洲華僑反帝大同盟 in 1929 and moved to New York City in 1930.[9] It was active and vociferous in nationwide anti–Chiang Kaishek demonstrations in July 1929. According to Fee, "The demonstration was organized by the Anti-Imperialist League and the Friends of the Soviet Union. The position we took was, the KMT is doing the bidding of the Japanese in order to strengthen her hold on Manchuria and use it later as a springboard for further aggression. It was then a touchy subject. I

Benjamin Fee (Zhang Hentang) 張恨棠 (1908–78). (Courtesy Virginia Fee Dip)

got beaten up in one of the street meetings in Chinatown by the Sanminding 三民鼎 toughies." Years later Fee reflected: "It is very difficult to evaluate whether these demonstrations accomplished their objectives. One can only take a long view on history and judge their consequences."[10] The demonstrations subsided after the right wing gained the upper hand.

Fee first demonstrated his leadership qualities during this period. The Young Communist League (YCL) of the American Communist Party (CPUSE) was encouraging members of the left in the Chinese community, notably Xavier Dea, to organize youth as part of the party's anti-imperialism activities. Both Dea and Fee joined the YCL in 1927.[11] Dea, Fee, and other young radicals founded the San Francisco Chinese Students Association (SFCSA) 三藩市中國學生會,

> which was formed around the end of 1927 and lasted until the early part of 1929. I was its founder and president during its whole existence. At its height, the club had a membership of more than three thousand, governed by a delegated body composed of representatives from every Chinese school, junior high and high school. Its main activities were to take over the leadership of the anti-imperialist struggle from the Chinese Six Company and its affiliates, sensing its tendency to side with Chiang Kai-shek in selling out the Chinese Anti-imperialist Revolution. It has conducted some of the most memorable mass demonstration and parades. In fact, it completely "took over the streets of Chinatown." Its dissolution was partly the result of the changing status of some of its key leaders and the combined suppression of the KMT and the Chinatown Red squad, headed by that infamous sergeant Manion.[12]

Fee then became a member of the Kung Yu Club that became active in San Francisco. Fee recalled, "The Kung Yu Club 工餘俱樂部 was founded by me and Xavier Dea 謝創, as an early attempt to organize the Chinese restaurant workers. It published a monthly labor pamphlet, called 工餘月刊. It is definitely left."[13] In 1929 Fee became a CPUSA member. That June he was also elected to the executive committee of the All-American Anti-Imperialist League (AAAIL), California Section. His activism and demonstrated leadership ability encouraged the party to send him to study in Moscow's Lenin School in 1930.

After Fee returned from the Soviet Union in the fall of 1931 he married fellow activist Eva Chan. He also resurrected *Qunsheng* 群聲 (the *Resonance*), originally a publication of the SFCSA and published using a mimeograph machine and facilities at the Nam Kue Chinese School. When this unauthorized usage came to the attention of the school authorities, they banned the publication and disciplined the students involved.

The publication soon attracted the attention of the anti-Communist right wing. In 1934 Elizabeth Dilling's *The Red Network: A "Who's Who" of Radicalism for Patriots* listed "Chu Sing Youth Association, Chinese Communist Subsidary; headquarters, H. T. Chang, P.O. Box 24-54, San Francisco, California." According to Fee, Chu Sing "must be the misspelling of *Chuen Sing* (the *Resonance* 群聲週刊), the youth publication of which I was the publisher and editor. H. T. Chang was my Chinese name 張恨棠."[14]

From the start the four-page publication struggled to survive. Conservative Chinatown leaders excluded its staff from using Chinatown printing facilities, thus forcing them to typeset and print at the Japanese American Golden Gate Printing Company, which was sympathetic to the left. Despite their zeal, it was difficult for the young Marxists to sustain this journalistic effort, which claimed a circulation of five hundred in 1931. It stopped publication for good in the mid-thirties.[15] An anecdote in connection with it shows the independent streak that eventually led Fee to part ways with the Communist Party:

> I remember the first editorial was in regard to the kidnapping of Charles Lindberg's son. The editor for the last or next to last issue was the controversial one on policy toward the People's Government of Fukien province, sponsored by the generals of the 19th Army Tsai Ting-kai 蔡廷鍇, Jiang Guangnai 蔣光鼐, Chen Mingshu 陳銘樞. That took place on the eve of the Fifth Anti-Communist campaign of Chiang Kai-shek against the Soviet territory. I wrote the editorial criticizing the Chinese party for not affecting a united front with this anti-Chiang government. It was my intention that if such unity could be achieved, we could turn back the right flank of the Chiang campaign and make the fifth campaign impossible. This stand was severely condemned by the Chinese leadership in this country. I was ordered to publish a retraction to the editorial or cease publication. I defied this order, and soon afterward *The Resonance* closed. I have read some historical document lately, and discovered to my satisfaction that Mao was severely criticized on that score, and it was one of the reasons why he was deprived of political power for a period of more than three years.[16]

During this period, as Japanese militarists continued their aggression in China, Fee spent part of his time applying his literary talents to political propaganda against them. In 1936 he worked with Japanese CPUSA member Karl Yoneda to issue the publication *Mon Kow* 文求 for the San Francisco branch of the Friends of the Chinese People. After the Sino-Japanese War broke out in 1937 Fee published *War of Resistance* (*Kangzhan* 抗戰), but soon had to cease publication due to lack of funding.

LABOR ORGANIZING

During this entire period Fee devoted much time to labor organizing. He joined the Seamen's Union around 1933–34 and strove to persuade the union to admit other Chinese as members. In 1934 he was among members of the Chinese left who participated in the San Francisco general strike. In 1935 he was hired by the International Ladies' Garment Workers' Union (ILGWU) as a union organizer and proceeded to organize workers at the National Dollar Stores factory, the largest in San Francisco Chinatown. Fee's interpretation of these events differs strikingly from that of Jennie Matyas, possibly as a result of their different attitudes toward the Communist Party.[17] Fee recalled,

> The real genuine attempt to organize the Chinese garment workers was aimed at the National Dollar Co. shop under the I.L.G.W.U. I was then its organizer. In fact, I met my wife in that shop. It followed a long period of activity with not little help from the W.P.A and the N.R.A. It was easily the first big Chinese union shop in history. Of course, I was betrayed by the treacherous and red-baiting I.L.G.W.U. leadership, and had handicapped the whole process of organizing that industry in the period to come. The most dramatic event was, when the workers of this shop stopped the Japanese Goodwill delegation from landing in San Francisco and parade up Market Street as the guest of Mayor Rossi.[18]

In another letter Fee elaborated further:

> The person Jennie Matyas referred to was someone you should guess by now [Fee himself]. Since this person is now working again for the ILGWU, it is important not to name him. The process of dismissal was quite disgusting. This certain person was organizing the National Dollar factory for them. The ILG ordered that a strike should be called. While this person was organizing the strike for one morning, Jennie Matyas went to the employer on the evening before and informed them of the strike plan and made the following proposition. In substance, she told the employer that his workers were preparing a strike the following morning and it would be a successful strike. But should that come about, this Communist person would have enjoyed great prestige among the Chinese workers, and it would cost no end of trouble to all the Chinese employers. If he signed a contract now without giving the workers and that certain person a successful strike, she will be able to confront this person and the workers with an accomplished fact, and denounce this person for incompetence as well as calling a strike to put the interest of the workers in jeopardy, and I will dismiss him forthwith. She got her yellow dog contract. The other person was not fired, because the left in the ILG succeeded in exposing this treachery. It was later that this person resigned in disgust. If things broke differently, it might have been possible to have the whole garment industry in Chinatown organized. On hindsight, one can

say that this person should never have resigned, but I know he was attracted by the opportunity to organize the S.F. waterfront, and later on the Chinese workers in that industry (the cannery, sailors, cooks and stewards, etc.). An earlier attempt failed mainly for the reasons you had advanced in your article.[19]

At this time Fee also played a leading role in the unionization of salmon cannery workers; helped found the Chinese Workers Mutual Aid Association (CWMAA) 板加省華工合作會, which connected Chinese workers with the mainstream American labor movement; and was elected to be the group's first secretary. However, his extramarital affair, divorce of Eva Chan, and subsequent marriage to Amy Lee in November 1938 damaged his working relationships with fellow progressives and party members. This led the CPUSA leadership to place Fee's party membership on probation,[20] and he had to relinquish the position of CWMAA secretary to Happy Lim.

In 1939 he moved to New York, where he became a translator at the Chinese Communist newspaper *National Salvation Times*, which had moved to New York from Paris due to the impending European war. However, he did not get along with the editor, Zhao Jiansheng 趙建生 (Rao Shushi 饒漱石), who was the Chinese Communist Party's representative at the Comintern. The CPUSA leadership apparently did not allow Fee to be active in party activities in the New York Chinese community, for he does not appear to have played any role in the founding of the *China Daily News* 美洲華僑日報 in New York City in 1940. However, he evidently was a regular reader of the paper and remained on friendly terms with it. His collected poems include a poem in memory of *China Daily News* chief editor Eugene Moy 梅参天 (1957) and poems commemorating the nineteenth (1959) and twenty-first (1961) anniversaries of the founding of the newspaper.[21] Fee apparently left or was expelled from the party sometime in the 1940s or 1950, thus ending his participation in the Communist movement.

FEE'S EVALUATION OF THE MARXIST LEFT PRIOR TO WORLD WAR II

When this writer asked Fee for his comments on the article "A Historical Survey of Organizations of the Left among the Chinese in America" in 1972,[22] his response gave his views on the Chinese left in America, based on some three decades of hindsight. This may be considered his evaluation of the left as he had experienced it before World War II. Fee stated:

I was more than glad to receive your copy of the CCAS Bulletin, for such an article on that subject matter is long overdue. I was also impressed by the efforts you put into its research.

Putting all formalities aside, I like to make a few observations. First, I wish to compliment you for emphasizing in various sections the basic thesis that the interests among the members of the working class regardless of ethnic groups are identical and that cooperation with groups outside the Chinese community was essential to help effect changes in Chinatown and to improve workers' conditions. However, fine these principles might be, I find an important flaw in them. This is the fact that we posted the Chinese left and left-wing elements in the American Labor movement as a separate and independent force, while they should be part and parcel of the same force. The central question is not "collaboration" but unity. When we drew up the constitution of the CWMAA, the chief and foremost aim was to help the various unions to educate their Chinese members on trade unionism as well as recruit them into the ranks of organized labor. Support of the Chinese revolution, while it is an expression of proletarian internationalism, was never itself the main aim. The problem confronting the Chinese Community can only be solved in the general frame work of struggle against capitalism. A viable and enduring left movement in the Chinese community, in order to withstand the combined onslaught of the U.S. imperialists, the Chinese capitalistic and feudal elements, must itself became an integral part of the American left, and not only seek safety in numbers, but protect by its stronger organizational structure. Had this been done, our reversal during the McCarthy and post-Korean period would have been much less damaging.

Second, the Chinese left suffered not inconsiderably because of its highest leadership has always been in the hand of university students and persons from the northern provinces, persons either have roots in the community or have but transitory interests in its well-being. "We live but for the day of the victorious Chinese revolution, then we shall return to China to do something big and significant." This kind of thinking soon found itself in the expression that the American revolution is "small" and insignificant, and that the Chinese community, in line with our thinking, will change completely to the support of the Chinese Revolution in a matter of at most three to five years. While this prediction of spontaneous response did not materialize, it is easy enough to shrug it off with such remarks as "Why bother? The whole Chinese Community in either San Francisco or New York City is no larger than that of a large village or a fair size commune." It has been these revolutionary "sojourners," more than any other factors that were responsible for the lack of enduring cadres, stable organization and continuous leadership to help the Chinese left to weather some of the storms of the past.

Third, there has been a strong opposition to the policy of turning to the working class for the mass basis of the Chinese left. This is most obvious on the East Coast. Due to the petti-bourgeois character of the leadership as well as its mass basis, the Chinese Left in New York never succeeded in re-orienting itself toward the Chinese workers. As a matter of fact, the small laundry owners of the CHLA strongly resisted the unionization of the wet-wash laundry and shirt laundry workers. Its policy of fraternizing with the restaurant owners and the feudal societies greatly alienated the restaurant workers and the Chinese youth. The *China Daily News*, increasingly a mere Xerox machine for statements and news from China, failed dismally to reflect and lead the struggle of the Chinese community. By following a policy of not expressing any editorial opinion, it hoped to avoid prosecution of the U.S. Government. "We just reprint things that are public records." Surely, this will not be able to substantiate a revolutionary organ as such.

Fourth. While the term "Left" has been treated as some loose and chancy development, it was not really the case. Ever since the latter part of 1927, the establishment of the first Marxist groups in San Francisco and Philadelphia, have furnished continuous guidance and leadership to all the left developments, almost without exceptions. Every grouping, every new advancement had been conceived and planned, mistakes and errors not withstanding.

Fifth. Your article had been particularly weak in dealing with the literary left in connection with the Chinese Youth movement. A case in point was the Chinese Literary Front 華僑文陣 in New York City and its offshoot the "New Shoot" 新苗. A number of left youth literary groups had sprung up under its influence. It is hoped that a future study will remedy this omission.[23]

Six. The most significant Chinese participation in American struggle was the participation of Xifutang in the San Francisco general strike. This one act had won for the Chinese workers the great respect and sympathy of the American labor movement. Chinatown was shut down for three days, with but two inexpensive restaurants . . . allowed to operate for the sake of the single workers.

San Francisco was fortunately to start its leftward development through the youth movement, thereby guaranteed its continuity in leadership and development and somewhat curtailed the petti-bourgeoise tendencies.

Most of the leaders of the Chinese left were not just Chinese leaders as such, but also leaders of the general left movement in their own rights. They played a leading role in the Scottsboro case, the Sacco and Vanzetti case, the Tom Mooney case, the buying of tractors for the U.S.S.R., support of Loyalist Spain and various form of struggles. They also took an active part in the Hunger March to Washington.

Seventh. The most significant expression of Chinese and American solidarity (not limiting to the left) took place after a series of trade union actions in Texas and California ports in flouting the shipments of scrap iron to Japan. In its annual spring feast Maritime unions are invited as honor guests in Chinatown and the New Year lion dance rerouted itself and danced in front of the maritime unions on the water front. Not long afterward, I was sent as an official delegate to the National Conference against War and Fascism in Pittsburg representing the Lǔ-Mei Huaqiao Yijuan Jiuguo Zonghui 旅美華僑義捐救國總會.[24]

FEE AND THE LEFT'S LITERARY MOVEMENT

Fee was an active participant in the literary movement of the left. But even though he edited and contributed to publications from the late 1920s up to the outbreak of the War of Resistance against Japan, most of these writings were meant to meet the political objectives of the moment. His collected poems include only one work from this period, "On the Shore of the Black Sea" (1931).

The Sino-Japanese War, however, stimulated the rise and blossoming of a literary movement of the left. Fee was drawn to it, perhaps in part because he was not involved in the left-wing political activities in the New York Chinese community.[25] Fee claimed to have had hundreds of his poems published in the *China Daily News*, the *China Salvation Times*, and *East Wind* 東風.

Fee described the background and development of the literary movement of the left as follows:

During the Second World War, I was the managing editor of the *Chinese American Weekly* 中美週報, the forerunner of the present day *United Journal* 聯合日報. It started on the premise of uniting the overseas Chinese in the U.S. to support the War of Resistance to the Japanese invasion. During my tenure, I paid particular attention to its literary section, and succeeded in rallying around it a sizable number of young left-wing writers, most

of them were then served in the U.S. armed forces stationing in China, particularly in the Burma theatre and occasionally in Shanghai. On their return from service, they organized a literary society called *The Overseas Chinese Literary Front* (華僑文陣), with the avowed purposes to carry on the left-wing literary tradition of China, which was under severe handicap and to create a new form of overseas Chinese literature, deep into the local people and speaks their languages. The project was quite ambitious and at times almost presumptuous, as it professed to someday revive the literatures of China itself. The guiding light of this group were the two Won brothers Wen Quan 溫泉, Wen Ming 溫明, Jack Lee 李澤, and Chee Shing Lee 李志誠 and others. Known as Muyūn 木雲, I was its poet laureate (pardon the presumption, please) and occasionally I wrote some short treatises under the pseudonym of Yi 毅. When Chiang Kai-shek turned against the united resistance and waged that infamous attack upon the New Fourth Route Army, the *United Journal* changed its position and I resigned as a gesture of protest.[26]

It is not easy to pinpoint the cause for the decline of this overseas Chinese literature movement. All I can do is to give you some of my understandings. From the very beginning I sensed one basic weakness of this movement, at least on part of their leading lights. This is, while they professed a goal of establishing a literature of overseas Chinese, deep under, they still nurtured the ambition of return to continental China and help to "revive" the tradition of people's literature in the new China. One cannot help to detect that in their writings, while present some local idiom and touched upon some special overseas Chinese issues, they were rather superficial, with a lot of gestures but no hearts. Another disappointment to me was the form they chose. Instead of prose and poetry, they selected the most difficult medium, that of short and medium length fictions. But the crushing blow was the reception they received from the literary authorities of the new regime. During the period preceded the liberation, these overseas Chinese writers have done considerable favor to the underground writers in way of material and moral assistance. On returning to China after the liberation, they felt they have been cold-shouldered by these people. I have disagreed with their viewpoint that they should received special considerations just because they had done some good deeds. But I did believe that as overseas writers they should receive some attention, because 1. It should be foreseen that the overseas Chinese communities could very well be the mainstay of the tottering KMT regime and therefore the sustaining of its writers are of long-term interests and 2. A carefully guided overseas Chinese literature could serve the important purpose of bridging the two cultures, the American and Chinese cultures. I have always insisted that the correct form of overseas Chinese literature should be one that not only drawing its wealth from the culture of the new and old China, but also that of the United States. An overseas Chinese literature satisfying of only reflecting the lives of the Chinese communities abroad of necessity has a very limited horizon and lack of sustaining force. A secondary reason could well be that these writers, almost to a man, were not Marxists. They easily fell into the humdrum of making a living and a family. Their vigor and freshness soon dissipated up against the hard struggle of life. Of most of these writers, I, almost alone, continued writing and mainly because I still could draw inspiration from events all over the world and experienced no anti-climax. A third reason was, with the disappearances of all left wing publications, most of these writers can no longer have their works published. Of course in the late fifties and early sixties, there appeared in the Canadian horizon such left-wing publications as the Weekend Express (週末快訊) of Toronto and later on the Eastwind (東風) of the same locale. But they are limited in scope and provincial, and paid very little heed to the literary sector.[27]

Although Fee left the Communist Party organization, his poetry shows that he remained sympathetic to its principles and goals. Many of his poems touched on such subjects as the Chinese revolution, the Soviet Union, the Korean War, the Cuban revolution, the fight against imperialism (such as the murder of Patrice Lumumba), the Civil Rights movement, the execution in Mississippi of William McGee for allegedly raping a white woman, the assassination of John F. Kennedy, and the peace movement. Fee visited Hong Kong in the 1970s to have his *Collected Poems of Mu-yün* 木雲詩詞集 published by Hong Kong's Chih Luen Press in October 1974 with a preface by Sima Lu, the manager of the press. Sima was noted as being an expert on Chinese Communist Party history, and the Chih Luen Press was noted for publications critical of the party.

NEW START IN NEW YORK AFTER WORLD WAR II

Benjamin Fee's life in New York after World War II was strikingly different from his life before the war. He adopted a new Chinese name, M. T. Chang 張明之. Many details on this second half of his life remain to be developed. However, he could not completely escape from his past political affiliations, for the FBI kept him under surveillance as a possible "subversive." In 1960 he was said to have become a partner in a printing shop at 98 Bayard Street in New York City. In the 1950s he became the first Chinese organizer in ILGWU 23-25, which had numerous Chinese members, and then its business agent. In 1957 the union local advertised its benefit program in China Daily News; in 1960 Fee helped the local issue its first handwritten Chinese edition of Local 23 News. He also helped establish English classes for immigrant members.[28] Fee retired from the union position at the end of 1967.[29] He remained active in improving the Chinese community, in April 1976 leading a voters' registration drive in New York Chinatown with the slogan "For Better Wages, Vote." In early 1977 he was honored by New York's Chinatown Planning Council as "Man of the Year."[30]

Fee passed away in New York City in July 1978. His obituary in the *New York Times* on July 9, 1978, read simply: "FEE—Benjamin (M. T. Chang)—born Sept. 30, 1908, Canton, China. Father of Maxine and Clifford. Fighter for progressive causes & international socialism. Union organizer, poet, author and teacher. Died July 3, 1978. Memorial Service to be held on Thursday, July 13, at 6 PM, at PS 124, 40 Division St, NYC."

Benjamin Fee, recently retired as one of the ILGWU local's business agents, honored as "Man of the Year" by the Chinatown Planning Council. (*Local 23-25 News*, March 1977. Courtesy Him Mark Lai.)

He's Man Of The Year

Ben Fee, who recently retired as one of the local's business agents, was recently honored as "Man of the Year" by the Chinatown Planning Council.

Manager Shelley Appleton said that Brother Fee had been a dedicated union officer as well as a dedicated member of the Chinatown community.

He said that, in honoring Brother Fee, the council was also honoring Local 23-25.

In photo above: Brother Fee receives award from Henry Tang, chairman of the CPC Executive Board.

NOTES

1. Fee's obituary in the July 9, 1978, *New York Times* stated that he was born on September 30, 1908; however, his sister Virginia stated in a June 24, 1990, interview with the author that Fee was born on August 31, 1909.
2. Federal Bureau of Investigation files on Benjamin Fee, Josie Fowler Collection, Department of Special Collections Manuscript Division, UCLA Library (hereafter cited as FBI files on Benjamin Fee). Information from these files should be used with caution since much of the information from informants was based on hearsay.
3. Xie Chuang (Xavier Dea), *Chongyang nan zu baoguoxin* [Seas and oceans cannot block an intention to serve the nation] (Guangzhou: Hua'nan Shifan Daxue Yinshuachang, 1993), 1–9.
4. Benjamin Fee, preface to *Collected Poems of Mu-yün* (Hong Kong: Chih Luen Press, 1974).
5. Ma Dianru, "Zhongguo Guomindang zhu-Mei zongzhibu chengli jingguo" [The establishment of the General Branch in the United States of the Nationalist Party of China], in *Commemorative Album for Sixth Anniversary of the Chinese Nationalist Daily of America* (San Francisco: *Kuo Min Yat Po*, 1933), 25–49.
6. Benjamin Fee, letter to author, February 18, 1973. The *Chinese Guide in America* apparently began publication before 1926 since issue 11 was dated February 11, 1926. Josephine Fowler, "'To Be Red and "Oriental"': The Experience of Japanese and Chinese Immigrant Communists in the American and International Communist Movements, 1919–1933" (PhD diss., University of Minnesota, 2003), 415 (hereafter cited as "Japanese and Chinese Immigrant Communists").
7. Benjamin Fee, letter to author, February 18, 1973. The Wuhan government broke with the Communists in July 1927. The assassinations in Vancouver occurred in August 1927. Chen Boxing, Zhu Guanri, and Zhou Huisan were all members of the left-wing faction of the Kuomintang who were connected with the *Chinese Nationalist Daily of America*. Chen was an important financial backer.
8. After the Wuhan government dissociated itself from the Communist Party, the Communists managed to hang on precariously in San Francisco's *Chinese Nationalist Daily of America*. But they were ousted in early 1928 when the Kuomintang-led regimes in Nanjing and Wuhan merged.
9. Peter Kwong, *Chinatown, N.Y.: Labor and Politics, 1930–1950* (New York: Monthly Review Press, 1979), 50.
10. Benjamin Fee, letter to author, February 18, 1973.
11. Xie, *Seas and Oceans*, 9; FBI files on Benjamin Fee.
12. Benjamin Fee, letter to author, February 18, 1973; "The San Francisco Chinese Students Association," *Chinese Students' Monthly* 24, no. 4 (February 1929): 190. In fact Fee was not always president of the SFCSA, but he was always on its executive board, albeit in different capacities during different years. There is no doubt that Fee was an influential leader within the group.
13. Benjamin Fee, letter to author, January 23, 1973.
14. Benjamin Fee, letter to author, July 29, 1973.
15. Benjamin Fee, interview by author, March 28, 1975; Fowler, "Japanese and Chinese Immigrant Communists," 161–62. Fowler interpreted archival documentation as indicating the existence of two youth publications, *Qunsheng* and *Resonance*. However, Fee stated in his interview that *Resonance* was the English name for *Qunsheng*. Considering the low membership of the youth association, it is unlikely that it supported two separate publications.

    Resonance was constantly plagued by insufficient funds (*Chinese Vanguard*, November 15, 1933). After producing a special edition to commemorate the October Revolution in 1934, it ceased publication until April 27, 1935 (*Chinese Vanguard*). On May 11, 1935, *Chinese Vanguard* published a message from the *Resonance* congratulating the former on its fifth anniversary, but a similar message apparently was not sent for its sixth.
16. Benjamin Fee, letter to author, July 29, 1973. Charles Lindbergh's son was kidnapped on March 1, 1932. Tsai, Jiang, and Chen were some of the anti–Chiang Kai-shek leaders who led the establishment of the Fujian People's Government on November 22, 1933. The Chinese Soviet base in neighboring Jiangxi decided not to support this anti-Chiang effort. By the end of January 1934 the Fujian government had been overthrown by Chiang Kai-shek's superior armed forces.
17. See Matyas's recollections in Jennie Matyas and Corrine L. Gilb, "Jennie Matyas and the National Dollar Stores Factory Strike in San Francisco Chinatown," *Chinese America: History & Perspectives, 2008* (San Francisco: Chinese Historical Society of America, 2008), 33–42, reprinted by permission of the Director of the Institute of Industrial Relations, University of California, Berkeley.
18. Benjamin Fee, letter to author, January 22, 1973. Fee refers here to his second wife, Amy Lee (FBI files on Benjamin Fee); at the time he was married to Eva Chan.
19. Benjamin Fee, letter to author, 1973.
20. FBI files on Benjamin Fee.
21. Fee, *Collected Poems of Mu-Yün* (Hong Kong: Chih Luen Press, 1974), 105, 152.
22. *Bulletin of Concerned Asian Scholars* 4, no. 3 (Fall 1972).
23. This omission was partially remedied in Him Mark Lai, "To Bring Forth a New China, to Build a Better America: The Chinese Marxist Left in America to the 1960s," *Chinese America: History & Perspectives, 1992* (San Francisco: Chinese Historical Society of America, 1992), 3–82.
24. Benjamin Fee, letter to author, 1973.
25. Him Mark Lai, "To Bring Forth a New China."
26. Benjamin Fee, letter to author, January 16, 1973. A power struggle within the Kuomintang in New York resulted in the 1942 ouster of Wu Chin-foo as chief editor of *Mun dHey*, the party organ there. Wu then founded *Chinese American Weekly* (1942) and the daily *United Journal* (1952).
27. Benjamin Fee, letter to author, July 29, 1973.
28. Xiaolan Bao, *Holding Up More Than Half the Sky: Chinese Women Garment Workers in New York City, 1948–92* (Urbana: University of Illinois Press, 2001), 153.
29. Fee, *Collected Poems of Mu-Yün*, 225.
30. *Local 23-25 News*, March 1977.

Selections from *Collected Poems of Mu-yün*

Benjamin Fee

TRANSLATIONS BY ELLEN YEUNG AND HIM MARK LAI

"The Life and Times of Benjamin Fee" by Him Mark Lai also appears in this volume, page 12. The first English translation, by Ellen Yeung, of Ben Fee's 1935 report "The Chinese American Garment Industry" appeared in the 2008 special issue of Chinese America: History & Perspectives, *"Labor and San Francisco's Garment Industry."*

AUTHOR'S PREFACE[1]

I left China to come to the New World at thirteen. My first acquaintance with poetry occurred when I was sixteen or seventeen when I, together with Miss Luo,[2] daughter of a Cantonese revolutionary martyr, translated the second verse of the "Internationale" from English to Chinese. I still remember the first four lines:

> No savior from on high delivers;
> No faith have we in prince or peer.
> Our own right hand the chains must shiver:
> Chains of hatred, greed, and fear.

Since then I have written over a thousand poems, ranging from free verse to metrical poetry of varying line lengths, tonal patterns, and rhyming schemes. Over half of these have appeared in overseas publications. I have never regarded myself as a poet; therefore, I have always included subjects that are not normally considered appropriate for poetry. And indeed, quite a few overseas Chinese literary connoisseurs have criticized my work for poor choice of words and lack of classical allusions. I have never defended myself because I do not believe language should be allowed to subvert meaning. The only claims I can make about this anthology are as follows: (1) In general, my writing is a natural expression of what I feel, without too much effort at polishing or reworking. (2) My poems exhibit a consistent ideology without resorting to catchy revolutionary slogans. (3) I have not adopted any nationalistic platform. I focus on objective reality and confine my discussions to the issues at hand. (4) I stay away from social verses celebrating birthdays and weddings. I consider them meaningless. You also will not find in my works any sentimental odes, melancholy laments, or self-pitying moaning. (5) I believe there is no greater people than the Chinese people.

Finally, I wish to express my gratitude to Mr. Sima Lu 司馬璐 and his wife, Madam Jü Baiyi 居白易, for all their editing assistance.[3]

Mu-Yün 木雲
July 4, 1974
New York City

DEPORTATION OF CHINESE AMERICANS

March 27, 1962

*(The original has forty lines of five characters/syllables,
with even lines using the same rhyme throughout.)*

Living under another's roof is difficult,
Like chrysanthemums at the foot of a fence.
They grow wild in autumn,
Mixed in with common weeds.
There is no Tao Yüanming in this alien land.[4]
Who, then, knows how to appreciate the yellow flowers?
Spring arrives, so does wild grass.
No better time to cut everything down.
It's only a square inch of land,
Yet even that is too much space.
No matter if the roots are deep and long.
No matter if the stems are young and single.
Fragrance elicits no mercy.
Solitude brings mistreatment.
Alas we Chinese Americans,
Our fate is worse than that of the flowers.
Year after year we experience exclusion.
Place after place we suffer expulsion.
Thousands and thousands live in constant fear.
Hundred and hundreds are in prison.
Which family still has intact eggs,
When everywhere you see toppled nests?
Worriedly waiting for the deportation vessel,
Fearfully anticipating Immigration's orders,
The strong plan protests.
The weak threaten suicide.

We are separated from China by thousands of miles.
    We live lives of prisoners in the New World.
The masters are quick with glib defenses:
The harsh laws are far from cruel.
Out of all Chinese Americans,
We deport but 56 annually.
Compared to the entire Chinese population
It's just one grain from a whole granary.
Such an argument mocks our intelligence.
Containing our anger is an impossibility.
This is such a big country,
With spacious land and rich resources.
56 people should be easy to accommodate.
Why subject them to such suffering?

DEPORTATION OF CHINESE AMERICANS

拘撥華僑　　三，二七，六二

寄人籬下苦，
苦若籬下菊，
秋至任叢生，
莠草相雜俗，
異域無淵明，
黃花誰賞目.
春至同野草，
刈除恐不速，
籬邊方寸地，
未許或寄足.
不問根深長，
不問枝幼獨.
芬芳難邀恩，
孤清反受辱.
悲哉我華僑，
運比黃花蹙.
年年受排擠，
地地被驅逐.
萬千常自危，
百十紛下獄.
何家有完卵，
到處巢傾覆?
愁待撥僑舶.
怕聽移民局.
強者計抗議，
弱者脅剖腹.
萬里隔神州，
一世羈新陸.
主子作辯忙，
虐政非云酷.
芸芸僑眾中，
年撥僅五六.
以此衡全僑，
實太倉一粟.
以此質明智，
忿怒更難束.
斯是大國度，
地大物富育.
五六本易容，
何竟加荼毒?

THE GIRL NEXT DOOR

April 8, 1959

*(The original has sixty lines of five characters/syllables,
with even lines using the same rhyme throughout.)*

The young girl next door
Is barely ten—a tender age—
With peachlike face and rosy cheeks,
Blond hair and eyes of blue.
A girl who looks intelligent,
She deports herself with grace.
We pass each other daily,
Chat casually and freely.
Children learn from their parents.
The fruit   doesn't fall far from the tree.
Her mentality is shallow,
Her conversation superficial.
She doesn't say "chop suey"
But she eats food that is "chink."
Several times I admonished her
About this disrespectful term.
My words passed like a breeze through her ears
Fading, without changing anything.
One evening she was at my door,
Her face worried and fearful.
"Yesterday my father said
China is becoming strong.
In another 50 years
America will be destroyed.
When that time arrives
Will you show me mercy?"
Her words alarmed me at first.
Then I was angry and hurt.
What was her father thinking?
Such sensational statements cause panic.
Once there was the "yellow peril"
A ridiculous invention, hard to verify.

Yet it became a pretext for invasion
By nations with imperialist intention.
Gnawing like a feeding caterpillar at S.E. Asia,
Their ugly faces revealed, Japan and America.
To seek the liberation of mankind,
Both yellow and white races are in the same camp.
The two nations, America and China,
Enjoyed a fraternal relationship, like brothers.
If peacefully existing together,
A wonderful future both can expect,
With cultural exchanges flourishing,
And the two economies thriving and booming.
When no evil intentions are harbored
What need is there for constant vigilance?
Gently I assured my young friend.
"The rumor is unfounded.
Good neighbors, China and America,
Just like we two are.
To cultivate friendship, there is barely time.
Why then should we act like charcoal and ice?
If we show mutual respect,
And treat each other with sincerity,
Our friendship will last as long as the pine,
Growing greener and greener with each year."
The girl nodded with understanding,
Her face lit up with a smile.
Our hands clasped in a long shake.
The fog has parted and the sun is beaming.

THE GIRL NEXT DOOR
鄰家女　四，八，五九

鄰家有少女，
芳年僅十齡，
桃腮玫瑰頰，
金髮藍眼睛.
外表似聰慧，
儀態尤娉婷。
日夕相過從，
談笑多不矜.
父母富陋習，
子女相襲承，
意識常膚淺，
出言浮且輕.
不云食雜碎，
偏喜說食「清」，
戒之再而三，
斯名殊不敬，
言如風過耳，
泯泯難通靈.
一夕忽造訪，
面色憂且驚：
「昨聽老父言，
中國方崢興，
只消五十載，
美　國將被平.
斯時君對我，
手下可留情？」
聞之初愕然，
再念怒難名.
伊父何居心，
危言聳觀聽？
前人倡「黃禍」，
荒誕不足徵.

帝國主義者，
遽藉此侵凌.
蠶食東亞洲，
日美同猙獰.
求人類解放，
黃白同陣營.
中美兩民族，
情誼本弟兄.
倘和平共處，
偌大好前程。
文化互交流，
經濟共繁榮.
要非藏禍心，
何須長戒警？
溫言慰小妹：
「傳說原不經，
中美應親鄰，
正如我與卿.
修睦且不暇，
何來炭與冰？
苟能相敬重，
待遇由衷誠.
友誼若松柏，
歲歲長菁菁！」
聞言女點頭，
開顏笑盈盈，
伸手作長握，
撥霧見晴明！

BATTLE IN HARLEM

August 3, 1964

*(The original has twelve sets of four lines, with the first two lines
rhyming. Each line has seven characters/syllables.)*

New York is famous for its unmatched prosperity,
But is also known for its infamous ghettos.
The poor neighborhoods are integrated,
Except in Harlem where it is still segregated.
Even sudden wealth sometimes comes to a ghetto.
Pockets filled to the brim, the lucky ones relocate,
Except for the blacks whose luck never turns.
Here, generations of lives are confined,
A small area measuring three miles across,
A population crammed together three hundred thousand
     strong,
Roofs leaking, walls crumbling, and rents rising,
Knees touching, elbows brushing, and bodies pushing.
Huge rats scamper in daylight, bold as brass,
Gnawing on babies when the kitchen is bare.
Housing is rare, property owners corner the market.
Salary is low, in vain the people labor.
In rags and in hunger, shivering children go to school,
Sitting in ill-equipped buildings and taught by ill-prepared
     teachers,
Thus graduating without learning.
Who can blame them for the wrong path they're taking?
Second-class citizens in bitterness wallowing,
Death and disease relentlessly attacking,
Vicious hoodlums constantly preying,
Good people forced into crime, succumbing.
Brutal police would only cast their nets,
Ignore the causes but treat harshly the symptoms.
Human lives, to them, are just worthless weeds.
Women and children, old and young, make no difference.
And so it happened—a black boy barely seven
Killed for nothing, public anger inflaming,
Clamors for justice resolutely rejected.
A single spark can start a prairie fire.

Harlem is in flames.
Glass and bricks are flying.
Now they know a struck flint produces fire.
People are arming themselves for self-protection.
The wolves in power are worried sick,
Mobilizing and deploying forces, all in a panic.
But all they do is repeat the same mistakes, in vain,
Northern and southern states follow the tired old tactics.
They array themselves as if facing a massive army.
The air rings with sounds of bullets flying.
Blood runs on the street, teeth are gnashing,
But before the enemies, not a single soul moaning.
Uncle Toms and turncoats are trembling in fear.
Honeyed words can no longer stem the raging waters.
The people anxiously wait for the coming of the east wind
To disperse the gloomy shadows and reveal the sun.

BATTLE IN HARLEM

哈林區搏戰　　八，三，六四

紐約繁華誇無匹，
兼誇無匹貧民窟。
貧民窟也無種分，
獨哈林區限色別。

貧民 間有暴富時，
囊豐載滿立他移。
唯有黑人運最厄，
世世代代囚於斯！

方橫三里彈丸區，
卅萬生靈苦跼居。
漏瓦頹垣租倍蓰，
捉膝接肘肉相堆。

碩鼠欺人白晝狂，
廚空乏食嚙兒郎！
地主居奇賈佔市，
薪低工賤枉勞忙。

襤褸飢寒人就學，
校設不完師道惡，
學成依舊業無成，
誰怪青年多墮落？

次民地位幾酸辛，
死亡疾病兩交侵，
匪類歹徒魚肉慘，
被迫良民變罪民。

暴警唯知佈網羅，
無心治本治標苛，
民命視乎如草芥，
婦孺老幼同災磨。

適有黑童僅逾髫，
無辜被殺恨難消，
群求伸雪遭嚴拒，
星星一火野原燎！

哈林區上烈炎揚，
玻璃磚塊請君嘗，
始知擊石終成火，
武裝自衛旌旗張。

當道豺狼盡戰驚，
動員調警又忘形，
舉直措枉行如故，
美南美北習相承o

佈陣一如大敵臨，
橫飛子彈擘空音，
浴血街頭人切齒，
敵前沒個再呻吟！

譚叔〈註〉漢奸心膽寒，
蜜言難復阻狂瀾。
愁看東風薰沐處，
沖破霾陰一片丹！

〈註：譚叔，Uncle Tom，指出賣黑人自身利益之叛徒〉

VISIT TO THE LINCOLN MEMORIAL

Lincoln's Birthday, February 12, 1947

(The original is in free verse.)

In the middle of New York Harbor,
At the mouth of the Hudson River,
The colossal Statue of Liberty
Stands at the edge of Bedloe's Island,[5]
Her right hand holding aloft a flaming torch,
Her left hand grasping the Independence Declaration tablet,
Announcing to the masses fleeing to the New World,
 "Here is the land of freedom.
This is the path to light.
These are the steps to happiness.
Those who seek liberation,
Throw yourselves into my bosom."

And yet,
In the humble alleys of Mexico City,
In the urban streets of Bangkok,
In the wilds of South Africa,
In the splendid city of Paris,
People are testing the limits of freedom.
People are climbing the steps to democracy.
This dark bronze goddess,
Standing resolutely in the wind,
Is she what they're seeking? No!
She is a great symbol,
But she cannot symbolize greatness.

"Give me liberty,
Or give me death"
What an emphatic declaration!
"Right or wrong,
Still my country!"
What a patriotic exclamation!
And yet,

In the humble alleys of Mexico City,
In the urban streets of Bangkok,
In the wilds of South Africa,
In the splendid city of Paris,
People are taking up the call for democracy.
People are echoing the roaring cry for liberty.
Are they seeking only self-expression
And have no time for other honest sayings?
No!
Those words struggle to be symbols.
But they do not symbolize struggle.

White-hot lava did not shape his skeleton.
Divine tools did not sculpt his features.
His body was not draped in a flowing robe.
His head was not covered with an eight-point wreath.
He was such an ordinary man.
He came into this world in a humble cabin.
His feet were firmly planted on the grassland.
    His appearance was not dignified or refined,
    His face plain looking but kind,
    His high cheekbones like burls on a branch,
    His long skinny legs like coiled roots of a tree,
    His thick beard like wild grass on the prairie,
    His sharp bright eyes like stars of late autumn.
    His stovepipe hat has collected a lot of dust and grime,
    His black woolen jacket covered with numerous
    wrinkles.
He was the model of simplicity,
A common man who achieved greatness.
Yet he had
    A deep and encompassing love,
    A sincere heart,
    A noble soul.
Though the superficial jeered at him for being uncultured,
Though the despicable tried to secretly plunder his remains,
Though the vicious tried to destroy his corporeal body,
And yet,
Hundreds of thousand years later,
    Handsome men turned to hideous skeletons
    Grave robbers trod on their own graves
    Assassins were reviled in the annals of history
People were like giant waves on the beach,
At times roaring, at times surging.
Only our Lincoln
Remained calm and true.
He never raised his voice with indignation.
He never pledged death for exaggeration.
Yet on his two thin narrow shoulders
Sat the burden of emancipation,
Lay the destiny of a free Union,
Rested the ardent wish of countless people.

VISIT TO THE LINCOLN MEMORIAL
訪林肯紀念堂

在紐約灣的中流，
在哈德遜河的河口，
自由女神的巨像，
屹立着比魯斯島的水涯，
她右手高擎着指天耀日的火炬，
她左手牢握着獨立宣言的方牌；
宣示給千百萬投向新大陸的災黎：
「這是『自由的國度』呀！
　　是『光明之路』，
　　是『幸福之階』，
　　追求解放的赤子喲，
　　請你投入我的慈懷！」

然而呵，
在墨西哥城的陋巷，
在曼谷的市街，
在荒野的南非，
在華麗的巴黎，
人們測量自由的指尺，
人們攀登民主的梯階，
是這銅色黝然，
臨風聳立的女神嗎？
不是呀！
她只是偉大的象徵，
她不能算是象徵的偉大。

「不自由，
毋寧死！」
那是多麼堅強的誓詞？
　「是與非，
　仍是我們的祖國！」
那是多麼忠鯁的警句？
然而呵，
在墨西哥城的陋巷，
在曼谷的市街，
在荒野的南非，
在華麗的巴黎，
人們宣揚民主的號召，
人們呼籲自由的叫吼，
是這樣的祇求自己的解脫，
不管他人枉直的名言嗎？
不是呀！
它們祇是爭鬥的象徵，
它們不能算是象徵的爭鬥。

白熱的熔巖沒有鍛鍊出他的骨骼，
神工的刀斧沒有鑿鑿出他的器官，
他身上沒有穿着衣帶飄然的神服，
他頭上沒有帶着八起稜尖的桂冠；
他是這樣的平凡，
他在粗木屋裏降入了人寰，
他在草根頭上站定了腳跟，
　　他沒有尊嚴文彬的儀容，
　　他祇有寡陋慈祥的面孔：
　　高聳的兩顴像是樹幹的瘤節，
　　瘦長的兩腿像是樹底的盤根，
　　茸茸的鬍鬚像是荒郊的野草，
　　烱烱的眸子像是晚秋的寒星，
　　煙囪帽積了不少的污痕，
　　黑呢衣起了無數的皺紋，
他是簡樸的典型，
他是偉大的平凡，
但他有
　　淵博之愛，
　　誠摯之心，
　　高潔之魂。

皮相的儘管嘲笑他的粗野，
卑污的儘管偷掘他的遺骸，
狼毒的儘管毀滅他的肉身！
然而
千百年後，
　　麗男子都變作了猙獰的髑髏；
　　盜墳賊終被踐踏了自己的孤墳；
　　行刺暴客永成了萬古的罪人。

人們是像海邊的巨浪，
不時怒發和疾騰，
獨有我們的林肯，
永是鎮靜和純真。
他沒有激昂的呼叫，
他沒有誓死的誇張；
然而他的瘦削的兩膊，
卻擔負着一個少數民族的解放，
維繫着一個自由聯邦的興亡，
寄托着無數平民的熱望。

He had the heart of a martyr.
But he loathed to put on a martyr's airs.
    "God must have loved common mortals.
    Or why else
    Would He have created such a multitude?"
And so with mildness
He opposed the powerful and the rich.
He glorified the ordinary.
He spread his belief in universal love to the world.

The traces of blood at the battlefield of Gettysburg
Had not been completely washed away by the years.
A few bare and aging trees
Sheltered the rows and rows of soldiers' graves.
    The sky was dark and gloomy,
    The mourners sad and sorrowful,
    The landscape silent and remote.
Five years of Civil War, of pain and suffering,
Pressed heavily on the hearts of Americans.
    The victors swaggered in arrogance,
    And the defeated hid their hatred.
The slaves liberated
    Threw off their shackles,
    But could not find a place to set their feet.
Soldiers who sacrificed their lives
    Left behind widows and orphans,
    But still lacked a place to rest their spirits.
Ah, dear Lincoln,
How did you comfort the anxiety-ridden?
    "To our soldiers who died for us
    We should dedicate our lives.
    We should devote ourselves to the task left unfinished by
    them.
    We should dare to make the ultimate sacrifice just as they
    did,
    So that this nation conceived in liberty
    Will have a new birth of freedom,
    That this government of the people, by the people, and
    for the people,
    Shall not perish from the earth."
No indignant shouts.
No exaggerated pledges of death.
No overblown oration.
No artful lies.
And yet
His sincerity
    Touched every heart.
His genuine tears
    Filled every eye.

Thirty-six Doric columns,
Thirty-six free states,
Hold up this imposing edifice.
A symbol of your extraordinary life.
The slaves walk up the many steps one by one
    Their brows flaring.
The oppressed stand in front of your marble throne
    Their heads held high.
In the middle of New York Harbor,
At the mouth of the Hudson River,
Stood the Statue of Liberty
But it is on the bank of the Potomac River,
    In Washington, D.C., the capital,
    In this imposing building,
That the Great Spirit of Freedom and Democracy lies.

他有殉道者的心;
但他不屑擺出了殉道者的模樣!
「上帝一定很愛平凡的人,
　　不然唰,
　　為甚麼他創造了這大多的一輩?」
就這樣的平淡,
　　他對權貴抗衡,
　　他光大了平凡,
　　他把博愛的信念遍洒了人間。

吉特斯堡戰場上的血痕,
還沒曾給歲月洗去了斑斑,
幾株枯秃了的古樹,
蔭庇了座座戰士的土墳。
　　天是陰沉,
　　人是淒黯,
　　景是幽森,
五年多內戰的慘痛,
重重地壓着美國人的心;
　　戰勝者的驕橫,
　　戰敗者的暗恨;
被解放了的奴隸,
　　擺脫了枷鎖,
　　卻沒處兒站定腳跟;
被犧牲了的戰士,
　　遺留了孤寡,
　　卻沒空兒憩息陰魂。
呵,親愛的林肯呀!
你怎樣的慰藉這焦灼的一輩呢?
「戰士為我們而死,
　　我們應為他們而生,
　　我們要繼承先烈的遺志,
　　我們要敢作後死的犧牲,
　　要使這個自由的國土,
　　真的自由新生,
　　民治,民有,民享的政權,
　　永久的存在人間。」
沒有激昂的呼叫,
沒有誓死的誇張,
沒有滔滔的雄辭,
沒有詭譎的說謊。
然而呵,
他的至誠
　　透進了每一個人的心房;
熱情之淚
　　充滿了每一個人的眼眶。

三十六根古希臘式的圓柱,
三十六個自由的州,
支持着這所巍峨的大廈,
象徵着你的偉大的一生。
奴隸們拾級升上你的長階,
　　個個都揚起了他的眉毛;
被壓迫者面臨着你的大理石寶座,
　　個個都抬起了他的頭顱。
在紐約灣的中流,
在哈德遜河的河口,
那裏起屹立着自由之神。
但在普他麥河的河濱,
　　在哥林比亞的首區,
　　在這一所巍峨的大廈,
才憑寄着偉大自由民主之魂。

ON THE SHORE OF THE BLACK SEA

July 26, 1931

(The original is in free verse.)

Several hundred friends were watching a comic skit.
I, who knew no Russian,
Slipped in with them, laughing when they laughed.
Isn't that funnier than the play itself?

Go and sit on the shore of the Black Sea
Said my trembling heart.
And so I left the boisterous scene,
But could not evade the couples by the water.

Is this the Black Sea which I have long admired?
This sweeping gray expense of water.
But it's all one color.
Where is the sea?
Where is the sky?

The ambitious plans of Peter the Great
The numerous battles of Mohammed's disciples
The blood of thousands and thousands of fighting men
The flames of war of many centuries
Should have painted this Black Sea
And turned it to red.

In the day it is green like colored glaze
At night it is gray like brick and gravel
It made me wonder,
How did the name Black Sea originate?

The sun has long set,
A lingering ribbon of red light
Adroitly, all by itself,
Divided the western sky and water.

The new moon nearing the end of the quarter
Hung lopsided at the edge of the dusky sky.
Shy and fearful, it emitted little light,
Casting but a few specks of silver on the surface of the sea.

The gentle waves,
Compared to the roaring breakers by the Golden Gate,
Are truly weak and insignificant.
But when they crashed on the reefs,
They made their own distinctive sounds.

Oh, waves of the Black Sea,
You, idly and foolishly,
Beat at the reefs of Sochi in the morning,[6]
Splashed against the grounds of Constantinople at night.
And yet
Have you ever the two worlds
Compared and scrutinized?

There lies the paradise for workers and peasants!
Heroes of socialist construction,
Soldiers of special operations,
Come here to enjoy your summer vacation.[7]

You can rant and rave as if there is something to shout about,
Make accusations that are totally baseless.
You can ride a horse and bend a bow to your heart's content,
Raise the wind and stir up the waves.

Here stands our solid rock in the turbulent stream.
The Five Year Plan will surely succeed.[8]
It stands high above the mortal world
Looking with disdain on the puny wind and waves,
Smiling.

ON THE SHORE OF THE BLACK SEA
黑海傍　七，廿六，三一

幾百同伴都在看滑稽劇，
不懂得俄文的我，
混在裏面隨人歡笑，
這不是比劇情還滑稽麼？

獨到黑海傍坐吧，
說我微顫的心弦，
就這樣脫離了煩鬧的劇場，
可是還躲不了海傍的雙雙伴侶。

這就是我所素慕的黑海咩？
灰色的汪洋一片，
混一色的，
恁的那塊兒是水？
　　那塊兒是天？

聖彼得大帝的雄謀；
謨罕默教徒的戰跡；
千萬健兒的血，
幾世紀的烽火；
早應把這黑海，
染成赤色。

白晝它綠似琉璃，
晚來它灰似磚礫，
這不由使我希奇，
黑海這名兒是怎樣起的？

日早落了，
一抹赤色鮫鮫綃似的迴光，
巧妙單獨地，
把西方的天和水劃分着。

快滿弦的新月，
斜掛在昏沉的天際，
嬌怯的起不了甚麼光輝，
衹在海面上撒下了幾掇的銀屑。

細細的浪潮，
比起金門港邊的掀然巨波，
也實在可憐的渺小！
但當它擊到石礁上，
卻自成異响。

黑海的波濤喲，
你愚騃騃地！
朝打着Sochi的石礁，
晚洗滌着君士但丁堡的園地，
但是呵，
你可曾把這兩個世界，
來比一比？

那兒是工農的樂土！
社會主義建設的英雄，
突擊隊的戰士喲，
到這裏來把炎暑渡。

恁你煞有介事的狂呼，
恁你毫無根據的攻訐，
儘地的盤馬彎弓，
儘地的興風作浪。

這裏是我們的中流砥柱，
五年計劃的必然勝利。
它矗立在塵寰高處，
睥睨着弱小的風浪，
笑微微地。

THE FIVE HUNDRED BRAVE MEN OF NANCHANG[9]

1939

(The original is in free verse.)

Enemy mounted troops have crossed the River Xiu.
Enemy open boats have surged up the River Kan.
The Wheelwrights Isle could not stop the advancing wheels of
    the enemy vehicles.
The Riggers Isle could not tangle up the mooring ropes of the
    enemy boats.[10]
The blue sky and blue water in front of the Tengwang Pavilion,[11]
Set off by the blood-drenched Rising Sun flag,
Have turned a greenish yellow,
Have turned turbid and impure.

Monster-like enemy tanks,
Rows on rows, baring their huge fangs,
Moving their lumbering bodies,
Grinding to dust our homes,
Crushing flat our fields.
Who will stop the spiked wheels of the enemy vehicles?
Who will provide cover for our retreating troops?
To buy us precious time
To scorch the earth and empty the fields,
And defend the cities of Gaoan and Wanzai.[12]

Is this an express command from a ranking officer?
No. This is a plea from a nation.
Take a good look.
The heroes of Sihang Cangku[13]
The stranded soldiers on Kuanglu Mountain[14]
What inspired them to fight on?
Was it the fervent zeal of patriotism?
Was it the burning hatred for the enemy?

Over the drill ground
Fluttered the blue, white, and red flag of China.
Within the ranks
Stood tall and resolute the five hundred brave men.

We grew up amidst gunfire in De'an and Ruichang.[15]
We were baptized by poisoned gas in the town of Wucheng.[16]
Tattered army uniforms,
Officers' attire we won through the hundreds of battles fought.
Smooth shiny scars,
Medals and insignia that will be kept by us forever.
We died yesterday but have been resurrected.
Today we are prepared to give our lives to the cause again.

Five hundred pairs of fists,
Five thousand fingers,
Extended,
Raised high,
Five hundred throats,
Five hundred open mouths,
Together,
Crying out.
"I will go. I … I … I, too, will go."
We are true sons.
For our people,
For our country,
We do not fear dying.
We defy death!

Nanchang is not France.
There is no Maginot Line.[17]
Neither is Nanchang Xuzhou.[18]
There is no Hindenburg moat.[19]
And yet
Nanchang has five hundred brave men.
Five hundred hearts pledged to die.
Five hundred bodies dedicated to people and country.
No need for machine guns.
No need for cannons.
Around our bodies of steel
We will wrap high-powered explosives.
Five hundred men.
Five hundred bombs of flesh and blood.

Down on hands and knees … creep forward.
Waiting for the right moment … spring into action.
Each one of us
is the Yue Fei who defeated the guaizi cavalry.[20]
Each one of us
is the Gao Chong who overturned the armored cars.[21]
FUCK!
We will blow you into smithereens.
Then we will see
Who is tougher?
Who is stronger?

THE 500 BRAVE MEN OF NANCHANG

南昌五百勇士

敵人的銕騎渡過了修水，
敵人的划子衝過了贛江，
軥轆洲拖抓不住敵車的軥轆，
打纜洲打捆不住敵舟的繩纜；
滕王閣前的一色水和天，
被那沾滿了血漬的太陽旗，
映得蒼黃，
映得混濁。

怪獸似的敵人坦克車，
成排成排地張露着巨牙，
要用牠的笨重身軀，
壓碎我們的老家，
輾平我們的田野。

誰去阻止敵車的齒輪呢？
誰去掩護我們後退的軍旅？
好讓我們多得點時間來，
實行「焦土」，「清野」；
佈防高安，萬載。

這是長官的明令嗎？
不，這是民族國家的請求呵！
你看吧，
四行倉庫的英雄，
匡廬山上的孤軍，
是誰鼓舞着他們的呢？
不是愛國的赤忱？
不是殺敵的熱火？

教場上，
高豎着青天白日滿地紅的國徽；
行列裏，
肅立着五百名頂天立地的勇士；
我們在德安，瑞昌的砲火裏生長，
我們在吳城鎮的毒瓦斯下洗禮；
襤褸軍服，
是我們百戰得來的上將衣冠；
光潤痕疤，
是我們永遠長留的襟章勳位 ••
昨日死而復生，
今日又準備成仁就義！

五百雙拳頭，
五千隻手指，
直伸，
高舉；
五百個嚨喉，
五百張口嘴，
齊聲，
共叫；
「我去，我去，我去 …….. 我也去！」
我們是好男兒，
為着民族，
為着國家，
我們不怕死！
我們敢死！

南昌并不是法蘭西，
沒有「馬奇諾」的碉堡；
南昌也不是徐州，
沒有「興登卜」的塹壕；
可是呵，
南昌有五百名勇士，
五百顆誓死的心，
五百具許了民族國家的肉體。

不要機關槍，
不要迫擊砲，
我們要在鋼銕似的渾身，
纏滿了爆發力強大的炸藥粉；
五百個人，
造成五百枚肉彈！

匐伏•••••• 爬行，
覓機 •••••• 潛動；
我們一個個，
是擊破拐子馬的岳飛；
我們一個個，
是挑起鐵華車的高寵：
待等我們挨近這些怪獸的肚皮，
他媽的！
定把你們轟毀炸翻！
那時看看，
誰比誰頑強，
誰比誰堅硬？

"Boom … boom … boom … boom"
Thunder-like explosions rocked the sky.
Scattered in the air
Flames that look like snakes,
Lightning flashes that look like pythons,
Blood that looks like blossoming flowers,
Flesh that look like meat sauce,
Pieces of steel,
Chunks of earth.
Ah! Weapons made of flesh and blood
Have finally halted the advancing wheels,
Blown apart the stomachs of the monsters.

You bandits who invade us! Listen! Think!
This thunderous boom,
Does it sound
Remotely like
The tune of someone proposing peaceful capitulation?

You bandits who invade us!
Look and see! Understand!
In Nanchang
Five hundred descendants of the Yellow Emperor Xuanyuan,
Vanguards of the liberation of the Chinese people,
Defenders of the righteous principle of humanitarianism,
Have exploded into five hundred blazing blossoms.
In contrast, there were your three courageous "human bombs"
Before the town of Miaoxing,[22]
Who wasted their blood at the hand of the executioner.
Who squandered away their flesh for the invaders.
The former
How noble and magnificent!
The latter
How pitiful and insignificant!

「隆•••隆•••隆•••隆」
打雷似的震天價响。
四處遍飛，
火蛇，
電蟒；
血花，
肉醬；
鐵塊，
泥土。
血肉造成的新武器，
呀！畢竟停止了敵寇的車輪，
炸碎了怪獸的腸肚！

侵略強盜們呵！你聽，你想，
這轟然的巨响，
可像
有半點
主降主和的音調模樣？

侵略強盜們呵！
你見，你曉；
南昌上，
有五百個軒轅的帝胄，
中華民族解放的前鋒，
人道正義的防衛手，
正爆發了五百朵熱烘烘的花呢？
比起廟行鎮前，
你們的「肉彈三壯士」，
血為劊子手白流，
肉為侵略者枉費。
前者呵，
是多麼崇高和偉大！
後者呵，
是多麼可憐而渺小！

NOTES

1. Translated by Ellen Yeung.
2. Luo Jingyi 羅靜宜, or S. S. Lo 羅素抒, came to America in 1925 and attended the University of California and Stanford University. She joined the Communist Party in 1927 and was sent to study at Moscow's Labor University, after which she returned to China in 1930.
3. Sima Lu (Smarlo Ma) was originally named Ma Yi 馬義. He joined the Chinese Communist Party in June 1937 and became a librarian in the Communist-controlled Yanan region. His experiences there soon led him to become disillusioned with the party, and he left it in 1943. After the founding of the PRC he moved to Hong Kong, where he became an expert on CPC history. He emigrated to New York City in 1983. Ju Baiyi was his first wife. After she passed away, he married author Geyang 戈揚, who had left China after the 1989 Tiananmen incident.
4. Tao Yüanming was a Jin-dynasty (fifth-century AD) official noted for his integrity, who had a special appreciation for chrysanthemums.
5. Bedloe's Island is the former name of Liberty Island.
6. Sochi is a Russian port and health resort on the Black Sea.
7. The author is referring to the USSR, which had gone through a revolution to establish the world's first socialist republic, supposedly as the first step toward the communist classless society.
8. Beginning in 1928, the Soviet Union initiated a series of five-year plans to build its economy in an orderly fashion.
9. The provincial government of Jiangxi was located in Nanchang. During the War of Resistance against Japan, the Japanese army sent a column that crossed the Gan River on the western side of the city to launch an attack on Nanchang on March 17, 1939. The battle raged for ten days, but at the end the poorly armed Chinese army was no match for the superior armament and air power of the Japanese. After sustaining more than one hundred thousand casualties to the Japanese thirteen thousand, it yielded the city to the Japanese, who occupied it until the end of hostilities in 1945. This poem tells of an incident during the battle for the city.
10. Wheelwrights Isle (Julu Zhou) and Riggers Isle (Dalan Zhou) are localities in Nanchang. The poet is playing the literal meanings of the geographical terms against descriptions of the enemy's armament.
11. The Tengwang Pavilion is a structure in Nanchang first built during the Tang dynasty. It was made famous by an essay written by Wang Bo in the *pianti* style (rhythmic prose characterized by parallelism and ornateness), which countless Chinese students learned to recite in schools.
12. Gaoan and Wanzai are counties in Jiangxi province west of Nanchang.
13. The Sihang Cangku was a reinforced concrete warehouse in Shanghai's Zhabei district just north of Soochow Creek. The structure was jointly owned by four Shanghai banks. It occupied an area of 20,000 square meters (64 meters in width by 54 meters in depth and 25 meters in height) and was built in 1931. Toward the end of the Japanese attack on Shanghai in 1938, when Chinese army units were withdrawing from the city, four hundred Chinese soldiers under the command of Xie Jinyuan tenaciously defended this point for four days and nights, thus effectively delaying the advancing Japanese so as to enable the main Chinese army to withdraw safely.
14. When the Japanese army attacked and captured Jiujiang, Jiangxi, in late May 1938, two regiments were assigned to protect the retreat route of the main forces of the Chinese army. After they retreated to Kuanglu Mountain, they held out against Japanese attacks. However, after the capture of Nanchang their position became untenable and they retreated safely, yielding the mountain to the Japanese on April 18, 1939.
15. De'an and Ruichang are counties in northern Jiangxi near the city of Jiujiang.
16. Wucheng Town is in northern Jiangxi near Jiujiang.
17. The Maginot Line was a series of fortifications built along the Franco-German border before World War II to defend against an attack from Germany.
18. After Shanghai and then Nanjing fell into Japanese hands by the end of 1938, the Japanese army launched attacks to control the Huai River and lower Chang (Yangtze) River basins. In mid-May, 1939, the Japanese army captured Xuzhou, the strategic transportation hub in northern Jiangsu.
19. The Hindenburg Line was a system of defenses in northeastern France during World War I that the Germans constructed in 1916–17 to defend against attacks by the Allies.
20. When the Nüzhen were attacking the Song empire, one of their most effective weapons was guaizi cavalry, where several horses were chained together. The momentum of the combinations was very difficult to defend against until Yue Fei figured out that killing or maiming one of the horses in the team would immobilize the entire team.
21. According to the *Story of Yue Fei*, Gao Chong was one of the noted fighters under Yue Fei fighting the Nüzhen invaders. He was leading an attack on a mountain when the Nüzhen ordered the battle chariots, weighing about 1,000 *jin*, pushed to roll downhill to halt Gao's attack. Gao was so strong that he managed to use his spear to overturn eleven of the chariots. But by then he was so exhausted that he was crushed and killed by the other chariots. This story was made into the well-known Beijing opera *Tiao Huache*.
22. Miaoxing is a town in Shanghai where the Nationalist army resisted Japanese attacks in mid-February 1932.

China Books and Periodicals
Extract from the Autobiography *China Born*
Henry Noyes

The story of the creation of China Books and Periodicals is reprinted by permission from Henry Noyes, "China Syndrome," chapter 4 of China Born: Adventures of a Maverick Bookman *(San Francisco: China Books & Periodicals, Inc., 1989). See also Him Mark Lai, "The Changing Roles Played by China Books and Periodicals," this volume, page 44.*

A CHALLENGE

The year 1959 was a turning point in our lives, a year when we were called upon to use all the ingenuity and experience we had accumulated in a lifetime. On 1 October, by coincidence China's National Day, our longtime friend Paul Romaine phoned me to say, "Henry, I hear you're no longer working at Pettibone Mulliken."

"That's correct. When I applied there three years ago for a job in the tool-and-die department, I neglected to put down my university education on the application form."

"They fired you for that?"

"No, not really. The real reason, I was a shop steward, filed and won too many grievances, and also locked horns with the works manager in bargaining sessions. Now I've had to file my own grievance with the Machinists' Union and the Labor Relations Board. But they're slow to act."

"You think you'll get your job back?"

"Not a prayer. The cards are stacked."

"Then I have something here that might interest you: a letter from Imported Publications and Products in New York. They supply me, as you know, with books and magazines from the Foreign Languages Press in Peking."

"What's the deal?" I was excited without yet knowing why.

"If you come down to the shop this afternoon I'll tell you more."

Paul Romaine ran the only independent bookshop in downtown Chicago. He handled bestsellers and popular fiction to pay the rent, but his chief interest was in progressive publications and his store was known as the best place in town for avant-garde books and magazines. Despite the inquisition of Senator Joseph McCarthy, symptomatic of the deepening freeze of civil liberties in the cold war period, Paul continued to handle radical writers of the 1930s: John Steinbeck, Agnes Smedley, Jack Conroy, Clifford Odets. As liberal leaders of the New Deal became McCarthy's special targets for political assassination, left-led coalitions and united fronts dwindled. In Chicago the Abraham Lincoln School was defunct. Henry Wallace's Progressive Party shrank to a holding operation of the isolated left before bowing off the stage of U.S. political history like earlier third-party movements. The American Peace Crusade had spent its energies in one giant rally at the Coliseum. The Congress of Industrial Organizations was being shredded from the top down by loyalty oaths and anti-labor legislation passed by an intimidated Congress. Romaine's bookshop was one of the few progressive institutions to survive the 1950s—the New Dark Age, as Paul called it—and he continued to handle *Moscow News*, *China Reconstructs* and the *Peking Review*; also to display them in his window on La Salle, the Wall Street of the Middle West. He had such an affable, pipe-smoking disposition that even officers of the law stopped in to browse and ask him questions like: "What the hell is Marxism-Leninism? And who is this Mao Tse-tung?"

Paul's wife, Marguerite, welcomed me with a cynical smile as she stood with arms akimbo behind the cash register: "You're a notorious character. Read what the *Chicago Tribune* writes about you, in case you missed it." The clipping she held out accused me, in usual *Tribune* style, of taking part in a worldwide conspiracy, and asked: "Why should a professor otherwise want to work in a machine shop?"

"Why indeed?" Marguerite mocked.

"Why not?" I took her up half seriously. "Gertrude and I decided to work with our hands to round out our characters. The days I could make a living as a freelance writer and organizer of large meetings for progressive causes ended with the New Dark Age. Besides, Chris and Nicky are great kids but they eat like pigs and need new shoes every three months. And seriously, I miss the day-to-day association with fellow-workers who usually say what they mean and mean what they say."

"Paul's got a proposition for you." Marguerite nodded up at Paul's office, a mezzanine pigeon loft from which he could keep his eye on customers and also watch the passing crowd of bankers, stockbrokers and lawyers in La Salle Street.

Paul was not a word waster. He motioned me to a seat with a twist of his pipe and handed me a letter. "From Margaret Cowl. She's a remarkable person. Single-handed she's organized the import of publications from the Latvian and Lithuanian Socialist Republics, the USSR, and also China. She has the right kind of guts. Her father died when she was only fourteen. She went to work in a garment factory, hid in the toilet when the child-labor inspector made his rounds, and for years supported her mother and younger brothers and sisters."

The letter invited Paul to take over the import of publications from China, since Margaret, at sixty-five, was about to retire and wanted to slim down her imports. "If you can't do it yourself," she wrote, "can you recommend somebody who's qualified?"

Paul came straight to the point. "You're the only person I know who's qualified, meaning that you are deeply interested in China and have wide contacts in the progressive movement." He gave me an encouraging smile. "You've used my China section like a library for years. You're a natural, China born . . ."

"But wait," I objected. "I don't know a thing about the book business, accounts, marketing . . ."

"That's easy. Marguerite and I can teach you the basics. What's it going to be?"

"First, a family conference."

"You'd be a schlemiel to turn it down." Paul spoke as if he had already made the most important decision in my life for me, and began to sort out a stack of invoices.

"Does Paul make all your decisions for you, too?" I asked Marguerite on my way out.

"He's right. You'd be a fool to turn it down," she said, with an urgency in her voice and eyes. "China's on the map to stay—800 million strong—in spite of the silence or abuse of the U.S. media. You could do both countries a favor in helping develop two-way understanding."

A FAMILY BUSINESS

Our family conference took place the following evening in the café of the Greyhound bus station. My trip to New York was an occasion of prime importance which required a group send-off. While Chris and Nicky were talking excitedly about taking canoe trips on the Grand Canal and riding camels across the Gobi Desert, Gertrude and I were discussing the pros and cons of transforming ourselves from proletarians to petty-bourgeois entrepreneurs. When my bus was called, Gertrude advised me in parting, "Investigate it all first before we make up our minds."

Twenty-four hours later I was sitting across a restaurant table from Margaret Cowl in the great American metropolis. She was a lively person for one soon to retire, with gray hair, glasses, and a youthful and alert manner. "Paul gave you a most favorable recommendation, which I value, since we are old friends. He wrote that you've been a machinist for ten years and before that the extension director of the Abraham Lincoln School. The Chinese will be specially interested in your experiences as a worker and teacher in people's education." Margaret was sizing me up with a friendly but critical eye, as if to make sure that I measured up to Paul's recommendation.

"But do you think the Chinese will balk at my missionary background?"

"Why should they? I'll send them a copy of Paul's letter. Your problem would be more with U.S. regulations. Since the U.S. Treasury bans export of capital to the People's Republic of China under the Trading with the Enemy Act, you wouldn't be able to send payments to Guoji Shudian. That's the firm in Peking from which I import Chinese publications. You would have to deposit funds owing in an account blocked by the U.S. Treasury." Since my eyes were blinking shut after an all-night bus ride, Margaret said tactfully, "So we'll talk more tomorrow."

After working for a week at Imported Publications and Products, I felt excited and depressed at the same time. How could we go into business with a zero-zero balance at the bank? But Margaret had avoided the subject. "This is not only a commercial business, it's building a bridge of friendship between two great peoples," she explained with pride. "An opening of doors and windows which Joe McCarthy and his cronies thought they had shut for ever. The American people need to know more about the people of China. By beginning to shape their own history, the Chinese will take the Western world back to school and teach us how to refashion an economy and morality that put humans first, not dollars. The American people can in turn supply the Chinese with science and technique to speed up their material development and help them raise their terribly low living standard." Then she asked me point-blank, "Well, what will it be?"

"I'll have to be frank with you. We haven't a dime to invest."

"You won't need it. You pay as you go. Every month you deposit what you owe to Guoji Shudian in a blocked account. You don't need capital."

"But what about you? After all the time and energy you've put into it? Margaret, you'd better find somebody else. We don't have enough dough to buy a decent typewriter!"

"Now you've considered all the negatives, what about the political importance?"

"You sound like my wife," I laughed.

"But seriously, you seem to have solved other problems in your life. Surely this is no more difficult than processing grievances, organizing Opera House meetings?"

"It's not the difficulty . . ." I began to object.

"I know. I'll be happy to give you every assistance, and there will be no exchange of money between us. You seem to be the kind of person who won't be in it for the money, with your interest in the Chinese people. There are half a dozen progressives here in New York who want the business, but they are concerned only with politics. If China's line should change or the USSR and China should follow different lines, they would jump ship and follow the Soviet line. The Chinese people deserve somebody like you."

I was overwhelmed. I called Gertrude to explain. "Margaret's made me an offer. How can I refuse?"

"You can't," said Gertrude, with gung-ho enthusiasm. "I've been thinking about it all week. Let's do it!"

Margaret Cowl was one of the few selfless people I have ever met. She transferred the whole import business of Chinese publications to us as promised and refused any remuneration with a curt, "There's no bottom line with us!"

When I came back to Chicago with the news that a new import firm to be called China Books would soon supply Romaine's with its publications from China, Paula and Marguerite congratulated me with a three-sided embrace. Marguerite said, "You're in on the ground floor," and Paul, "You're lucky, while it's still a small business, to get your basic training. But make no mistake, this is just a beginning. Relations between the U.S. and China are bound to open up ahead. There's already a firm basis of friendship between the Chinese people and ourselves—always has been. You'll find millions of Americans interested in the New China once you get rolling. In the meantime, come and work with us. We promised to show you the ropes—and we will. To begin with, you should read the latest arrivals. Here's Felix Greene's brochure on his 1957 trip to the PRC, which City Lights in San Francisco has just published. Also, you should read Rewi Alley's *The People Have Strength* from New World Press in Peking—the best account so far of China's reconstruction after the Civil War. You'd better do your homework now, because once you get into the book business you'll have no time to read!"

As Paul climbed back up the stairs to his mezzanine office, Marguerite handed me a slim lemon-colored book, *Red Flood Over China*, by Agnes Smedley. "A present for you to celebrate the opening of your new enterprise. Edgar Snow gets all the credit for publicizing the Chinese revolution, but a woman journalist beat him to the draw. Three years before *Red Star Over China* appeared, Smedley published her account of the setting up of the first Chinese Soviet Republic. It's rare. Treasure it, and it may bring you good luck!"

Six weeks later, we received a letter from Guoji Shudian offering to open commercial relations based on the strong recommendation of Margaret Cowl. Since our family budget made no provision for renting a store or office, we tacked up a small shingle on our front door and registered ourselves with the record office as China Books & Periodicals, CB&P.

Our next problem, serious though not crippling, was to deal with restrictions imposed by the U.S. government under the Trading with the Enemy Act. Under the First Amendment of the Constitution, Americans were guaranteed the right to read even publications originating in a communist country. But all trade with China had been cut off in 1951 and import of publications was possible only under Treasury license. The

Treasury kept us on hold for several months before finally responding favorably to our application, but its conditions were onerous. Since we were forbidden to pay Guoji Shudian, we were required to deposit funds owing in a blocked account in a U.S. bank.

When I went at bank opening time down La Salle Street into the canyon of the Midwest empire of banks, brokerage and insurance firms and asked for the foreign department at the Continental Illinois National Bank, which was then the most prestigious institution in Chicago dealing with foreign moneys, the young people in the department were amazed and delighted that a normally dull Monday morning could turn up such a unique problem, never faced by this bank before. "Hmmm! Open a . . .?" After palaver back and forth that eventually went up to a vice-president on the fifth floor and an afternoon appointment, the young bankers and their secretaries went flocking off to lunch, wishing me good luck. The senior vice-president of the Continental Illinois showed a deadpan, bloodless face with an abrupt, flat-backed skull, heavy shoulders mounted in opposition to new things, facing me across an acre of polished desk.

"*Open* a blocked account? It's impossible, a contradiction in terms." Then he allowed his negative banker's logic full play: "We can block or freeze assets already deposited under the Trading with the Enemy Act. But *open* a blocked account? It's impossible. Besides, I doubt if it is strictly legal." That was it. He was dismissing me after five hours of futile negotiation that had reached the top and had nowhere else to go.

"Do you think," I asked heatedly, "that the U.S. Treasury would oblige me to do something that was not strictly legal?" He held his palms up. The interview was over.

I took my hot head over to Irv Steinberg's office on the run. Irv was about as cool and militant a lawyer as you could find in Chicago. "You seem to be upset," he said, to cool me down. "So what if the Continental Illinois doesn't want your money!" He held his hand up, since further details were not of substance at the moment, as he dialed the Exchange National Bank. "Mr. Tinucci, please . . . How are you, my friend? This is Irv Steinberg. I have a client here with a problem. Something new. He has a Treasury license to import books from China. Yes, I said China—the People's Republic, not Taiwan. He is required to deposit funds owing in a U.S. bank since he can't send them to China right now because of Treasury restrictions. So what we need is for you to open a blocked account for these funds."

I couldn't hear Vice-President Tinucci's words, but gathered he was putting up the same kind of argument as the Continental Illinois. "There's no time to worry about all the buts," Irv reassured him. "All you have to do is say 'blocked by Tinucci' and the Treasury will back you up. After all, it's what *they* legally require." So the blocked account was actually *opened* at the Exchange National Bank, a first for the City of Chicago.

In August, we were advised by the U.S. Customs Department that they were holding a shipment of some two tons of books from "Red China" and that we should make arrangements to clear them. I learned from Margaret Cowl that, with bonding, an importer could clear shipments without using the services of a broker and save about $200. I went to Customs and filled out three preliminary entry forms; then I went to the Hartford Insurance offices, put down $40 and got myself bonded.

The Customs House had ten floors. In the next three days I was shunted from one to another, up and down, back and forth. A lot of this was deliberate because superintendents and clerks had their own favorite brokers and were setting up stumbling blocks to force me to use their services. Finally, I cut or broke through all the red tape and the shipment was released on condition that I would have Guoji Shudian fill out a special Customs declaration on official US stationery. The books came sacked, filled our two front rooms at 334 W. Schiller Street, and made the floor sag dangerously. We filled a hundred pear boxes, lining the walls with books title out, and opened the store to the public. Three months later we received a letter from Guoji Shudian advising that it was not appropriate for their firm to fill out a US official Customs declaration. The implication was obvious: this would be a violation of protocol. The US Customs then retaliated by slapping a $1,200 fine on CB&P for failing to comply with US government regulations. By some standards this would not seem a large sum, but with sales running $200 the first month and $500 the second, it was more than punitive—it was ruinous.

Again I hotfooted it down to Irv Steinberg's office. Irv was imperturbable, as usual. After hearing my breathless laments, he picked up the phone and called Customs. "You are asking my client to do something that is impossible. He has your notice . . ." and Irv went into details, concluding, "Since there are no diplomatic relations between our two countries, we cannot expect the Chinese to recognize or sign official US documents. You understand," he added, in his best pacifying voice.

Silence, then a new proposal: "They agree to reduce the fine from $1,200 to $12." Irv held his hand over the mouthpiece. "Do you agree?"

"No, why should I pay a cent?"

Irv commanded silence. "My client agrees." He put down the receiver before I could protest. "Don't you see, we've won a victory? They've admitted it, but they have to save a little face. You can't be a hothead about these things. You've got to use diplomacy. You have to show willingness to abide by the letter of the law, even if you don't agree with it. You're not a civil rights organization, you're on your own. Remember, if things get rough, you are creating evidence of compliance in advance if we ever have to go to court. You need to bend over backwards to show how co-operative you've been."

"I'm not very good at piety never have been but I'll try," I assured him. "The most serious problem now is the license. I'm going batty with these reports to the Treasury. On every item I have to deposit 50 per cent of the sales price in the blocked account. It's insane!"

"You should go to Washington or, rather, New York, and talk to the Foreign Assets Control. You know, say you've given your full co-operation, but . . ."

"Margaret Cowl says to steer clear of the government," I interrupted. "I'll get worse, rather than better terms. Let sleeping bureaucrats lie."

"Margaret Cowl may be right for herself but wrong for you, Professor. Just be straightforward and sincere."

The next week, after another all-night ride on Greyhound, I was looking for the Federal Reserve Bank on Wall Street. The building itself was a substantial monument to American government and its financial operations.

Mr. Greig, in the office of Foreign Assets Control, was a short, energetic, fussy type of bureaucrat in spats and stylish gray suit and tie. His face came to attention, then seemed to go back into itself, turtle-like, so that it was hard to know when and if he listened. He was indifferent to my request to simplify my license until he found that I had been a professor of English. "I lecture on economics myself to various groups, mainly business, in Manhattan," he informed me, as if we were now in the same batting league. Then he batted questions in semantics at me, which I fielded to his satisfaction. For half an hour we compared notes on how best to keep an audience awake for an hour. Our dialogue was interrupted by Mrs. Schwartz of the Treasury in Washington, calling to confer on a problem of foreign assets and then to exchange fried chicken recipes. Finally, Mr. Greig put down the receiver, carefully filed the fried chicken recipes, then turned to me with a smile.

"What was it you wanted? Something about your license? Oh yes, you find it unusually complex. Well, why don't you write me a letter saying you find it difficult to make a living and propose a simplification. I'll see you get it, don't worry." Concerned now with my livelihood, he went to his file and pulled out the cards of three British firms that imported furniture and art objects from China. "You can't make much of a living out of books. Why don't you open relations with these firms? There's a good sale for Chinese furniture, rugs and such of course, imported before the embargo of 1951."

Before I left New York, I wrote Mr. Greig a proposal that we deposit the exact invoice price of items sold. This was not only a more viable formula, but also consonant with normal import-export transactions. By the end of the month CB&P had an amended license valid until 1971, when license restrictions were terminated and U.S. funds could be transmitted to the People's Republic of China.

Our problems were not only with legal restrictions and regulations, however, but with political forces from right to left. Our preliminary base, inherited from Imported Publications and Products, consisted of the eight radical bookstores affiliated with the Communist Party. But one by one, these began to defect from supporting China to supporting the Soviet Union only. *Long Live Leninism* was actually the parting of the ways. Several articles, combined under this title, were featured in the *Peking Review* No. 17, 1960, which was the first publication we had received from China. We had hardly got over the excitement of opening the first packages, shipped airmail direct from Peking, when our phone started to ring. From left to right, callers wanted this issue. "It's controversial, you know." Why, I wasn't exactly sure at the time. It presented Lenin's well-known thesis on imperialism: that war was inevitable unless the peoples of the world were strong enough to prevent it, presumably through revolution. In supporting Lenin's thesis, the Chinese polemicists characterized the rearmament of Germany and Japan as U.S. imperialism's way of breaking down the peace and laying the basis for a third world war.

Several weeks later an airmail shipment of *Long Live Leninism* arrived in book form, with a white linen cover and a red jacket with Lenin's portrait in black and white. It became our first bestseller and was sold out in a month. I heard from Margaret at this time that a top-ranking Party official in New York was urging her not to handle the book because it was too controversial, besides being sectarian and damaging to the peace forces. When I asked, "What is your reaction?" she replied, "Who am I to decide between my Chinese and Soviet comrades?" Soon afterwards I had a call from the educational director of the Illinois State Communist Party, who said he wanted to bring a leading ideologist in his party out to the store. "Fine," I said, "I'll be happy to show you both our books. But if he wants to discourage me from handling *Long Live Leninism*, please tell him he'll be wasting his time." There was a hasty click at the other end of the line.

"Peace at almost any cost" seemed to be the new slogan of left-wing parties both in the United States and Europe. But Mao Tse-tung was telling the Chinese not to be intimidated. People made the atom bomb; people should agree never to use it, and then to destroy it once and for all. On the other hand, Khrushchev was saying that the atom bomb is not a toy for children, thereby justifying his refusal to share it with China and other fraternal countries and torpedoing the unity of the "socialist world."

The rift between China and the USSR widened through polemics that China first directed at the Central European communists and then at the USSR itself. Since the U.S. Communist Party sided with what the Chinese called Soviet revisionism, the radical bookstores we served showed less and less interest in handling publications from China, and then open hostility. "My people hate the Chinese," one of their managers blurted out when he cancelled his orders for Chinese magazines. "No, we don't want any more stuff from China!"

"Even the children's books?" I asked sarcastically. "How can a professed Marxist-Leninist hate a whole people, especially as many as 800 million?"

Political splinter movements from the CPUSA—the Provisional Organizing Committee, Hammer and Steel, and later, Progressive Labor—supported the Chinese side of the polemics, but their influence was limited and they could not fill the gap in book sales left by the departure of the communist bookstores. It was time for us to enlarge our market, or close our doors.

In Chicago our clientele was small, confined mainly to teachers and students. I decided to travel the country by Greyhound and investigate other possibilities, particularly the West Coast. On a $99 ticket I could travel the whole country as long as I did not backtrack. I decided to concentrate on the periodicals, since they carried the latest information about China and would play an immediate role in ending the myth that it was the "unknown." In five weeks, I lined up forty-three newsstands in major American cities to handle *Peking Review*, *China Reconstructs*, and *China Pictorial*: in Denver, Seattle, Salt Lake City, St. Louis, Los Angeles, Omaha, San Antonio, New Orleans, San Francisco of course and other cities.

I remember especially the bus trip across Kansas, all night pursued by an engulfing thunderstorm. Lawrence, Kansas, appeared and disappeared between lightning flashes. At last clouds sorted themselves out in the predawn over Kansas City and areas of daylight began to show through. The bus splashed into the station through streets flooded from backed-up sewers. During the fifty-minute breakfast stop, I waded through the downtown area to the two news dealers who handled out-of-town and international newspapers. They could both see a chance of making an extra buck and agreed to try out the Chinese magazines, though they could hardly believe that material from China would be in English and that it could actually be imported into the United States. That was our problem, I assured them, and boarded the bus for St. Louis. Two months later, Chinese magazines were on sale in both Kansas City and St. Louis and in some forty other cities.

In San Francisco, Louis Swift of L-S Distributors had agreed to handle the Chinese periodicals for wholesale distribution. Louis, a victim of polio, was a living example of how a disadvantaged person could overcome a serious handicap and help others in the process. He sat at his desk in the front office and shouted orders that could be heard in the back stockroom, and even in the basement. On his wall was the golden key to the City of San Francisco, which Mayor Christopher had presented to him as one of the city's most distinguished citizens. Louis Swift had a winning smile behind a rugged moustache and beard, gray hairs yielding only in patches to white. "San Francisco is the place for you," he advised, and at the same time commanded by inference that we should transfer CB&P to the West Coast.

I needed no persuading: San Francisco was my first American city. When the *Ecuador* docked there on 31 January 1919, we had stepped back on land after a violent crossing from Hong Kong. It was with nostalgia and admiration for this most beautiful of all cities in the United States that I wandered around its harbor and streets in the spring of 1963, forty-four years later. "It is the only city in the world," boasted a friendly bus driver, "where you have winter, summer, fall and spring all in the same day!" San Francisco is also one of the most tolerant and progressive cities in the United States and, facing the Far East, a city whose labor unions and business enterprises favored resuming trade with China. The harbor had once been the Golden Gate to China, and Louis Swift was confident that it was destined to become so again.

His confidence was so infectious that it inspired me to call home that night and surprise the family with a question, "How about moving to California?"

ONE MILLION LITTLE RED BOOKS

When I left San Francisco on my $99 Greyhound ticket, we had already decided by phone to move China Books & Periodicals to the West Coast. Gertrude approved. Chris thought it would be easier out West to work up into the big leagues as first baseman. And Nicky had seen so many Errol Flynn, Kirk Douglas and Roy Rogers films that she was sure she could ride a horse to college.

We had scarcely set up shop in San Francisco when Herb Caen, the best-known gossip columnist on the West Coast, came strolling in to inspect us and our books. Two days later we were given an official welcome in the Caenfetti Column of the *Chronicle*, which described CB&P as "Peking's foot in the door" and a firm that had ambitions to expand rapidly. The paper had only just hit the newsstands when we began to receive calls from enterprising realtors offering us whole buildings with railroad sidings to help us expand. The owner of the corner café, however, rushed in to say we should sue Herb Caen for libel. "Imagine calling you Peking's foot!" But Louis Swift, who had tipped him off about our arrival, called to say, "Send Herb Caen a thank-you note. Now you are kosher!"

Our new location in the heart of San Francisco's Mission District on 24th Street was at the epicenter of the Bay Area, convenient by freeway and bridge to the Stanford and Berkeley crowd and more locally to the many San Franciscans longshoremen, ex-members of the armed forces, overseas Chinese, students and teacher who had a personal or academic interest in the People's Republic. We also received orders, chiefly on the telephone or by post, from merchants, bankers and civic leaders who favored opening trade channels. Before World War II, 40 per cent of the docks in San Francisco Harbor serviced the China trade; a whole dockside area was still called the China Basin. Since the trade embargo of 1951 by presidential decree, many of these surplus docks were being turned into boutique complexes and amusement centers for tourists or closed. Robert Gomperts, President of the World Trade Association, who dropped by our store to welcome us to San Francisco, estimated that 90 per cent of the businessmen on the West Coast were pressuring the President to end the embargo. We received calls from textile importers, paint and varnish exporters, wheat merchants,

travel agents, all asking what our magic formula was for opening trade with China. They even offered us junior partnerships if we would give them a hand. Our reputation and clientele broadened out.

From 1964, the San Francisco Bay Area was the right place for us to be. It was a germinal period in American culture and we found ourselves at the center of new movements fertilized by a confluence of intellectual and political crosscurrents. Groups, as well as individuals, were interested in China's approach to socialism and many of them turned our store into a material resource center, beginning with the free speech movement. In Berkeley, Mario Savio and the "free speechers" were demanding a complete restructuring of the multi-university and the society whose interests it served. People came first, he insisted, especially the young. One of the first quotations from Chairman Mao to become current in Berkeley, three years before the Little Red Book arrived from Peking, was his tribute to youth: "The world is yours, as well as ours, but in the last analysis it is yours. You young people, full of vigor and vitality, are in the bloom of life, like the sun at eight or nine in the morning."

Why should students "full of vigor and vitality" waste four years in classrooms with five hundred other auditors listening to a professor reading lectures from fifteen- and twenty-year-old notes? A new incentive to change the old academic world brought students from all over the Bay Area to browse at CB&P and find ideological support for their campaigns— even the extremists who found in Mao's attack on stereotyped writing a justification for launching a free speech movement. "We're fed up with academic euphemisms. Four-letter words are earthy, gutsy, full of the life of the streets" so went the campaigns in the student press. "We're going to use 'fuck' in our papers whether the Board of Regents likes it or not."

At about the same time a group of seven "diggers," unbeknownst even to themselves, were launching the psychedelic movement, which was soon to embrace and overpower the free speech and four-letter-word campaigns and incite the nation's youth with incense, pot, hash, the Jefferson Airplane and much more. Taking their name from a communal anti-Establishment group in England a century earlier, the San Francisco diggers adopted a three-principle philosophy. They advocated peace on earth and, more immediately, the end of the Vietnam War and the withdrawal of American "advisers." They were ultra-democratic in practicing brotherhood and sisterhood of the Buddhist as distinct from the Christian orders, and they believed in smoking dope and baking brownies laced with marijuana. In their more sober moments they read books on the Chinese revolution, guerrilla warfare and communism, Psychedelic Shop on Haight Street near the intersection of Ashbury. Since they were always short of ready cash they felt no urge to buy, and as long as they didn't smoke dope or burn incense in our store, we let sitting diggers read. We, like them, were infected by the tolerant spirit of San Francisco's patron saint.

Peace, love, freedom, brotherhood and sisterhood were words put back into meaningful circulation. The media could only report their excesses. But new mimeographed handouts, New Age weeklies, poetry broadsides chanted in restaurants and distributed free on the streets, and rock music expressed the new way of life, the new Tao of freedom. If any section of the people was oppressed, how could any other section be truly free? Liberation—women's lib, sexual liberation, black and brown liberation—was a powerful wind blowing away old stenches and stereotypes.

In spring 1967 we received an airmail sample of the *Quotations from Chairman Mao Tse-Tung*. We had no notion at the time that this Little Red Book was to give a powerful boost to all the young liberation movements and our sales a great leap upward. We thought we were taking a big chance in ordering a thousand copies, the largest order for a single title we had ever placed with Guoji Shudian. Two days after we received airmail shipment, all thousand were sold. The Little Red Book became a status symbol for anybody opposing bureaucratic authority. Waving it was evidence that whoever owned a copy was at least a rebel, if not a self-styled revolutionary. Our store was flooded with status-seekers from all over the country. We cabled Peking to loft 25,000 more *Quotations* to us by air freight. They were gone in a month. We ordered 100,000 more. It was our big breakthrough into the book world. We sent a postcard announcement to every bookstore in the United States and received over a thousand orders. By the end of 1968 we had distributed over 250,000 and in the following fifteen years we were to sell over one million.

The extravagances of the "Great Proletarian Cultural Revolution" in China had already been served up by the media. The wild youth of China were shown night after night on prime news time in unruly mobs wielding the Little Red Book. Negative analysis on the radio and in the press, aimed by newscasters to discourage American youth from such outrageous behavior, backfired. Mao Tse-tung was the only national leader at the time encouraging youth to have confidence in their power to change the world. "Go ahead, bombard the headquarters of reaction," he was urging. And young people of the world were responding, "We hear you!"

It was a period of massive civil rights struggles in the South with sit-in strikes in drugstores, bus boycotts, the Supreme Court decision for equal rather than "separate but equal" education. Above all, however, it was a period of growing dissatisfaction with the war against the Vietnamese people and with the Establishment that waged it with the lives of young Americans. A disproportionate number of these, shipped home in flag-draped caskets, were black or brown. It was a period of peace marches, united fronts of diverse political and religious elements. It was a period when the Black Panther Party organized a new national movement which seemed to threaten the existing order of white supremacy with its program for peace in Vietnam, socialism in the United States and diplomatic relations with the People's Republic of China.

By the end of the 1960s, CB&P had become a model people's bookstore. In a dozen major cities, similar movement bookstores had been opened to meet the reading demands of a generation who was organizing new political associations and setting compasses for new social horizons. They shared a conviction that wars of aggression and nine-to-five subservience to money-making were not the way of life, the Tao, which they wanted to travel.

The Changing Roles Played by China Books and Periodicals

Him Mark Lai

Henry Noyes tells the story of the creation of China Books and Periodicals in the extract from his autobiography, China Born, *this volume, page 37.*

When Henry and Gertrude Noyes established China Books and Periodicals 中國書刊社 in Chicago in 1960, the U.S.-imposed embargo on the People's Republic of China (PRC) had been in effect for a decade and U.S.-PRC relations were close to their nadir. It had taken some time for the embargo to be effective, but after the government prosecuted and fined a few Chinese merchants for violating the ban and conducted massive investigations into Chinese immigration fraud, the Chinese community was cowed. In 1957 the Oasis Bookstore, the only bookstore in San Francisco Chinatown selling books published in China, had to shut down when U.S. Customs made it impossible for the store to import PRC publications from the PRC or from Hong Kong/Macau firms with ties to the PRC. The Chinese community was thus cut off from the flow of information from China except for accounts, often biased, that were published in the Chinese media dominated by the Kuomintang or the English-language U.S. media obsessed with the Cold War. China Books and Periodicals became a major U.S. bookseller importing publications exclusively from the PRC under a license granted by the U.S. Treasury Department.

China Books and Periodicals moved to San Francisco sometime in 1963.[1] At first it was located in a rented storefront on Gough Street near Market Street; not long afterward the Noyeses acquired and moved into the premises on Twenty-fourth Street that became its home for the next few decades.

When the store had opened in Chicago, I had ordered a subscription to *People's Daily* 人民日報. There probably were not too many Chinese names on its *People's Daily* subscribers list, and when I visited the Gough Street store just after it opened, Henry Noyes recognized my name immediately. He soon told me that he ordered his publications from Guoji Shudian in China and was interested in building up an inventory of books on all subjects not only in English but also in Chinese. However, he was stymied by his rather rudimentary knowledge of Chinese. With the anti-Communist hysteria

and federal prosecution of Chinese immigration fraud in full swing, many Chinese fluent in the language were understandably leery of association with a business connected with the left. However, I volunteered my services, and during the next few years I spent some time in the store, sitting beside Henry Noyes to translate each title and tell him the gist of its contents, so that he could place orders. As remuneration I could take any of the books for my own collection.

China Books and Periodicals gradually built up an inventory of Chinese-language books, and as the news spread in the community, Chinese customers began visiting the store despite the possibility of FBI surveillance.[2] I continued to help with translation for several years until the start of the Cultural Revolution around 1966, when the number of titles China exported decreased to a few items that were "politically correct." During this period business at China Books and Periodicals actually picked up as there was a great demand, especially among progressives, for publications on China's new revolution to ostensibly achieve an egalitarian society. The bookstore is said to have sold over a million copies of the Little Red Book (*Quotations from Chairman Mao* 毛主席語錄) since 1969.[3] By the 1970s the tension between the United States and the PRC was relaxing and it was not as difficult to find someone to translate Chinese-language catalogues. In the meantime I had become busy researching, writing, and teaching Chinese American history. However, I kept up my friendship with the Noyeses and still visited the store on occasion.

During the 1960s the Civil Rights movement, followed by the anti–Vietnam War movement, led to a reawakening of liberal and progressive forces in American society, including many in the Chinese community. There were increasing calls for Washington to end its ever more ineffective policy of isolating the PRC. By the end of the decade there were definite signs that this policy was poised for a change. China Books and Periodicals actively encouraged the change. In spring 1971 Henry and Gertrude Noyes, together with John Ong 翁紹裘 and Maurice Chuck 黃運基 of the Chinese-language newspaper *Chinese Voice* 華聲報 and activist Ann Tompkins, met to found U.S-China Peoples Friendship Association, which was intended to further better understanding between the people of the two nations. This group's successor, the national U.S.-China People's Friendship Association, was founded in 1974 and has over fifty chapters.[4] China Books and Periodicals introduced many in the community, including a number of Chinese Americans, to the activities of this organization.

By the late 1960s many of the Chinese-speaking people in America thirsted for more information from China. China Books and Periodicals assisted in the reappearance of Chinatown establishments marketing publications from the PRC. In early 1970 Chinese Americans from Asian Community Center, mostly English-speaking progressive youth, opened Everybody's Bookstore 大眾書店 in a storefront at the International Hotel at 840 Kearny Street, selling PRC publications provided by China Books and Periodicals.[5] The Chinese-speaking community was not far behind. Around 1971 a group headed by Roger Wong 余朝捷 established New China Book Store 新華書店 on a modest scale in Room B of 523 Grant Avenue in the southern part of Chinatown, targeting the Chinese-speaking community. Jimmy Lee (Lee Kam Wah 李錦華), the store manager, soon moved it to more spacious quarters in the heart of Chinatown.[6] At first China Books and Periodicals supplied publications for these pro-PRC booksellers, but relaxation of the U.S. embargo during the early 1970s soon allowed them to deal directly with suppliers in Hong Kong and the PRC.

With the relaxation of U.S.-PRC tensions and normalization of relations China Books and Periodicals soon lost its exclusive rights as a distributor of PRC publications. At the same time, with the launching of economic changes in the PRC after 1979, Chinese corporations began to look to expand abroad. Particularly important was the ideological sector, which included publications, and moves in this sector further affected the position of China Books and Periodicals.

In 1988, Joint Publishing 三聯書店, Commercial Press 商務印書館, and Chung Hwa Book Company 中華書局, three major Hong Kong publishers with strong connections to the PRC, established Sino United Publishing (Holdings) Limited (SUP) 聯合出版集團,[7] which spearheaded the thrust of the Chinese publishing sector abroad. In 1989 the group tested the market by establishing a bookstore in Vancouver, B.C.[8] Its next major move targeted the three major centers of the Chinese population in the United States: New York, San Francisco, and Los Angeles. In 1993 SUP purchased Oriental Culture Enterprises 東方文化事業公司[9] and Eastwind Books and Arts 東風書店,[10] major Chinese booksellers in New York and San Francisco, respectively. However, negotiations with Evergreen Bookstore 長青書局, the major Chinese bookseller in Southern California, fell through. Instead in 1994 Joint Publishing opened what it claimed to be the largest bookstore on the West Coast across the road from Evergreen Bookstore.[11] The same year a Joint Publishing bookstore also opened in Toronto, to be followed in 1998 by two additional stores.[12] Thus SUP established its presence in all five major centers of the Chinese population in North America.

In 1985 China International Book Trading Company (CIBTC) 中國國際圖書貿易總公司 of Beijing founded Cypress Book Company 常青圖書（美國）有限公司 in New Jersey and headquartered it in San Francisco, where it became a competitor of China Books and Periodicals.[13] But with the continuing interest in China, China Books and Periodicals managed to thrive. However, a slump occurred after the 1989 Tiananmen incident. Although the Noyes family held on tenaciously through the 1990s, they finally sold the business to SUP and China International Publishing Group (CIPG) 中國國際出集團 of Beijing in 2003.[14] One function undertaken by the new owners was distribution for Long River Press, a joint venture established by CIPG and SUP in San Francisco in 2002.[15] Thus China Books and Periodicals closed one chapter and opened a new chapter in its history.

NOTES

1. China Books and Periodicals was first listed in *Polk's San Francisco Business Directory* in 1964, which meant that it was in San Francisco sometime in 1963, when data for the 1964 directory were being compiled.

2. For example, the FBI noted the following: "On April 18, 1964, an Agent of the FBI observed a Chinese male with dark hair and wearing glasses in China Books and Periodicals. The Agent observed a 1962 Buick registered to MARK LAI parked in front of the book store." Document SF 105-1494 (January 4, 1965), p. 4, covering investigative period November 30, 1964, to December 4, 1964, on Lai, Him Mark. Obtained through Freedom of Information Act.

3. Sally Taylor, "China Takes over China Books: The Longer Story," *Publishers' Weekly*, November 10, 2003.

4. Xiong Guohua, *Meiguo meng* [American dream] (Guangzhou: Huacheng Chubanshe, 2002), 159–60; U.S.-China Peoples Friendship Association website, *www.uscpfa.org* (accessed July 19, 2008).

5. See Harvey Dong, "A Bookstore for Everybody," this volume, page 95.

6. New China Book Store was first listed in *Polk's San Francisco Business Directory* in 1972, which meant that it was established sometime in 1971, when data for the directory were being compiled. Soon after its founding the store moved to 1260 Stockton Street at the corner of Stockton and Broadway, and then to 642 Pacific Avenue.

7. "Fazhan lishi" [Historical development (of SUP)], *http://www.sup.com.hk/web/supsituation1.asp* (accessed July 21, 2008).

8. "Lianhe Chuban (Jianada) Youxian Gongsi" [Sino United Publishing (Canada), Ltd.], *http://www.sup.com.hk/web/suporg087.asp* (accessed July 21, 2008). The SUP Bookstore is located at 78 East Pender Street.

9. "Dongfang Wenhua Shiye Gongsi" [Oriental Cultural Enterprises], *http://www.sup.com.hk/web/suporg084.asp* (accessed July 21, 2008); "Dongfeng Shudian" [Eastwind Books and Arts], *http://www.sup.com.hk/web/suporg081.asp* (accessed July 21, 2008). Oriental Cultural Enterprises at 13–17 Elizabeth Street was founded by Liu Zhenyi 劉振翼 in 1976. It was one of the first major Chinese bookstores founded after the relaxation of the U.S. embargo against China.

10. Kathy Nguyen, "Food for the Mind, Body and Soul," *http://www.coastnews.com/sf/eastwind.htm* (accessed July 21, 2008). In 1979 thirty Chinese in the community pooled resources

to found Eastwind Books and Arts. Doroteo Ng 王達 became the manager. Later he bought out the other shareholders and became the owner. The current bookstore manager told the writer on August 4, 2008, that planning for the store took place in 1977–78. It opened for business at 1435a Stockton Street in March 1979. At its peak in the 1990s Eastwind had a branch at 633 Vallejo Street handling English-language publications (later this was closed and its inventory consolidated with that of the main store) and another at 1986 Shattuck Avenue in Berkeley (this was sold to Harvey Dong in 1996, per e-mail from Harvey Dong to author, July 21, 2008).

11. Liu Bing, *Wo de chuban yinshua ban shiji* [My half a century of publishing and printing] (Los Angeles: Evergreen Publishing Wenhua Gongsi, 2000), 124–29, 183–88; "Lianhe Chuban (Luoshanji) Youxian Gongsi" [Sino United Publishing (Los Angeles), Ltd.], *http://www.sup.com.hk/web/suporg068.asp* (accessed July 21, 2008). Evergreen Bookstore was founded by Bing Liu 劉冰 in 1978. By 2000 it had ten stores, mostly in Southern California. The main store, managed by Bing Liu, was located at 760 West Garvey Avenue in Monterey Park. The SUP Bookstore was located at 111 North Atlantic Blvd., #228, Monterey Park.

12. "Lianhe Chuban (Duolunduo) Youxian Gongsi" [Sino United Publishing (Toronto), Ltd.], *http://www.sup.com.hk/web/suporg090.asp* (accessed July 21, 2008). The SUP bookstores in Toronto were located in the suburban areas, one in Scarborough at 1571 Sandhurst Circle, Unit 127–29, and two in Markham.

13. "Cypress Books (US) Co.," *http://www.cypressbooks.com* (accessed July 23, 2008). The bookstore was at first located at 3450 Third Street, #48.

14. Taylor, "China Takes over China Books"; "China Books and Periodicals," *http://en.wikipedia.org/wiki/China_Books_and_Periodicals* (accessed July 20, 2008). CIPG was formed in 2002 by People's Press, People's Literature Press, Commercial Press, Chung Hwa Book Company, China Encyclopedia Press, China Fine Arts Press, the People's Music Press, DSX Book Company, China Translation and Publishing Corporation, Xinhua Bookstore, China International Publishing Trade Corporation, and China Book Import and Export (Group) Corporation. *http://www.china.org.cn/english/2002/Apr/30344.htm.*

15 "Long River Press," *http://www.longriverpress.com/aboutlrp.html* (accessed July 23, 2008). Cypress Book Company, Long River Press, and China Books and Periodicals are all located at 360 Swift Avenue, South San Francisco, #42, #48.

East/West
The Chinese American Journal
William Wong

Images from East/West *are found throughout this volume.*

In 1966 Gordon Lew's job was to translate English news articles into Chinese for the *Chinese Times*, one of four Chinese newspapers in San Francisco Chinatown. One morning when he arrived for work, he saw an astonishing sight—paper from a teletype machine flowing all over the floor. He immediately realized that either the machine had malfunctioned or there were major stories coming out of China.

The machine had not malfunctioned, and the story was the Cultural Revolution. Lew faced the considerable task of trying to make some sense out of the chaos in China and translate the stories on deadline for Chinese-literate readers in Chinatown and Chinese America.

That episode planted a seed that Lew and two Chinese newspaper colleagues, Kenneth Joe and Ken Wong, nurtured to create *East/West*, a bilingual weekly newspaper published out of San Francisco Chinatown for twenty-two years and nine months (January 1967 to September 1989). Lew became the publisher and editor, Joe worked in the Chinese section, and Wong was the principal writer in the English section.

East/West was born at a time of tumultuous changes in China and in the United States. These profound changes deeply affected Chinese Americans, and no publication was serving their need for focused, reliable information that was both wide and deep. The newspaper's founders wanted to give Chinese Americans news and views about the changing times in their own community and their ancestral country, speaking directly to their unique ethnic and cultural identities.

East/West fulfilled that goal by reporting and commenting on local community news. It also provided an invaluable forum for a wide range of Chinese American and Asian American views that shed light on historical and contemporary experiences. Stories from China and from the home front in the mid- to late 1960s connected in both direct and complicated ways to the Chinese American and Asian American communities emerging out of the shadows of segregation and discrimination since the mid-nineteenth century.

CHANGING POLITICS IN CHINATOWN

China's Cultural Revolution put into focus the internal politics of San Francisco Chinatown, whose purported leaders were loyal to the ruling Kuomintang (Nationalists) on Taiwan. These leaders of various Chinatown associations and organizations were rabidly anti-Communist. Chinese American progressives and activists challenged the conservative old guard on both the China front and the domestic front. The American chaos of anti–Vietnam War, Civil Rights, and countercultural movements in the 1960s and 1970s inspired young people and activists in Chinatown to examine critically what their own community was like and how its major institutions, controlled by the pro-KMT old guard, resisted grassroots demands for progressive changes.

The editorial—the newspaper's official position—in *East/West*'s inaugural issue (January 1, 1967), for instance, criticized the lack of leadership in San Francisco Chinatown. This was the first of many editorials that challenged the authority of old-guard family and district associations that held institutional sway in the community. "We are rocking the status quo, banging the drums, making noises, because Chinatown needs to be awaken [sic]," the editorial said.

Major changes started unfolding in the wake of the various political, social, and cultural movements. Federal antipoverty program dollars flowed into Chinatown. New activist organizations led by progressive Chinese Americans worked to address Chinatown's slumlike conditions. Chinese immigration began to rise in the post–World War II years, especially after Congress liberalized immigration laws in 1965. Many Chinese immigrants from Hong Kong settled in San Francisco Chinatown, exacerbating extant political and social problems.

The community issues to which *East/West* paid deeper attention than the mainstream newspapers ranged from grassroots protests of Chinatown's ghettolike conditions to the shocking rise of youth gangs, from opposition to school integration to demands for equal treatment, equal opportunities, and greater political power.

These issues pitted a younger generation of liberal and progressive Chinese Americans against the ruling conservative

Chinatown establishment that was more comfortable with old China-Taiwan politics. *East/West* recorded and commented on the many skirmishes in this battle for the soul and identity of Chinese America at the two-thirds point of the twentieth century.

Mainstream San Francisco newspapers didn't completely ignore Chinatown's problems in the late 1960s. In the summer of 1967, the *San Francisco Examiner* published a five-part series, "The Other Face of Chinatown," which focused on the community's slumlike conditions and alleged exploitation of workers. Included was the call to unionize Chinatown workers.

The Chinatown establishment objected to the *Examiner's* allegations. A Chinese Six Companies committee fought unionization efforts and protested the "lopsided" series. This committee later refuted the *Examiner's* findings and promoted a more upbeat vision of Chinatown.

East/West occupied a middle position. It lamented the community's social and living conditions and lambasted the Chinatown establishment for not doing more to help, and it was criticized by community progressives for being "wishy-washy." *East/West* responded to the *Examiner* series in news articles, community commentaries, and editorials. One editorial, on August 21, 1967, said it hoped the series stirred interest and inspired action to alleviate Chinatown's problems.

Labor issues and the battle to unionize Chinatown workers continued well into the 1970s. "We covered all of it," says Judy Yung, associate editor in the mid-1970s. "We were siding with the workers, of course, but we were trying to be impartial. By covering it, we were helping. These were exciting political times."[1]

PROTESTS

East/West covered San Francisco Chinatown's first major protest demonstration. On its August 28, 1968, front page, under a large headline, "Days of silence over/Demonstration ends Chinatown passivity," the main news story reported that some two hundred marchers had carried signs complaining about "intolerable social conditions in Chinatown." An editorial on the same date urged the Chinatown establishment to "awaken and realize that the times are a-changing and move with it."

The theme of Chinese American protests of general and specific social and political inequities was constant in *East/West's* coverage and editorials throughout its twenty-two-year history, especially during the politically volatile late 1960s and 1970s. That didn't protect *East/West* from criticism from within the community, however.

In a February 19, 1969, editorial *East/West* said, "We are being clobbered left and right by the lunatic fringe. The radicals think we're copping out and the conservatives feel we're too far out. We accept the tribulations as a hazard of the profession. . . . Sticks and stones hurt, but would you believe that we had had our window smashed, been threatened with a lawsuit and reported to the FBI as being communists?" The editorial said *East/West* favored peaceful protests.

CHINA-TAIWAN

In addition to the chaotic Cultural Revolution, the 1960s and 1970s saw some tectonic world diplomatic moves, most notably China's admission to the United Nations and resumption of U.S.-China relations at the expense of Taiwan. Mainstream American newspapers carried some news about China and Taiwan, but *East/West* brought a special dimension to its coverage because of the connections of some Chinese Americans with the putative homeland. *East/West* covered both the international China-Taiwan conflict and its complex local implications.

The leading pro-Kuomintang/Nationalist Chinatown organization was the Chinese Six Companies. Most San Francisco Chinese newspapers openly supported or were affiliated with the KMT. Chinese Americans sympathetic to Communist China were either fewer in number or less visible. Then there were those unaffiliated with either side.

The Chinatown establishment believed that anyone who didn't support the KMT was pro-Communist, says L. Lingchi Wang, a longtime writer for *East/West*. "This is where Gordon [Lew] became a problem for them because he refused to pledge loyalty to the KMT Taiwan government. He was not gung ho for the [Chinese mainland Communist government] either. He took a Chinese American position."[2]

Judy Yung recalls, "There was always a big fight in October between the Communists and Nationalists about who could use Portsmouth Square [the center of San Francisco Chinatown]. Who's going to have the parade? Who was going to protest each side? We were very conscious when interviewing people for stories as to whether they were pro-PRC or pro-KMT." *East/West* ran stories about the celebrations of both China and Taiwan, as well as stories and commentaries reflecting both sides. "We tried to be balanced," Yung says.[3]

The editorials also didn't choose sides. "When Nixon went to China, or when China entered the UN, and no longer recognizing Taiwan, we don't take a pro-Communist position. We are always advocating for the Chinese American position in our community first," Lew says.[4]

Some readers assumed otherwise. When *East/West's* Chinese section ran a photograph of the Red Guards, the young people who carried out the Cultural Revolution, some readers who didn't read Chinese concluded the photo meant *East/West* was pro-Communist. Lew calls that assumption "ridiculous." He acknowledges that *East/West's* editorial position was liberal, "but liberal does not mean we are pro-Communist or anti-KMT. We were not that at all."[5]

The KMT in San Francisco didn't like *East/West* because the newspaper didn't support a pro-Taiwan position. "They just found that we were not cooperating," Lew says. "I never

MISSION STATEMENT

In its inaugural issue, dated January 1, 1967, East/West *ran the following editorial statement on the front page:*

We hold high the torch handed down to us to light the path of the Chinese-American and humbly hope to uphold the tradition of honest and fearless journalism.

We are an unique creature, the Chinese-American. There is nothing quite like us on earth. We are fortunate to inherit the best of two worlds, the contemplative East and the kinetic West. There are some 200,000 of us living in the United States with more coming each day from the Orient since the liberalization of immigration laws in 1965.

The days of the inscrutable Chinese and its Fu Man Chu syndrome are over. From the coolie days of our forebears who borne "the heat of the day" in the 1880s laying tracks for the "iron horse" we have come of age to participate in the main-stream of the Great Society.

We have doctors, lawyers and engineers listed in "Who's Who." We have a senator in Congress and two state assemblymen, one in Arizona, one in California. In this enlightened era we have been singled out as a race of industrious, intelligent and trustworthy people. Yet, there exist among us poverty, ignorance and crime.

There are acute areas of potential conflicts. How do we relate with the Negroes and civil rights? Should Chinatown labor be unionized? Where do we stand should war break out between Communist China and the United States?

We shrink not from the controversial, not deliberately seeking it, but facing it headlong should it come our way.

We are committed to the propagation of Chinese culture. It is the mortar that held the Chinese together as a race the past 4,000 years. But we propose not to be stuffy. Nothing is more asinine than to be boring.

Our pages are open to all, from savants to dishwashers, to express their views. We may go broke in pursuit of the idealistic, but we will not compromise. Neither are we pro-Democrat or Republican, Peking or Taipei. There are no strings on us.

Finally it is our aim to chronicle the ups and downs and fulfillment of our fellow Chinese-Americans, their stories in black and white.

To these ends we pledge our talent and energy.

---

hobnobbed with them. I never attended their functions. I think the people in the know knew that our target was the Chinese American community. We were trying to stay away from the mainland and Taiwan conflict."[6]

Two *East/West* staff members, Kenneth Joe and Byron Mok, helped shield the newspaper from KMT criticisms. Both worked in the Chinese section and were KMT loyalists. "They worked with associations of the old Chinatown community, but they were both my friends," Lew explains. "It was almost like a friend protecting a friend. If they were there, at least we would not have criticisms or attacks from one side."[7] He explains, "This was how Ken Joe and Byron Mok played community politics. They are saying, 'Oh, they [*East/West* staff] are all right. We are keeping an eye on them. They are just young rabble-rousers.'"[8]

When the UN admitted the PRC, *East/West* ran the story on its October 27, 1971, front page, with a relatively brief nine-paragraph story under the headline "End of an Era: UN Admits People's Republic, Nationalists Expelled." The editorial in the same issue asked what was going to happen to the pro-KMT/Taiwan Chinese Six Companies. "Most people on the street are cautious in their comment on the change waiting for firmer ground to make a stand. Reporters found it was like pulling teeth asking for opinions. And this is a typical Chinese-American stance, 'Say nothing and you won't get in trouble.'"

An incident occurring at this time illustrates the delicate position of *East/West* in the China-Taiwan dispute. *East/West* sent Richard Springer and L. Ling-chi Wang to cover a 1971 press conference in Chinatown called by the Chinese Six Companies to denounce the UN's admission of the PRC. Just before the press conference began, Wang, who in *East/West* commentaries had supported the UN decision, was harassed, physically intimidated, and threatened. "Ling-chi went in a few minutes before me, and as I was going in one of the swinging doors, they were pushing him out the other and almost throwing him down the stairs," recalls Springer. "They [Six Companies officials] were angry about what he had been writing in the three or four years before."[9]

On the November 2, 1971, *East/West* front page, Wang wrote a personal account of the incident. Six Companies officials had demanded to see his press credentials and begun shoving him out. He had heard one official shout, "Kill him! Kill him!" in Cantonese. Wang had then held an impromptu press conference of his own. "I told the reporters they had just witnessed a common occurrence in Chinatown," Wang wrote. "'That was just one of the many ways the Chinese Six Companies uses to suppress dissent and put down demands for justice.'"

Springer's accompanying story highlighted Wang's ouster from the press conference. Springer wrote that he and other reporters were not asked to show their press credentials. He quoted a Chinese American professor saying *East/West* was leftist. He and Wang disputed that characterization, saying *East/West* held "moderate" political positions.

East/West did not escape criticism from Chinatown progressives. "The left was never satisfied," Springer says. "The paper had a sort of schizophrenic reputation." He noted the liberal English-language editorials were juxtaposed with pro-KMT writings in the Chinese section.[10]

EDUCATION

Education was another hot topic for Chinese Americans and *East/West*. Community concerns ran the gamut from improving the education of Chinese American students to better serving new immigrants who spoke little or no English. They also included demands for Asian American Studies on the college and university levels.

For the most part, *East/West* supported these community demands but advocated a more nuanced position. In an April 29, 1970, editorial, it expressed sympathy for the American educational challenges faced by Chinese immigrant students, but it also noted the deep divisions between American-born Chinese (ABCs) and the immigrants (called "fresh off the boat," or FOBs). *East/West* criticized Chinese American parents for not attending school district events designed to help their children. "Unless there is a greater grass root participation, the Chinese community will have to do with a second-class education for its children," the editorial said.

One education issue that aroused deep passions in the Chinese American community was San Francisco's plan to integrate its public schools. The plan called for, among other things, the busing of many Chinese American students away from their neighborhood schools to integrate schools in areas of the city that had a high concentration of African American children.

In the late 1960s and into the 1970s, the school integration issue ignited fury among some Chinese American parents and the Chinese Six Companies. Parents opposed to busing boycotted the city's schools and started an independent "Freedom School" in Chinatown.

Again, *East/West* took a moderate position. The June 9, 1971, editorial said, "Busing is not the issue at stake. Integration is. It is the law of the land to have integrated schools. Busing is but a means to achieve that end." And in her June 9, 1971, column Jade Fong (Judy Yung, who used this pseudonym before she became associate editor) said she had grown up in Chinatown surrounded only by Chinese and commented, "What this did to me was to make it extremely difficult for me to feel comfortable with people of other races. And when you finally leave the ghetto, you're going to find there's a hell of a lot of people in this country who are not Chinese and who are no worse for it, and you're going to have to learn to live with them."

East/West urged Chinese American parents to stop boycotting the schools. "It's time for all Chinese-Americans to learn to live with all the other Americans, with the majority and with the minorities as well," the October 20, 1971, editorial advised. Publisher and editor Lew, who had "insider" status as a teacher in the San Francisco Unified School District,

notes, "The central issue was better schools and not busing. But the community is so thick-headed and they keep this so-called parents' school at Six Companies for twenty to thirty years. . . . It's sad they kept this parents' anti-busing school going. Who are they hurting? They're hurting the children."[11]

GANGS

Another noteworthy community topic that *East/West* covered was alienated youth and gangs. The outbreak of juvenile delinquency in Chinatown perplexed community elders of all different political stripes.

The problem stemmed in part from the increased immigration in the 1960s of young people from Hong Kong and the subsequent difficult adjustments of both immigrants and the host community. But some native-born Chinese American youth were also disaffected and emboldened by the Chinese American/Asian American empowerment movements of the 1960s and 1970s. The alienated youth organized in groups, or gangs. Two of the most prominent were Hwa Ching for immigrants and Legitimate Ways, or Leways, for the American-born.

Sometimes these groups clashed; other times they coexisted. Sometimes they worked within the established political order, pleading for help from the Chinatown leadership and City Hall; sometimes they carried out criminal activities in Chinatown against merchants and tourists. Occasionally they clashed with and criticized the Chinatown old guard. Some youth made up the enforcement arm of Chinatown tongs, which were associated with Asia-based international criminal syndicates. Chinese American and Asian American activists formed organizations to help the troubled young people.

East/West expressed a moderate position regarding youth gangs and possible solutions, lamenting the criminal activities and urging Chinatown establishment groups to assist the troubled youth. It scolded the Chinatown old guard for promising action but doing nothing. "We are disillusioned by the Establishment. Not because of its apathy and inertia, but with its failure to deliver what it promised," the March 13, 1968, editorial said. And the March 24, 1971, editorial criticized the polarized positions—radical activists supporting the youth versus establishment figures pushing a hard law-enforcement line—and concluded, "We need to keep the line of communication open."

Despite its careful and nuanced position, *East/West* couldn't avoid being part of the story again, its role an uncomfortable and dangerous one. In the most sensational episode, *East/West* writer Ben Fong-Torres was beaten up by three gang youths in June 1970 for covering the gang story. "I had violated some code of silence that had insinuated itself in the Chinatown underground. . . . I retreated to the far safer, much more comforting worlds of rock and roll and *Rolling Stone*," he wrote in his memoir, *The Rice Room*.[12]

The beating and a cherry-bomb explosion at the front door of the *East/West* office cast a deep pall over Gordon Lew and his staff. From that point on Lew instructed his editors to cover the youth gang story indirectly by summarizing stories in mainstream newspapers. When Judy Yung became associate editor of *East/West* in the mid-1970s, she received direct instructions from Lew to not assign reporters to cover stories about gangs.

That strategy was still in place in 1977 when, over the Labor Day weekend, gang violence erupted in a massacre at the Golden Dragon Restaurant in the heart of Chinatown, killing five and wounding eleven tourists and ordinary San Francisco Chinese Americans. *East/West* readers didn't get any original reporting from the newspaper, which devoted ample space over several issues to the sensational crime but principally rewrote accounts from the mainstream newspapers.

CHINA DEMOCRACY PROTESTS, 1989

Another major China story that deeply affected San Francisco Chinatown and other Chinese American communities was the so-called prodemocracy movement in Beijing and other cities in the spring of 1989. *East/West* carried numerous articles and commentaries on that story and the implications for the local communities.

The May 4, 1989, issue was filled with articles about the significance of the May 4, 1919, movement in China, eight years after the fall of the Manchu dynasty. Gordon Lew recounted that movement in an article with the headline "The 1st Great Student Movement." The article said dissidents didn't feel that the Chinese people had much say in the new Chinese Republic.

The entire front page of the June 7, 1989, issue was devoted to the Chinese government's violent crackdown on June 4, 1989, on prodemocracy protestors in Tiananmen Square. *East/West* called it a "special China issue." There were two articles on the local Chinese American impact—"Grief and Outrage over Massacre" and "China Investors Hope for a Calm after the Storm." An editorial written by editor Serena Chen supported the protestors. The following issue, dated June 15, 1989, carried numerous follow-up articles and commentary on what was then being called the Tiananmen massacre.

At this time, Chen notes, *East/West* used a Chinese reporter who was a student in the United States. This reporter, using a pseudonym, wrote a column in both English and Chinese analyzing what the Chinese press was saying about the incident. *East/West* carried numerous articles, commentaries, and editorials about the democracy movement in China, highlighting Chinese American perspectives and angles. During the crisis, mainstream reporters and community members would visit *East/West*'s office, Chen says, to read the bulletin board that posted the latest news from China.[13]

CHINESE SECTION

East/West was published in English and Chinese and for many years the two sections had approximately the same number of pages, ranging from eight to twelve each. However, the English section was considered more important, former staff members say, and the Chinese section did not mirror it in content. The editorial and perhaps the main news article in the English section would be translated into Chinese. Otherwise, the Chinese section tended to focus more on culture, arts, and history, and it often reprinted articles from other sources (as did the English side).

Some of the English-section staff doubted the value of the Chinese section. Judy Yung says, "The impact of the Chinese section was nil. No way it could compete with the other Chinese papers."[14] Richard Springer says, "We would argue with Gordon: how could the Chinese section compete with the other Chinese newspapers? He would say: it is not a question of competing, but a matter of presenting a bilingual publication that gives a certain perspective that Chinese papers do not."[15] Lew says, "Our concern was basically to have more community news," as opposed to news from China, the staple of San Francisco Chinese newspapers of the time."[16]

STAFF

Operating on a shoestring budget, *East/West* had few paid staff members. Nonetheless, many people wrote, edited, and otherwise produced the newspaper.

Gordon Lew served as publisher and editor for most of *East/West*'s twenty-two years. Bilingual and biliterate, Lew oversaw both sections and worked on the Chinese side along with Kenneth Joe and Maurice Chuck in the early years.

Gordon Lew was born in 1934 in Canton (now called Guangzhou), the capital of Guangdong province, but he considers Hong Kong his hometown because he spent some of his school years there, where his grandfather had a construction business. He graduated from high school in Macau in 1951 and emigrated to Boston, Massachusetts, the next year.

U.S. Army service interrupted Lew's college career, but he graduated in 1959 from the New England Conservatory of Music with a BA in music education. He moved to San Francisco, where members of his family had settled. He got a master's degree in music education from the University of the Pacific in Stockton, California. Because of the yellow color bar, he could not achieve his goal of teaching music in the San Francisco public school system until about 1965 or 1966. He subsequently transferred to City College of San Francisco to start its Chinese language and culture department. Lew also became an ordained minister after studying at the Pacific School of Religion in Berkeley, California.

East/West was almost a hobby for Lew, one that took a great deal of his free time as well as his income. He and his attorney wife, Helen Y. H. Hui, financed the paper for much of its lifetime. "Gordon is such a giving person," says L. Ling-chi Wang. "Every issue came out of his own pocket."[17] "I have very fond feelings for Helen and Gordon," says Mary Castagnozzi, who worked for *East/West* from 1977 to 1982. "They are incredibly encouraging and supportive people."[18]

Apart from Lew there were seven main writers and editors in the newspaper's lifetime, most of them holding the title of associate editor. They were Ken Wong, Ben Fong-Torres, Richard Springer, Judy Yung, Mary Castagnozzi, Diane Yen-Mei Wong, and Serena Chen. Each editor brought his or her own outlook and experiences to *East/West* and subsequently went on to a fruitful career.

Ken Wong was an editor and writer in the English section in the early years. Using the pseudonym Manchester Fu, he wrote a lively "items" column that highlighted his love of puns, movies, theater, and entertainment. He joined the *San Francisco Examiner* in 1971, breaking the yellow color line at that newspaper.

Starting in 1967, Ben Fong-Torres wrote about community issues and injected a dose of the 1960s counterculture into his columns and some articles, as well as a flashier layout style. After leaving *East/West* in 1970, he became a writer and editor for *Rolling Stone* magazine, a radio personality, and an author.

In his twenty years with *East/West* Richard Springer showed versatility and a dispassionate nature. He wrote all kinds of news and feature stories as well as a column about films. Not being of Chinese descent, he didn't know Chinatown well when he began—a plus, he figured, because he didn't have a Chinese American agenda. After his departure in 1989, he worked as a freelance writer and then became a reporter for *India West*, which serves the Indian American community.

In the early to mid-1970s Judy Yung brought a curiosity about her native Chinatown, bilingualism, a thirst for social justice, and a breezy, progressive feistiness to her column. She left *East/West* to direct the Asian Branch Library in Oakland, then became an American Studies professor at UC Santa Cruz and an author of Chinese American women's history.

Mary Castagnozzi used her Mandarin Chinese, learned in college on the East Coast, to cover stories where that language, not the more common Cantonese, was required. She worked for *East/West* in different writing and editing capacities from 1977 to 1982. She then worked and traveled in China and became a Mandarin-language instructor in the San Francisco Bay Area.

Diane Yen-Mei Wong, the editor in the early 1980s, believed in social justice also, and wrote and assigned stories reflecting a broader Asian American and progressive perspective. After she left in the mid-1980s, she became executive director of the Asian American Journalists Association and of Unity, a coalition of minority journalism associations.

Serena Chen, *East/West*'s last editor, wrote and assigned stories that continued the newspaper's tradition of liberalism and civil rights advocacy and also wrote a provocative column. Chen went on to become an antitobacco advocate for the American Lung Association.

Reporters came and went. "First thing I did," says Lew, "was enlist college students to write for us."[19] For some young writers and editors, this provided an intense, exciting opportunity to practice community journalism when Chinese America and Asian America were emerging as self-defining communities in an America that was undergoing deep political, social, and cultural changes.

The young men and women Lew hired, most of them of Chinese descent, performed the main editing and writing functions for the English section. Most, if not all, also did "grunt work"—copy- and proofreading, dealing with typesetters and the printer, and picking up copies of the printed newspaper. Lew built teamwork and camaraderie by treating staff members to dinners in Chinatown on Tuesday nights, the heaviest production times.

"I remember there were a lot of students that came through *East/West*," Lew says. "They may have written a few articles for us, then they graduated. We didn't see them again. Although we paid them, it was so little, like $20 an article."[20] While some freelance writers were earnest and worked hard, others were "characters," in the words of Springer, who in his twenty years with *East/West* saw a wide range of people come and go. Some, for instance, "sold articles they had written for us to other magazines or publications without telling us. They tried to get involved in covering gang stuff when Gordon told them deliberately not to. They had an axe to grind. They would interview people and not turn in the stories, which made [Gordon] lose his top."[21]

"I went through agonizing years," Lew says in reflecting on these "characters." One of them was an FBI agent assigned to Chinatown during the early years of the Cultural Revolution. The agent apparently was interested in the loyalties of Chinatown residents. He was "very friendly to the Chinese," Lew says. He attended a Methodist church favored by San Francisco Chinese. "He developed his own eyes and ears in the community." He even wrote a few articles for *East/West*—"a couple of Christmas articles," Lew recalls. "Can you imagine? An FBI agent writing for *East/West*?"[22]

Two Chinese American scholars, L. Ling-chi Wang and Him Mark Lai, wrote for *East/West* for many years. While they had no staff titles and didn't get paid, they were highly regarded by Lew and his editors.

Wang, a University of Chicago graduate student, had come to San Francisco a year before *East/West* began. San Francisco was the hometown of his girlfriend, later his wife. He became fascinated with Chinatown and decided to transfer to UC Berkeley to complete his studies in ancient Middle Eastern languages.

East/West became an ideal vehicle for Wang's prolific writing, intellectual curiosity, and passionate activism. He wrote front-page news articles on community issues, opinion articles, and unsigned editorials. Also, as an activist and scholar, he advocated for liberal and progressive policies. Because of these pursuits, he was often a source in *East/West* stories.

Wang moved up the academic ladder, becoming chair of the Ethnic Studies Department at UC Berkeley, and has continued his community activism since his academic retirement.

Him Mark Lai was an engineer for Bechtel Corporation, an international company based in San Francisco. In his spare time he was a student of Chinese and Chinese American history, avidly reading and analyzing Chinese newspapers. When Maurice Chuck joined *East/West* to write for the Chinese section sometime during its first year, he invited his friend Lai to help proofread Chinese articles and write about Chinese American history in English.

"I hemmed and hawed," Lai says about Chuck's invitation. "I considered myself an engineer, and engineers are lousy writers."[23] In fact, Lai penned many Chinese American history articles for *East/West* and is now considered the dean of Chinese American historians.

CHINESE WORD-A-DAY/ MISS CHINATOWN

Two topics won regular space in *East/West*. One was Gordon Lew's popular "Chinese Word-a-Day." It occupied a corner of an inside page throughout the years. Lew featured one word per issue, telling the story of the word's origins and drawing his own illustrations.

The other was beauty contests and photographs of pretty young Chinese American women. Every year *East/West* covered the Miss Chinatown pageant run by the Chinese Chamber of Commerce during the Chinese New Year celebrations. At other times the newspaper sprinkled its pages liberally with photos of beauty contestants.

"We never covered the old Chinatown organizations other than the Miss Chinatown contest," Judy Yung says. The photos "sold papers. It's not what I wanted to do, but I never questioned it. Pretty pictures, pretty faces. But I also did some columns on why beauty contests were sexist. Gordon didn't question that."[24] On occasion *East/West* also criticized the Miss Chinatown pageants. For example, on February 26, 1969, it called that year's contest "sloppy, dull, and confusing . . . a long, dragged out affair."

BUSINESS

The founders of *East/West* didn't think about it as a business. They were journalists and educators, not entrepreneurs. They were motivated by intellectual ideas, not making money. For most of its twenty-two years, Lew and Hui covered those of the newspaper's expenses that weren't paid for through advertisements and paid circulation. While the expenses weren't high, the newspaper usually operated at a loss, according to staff members, meaning that Lew and his wife subsidized it for many years.

"People asked me, 'Did you try to sell stock or ask somebody to come in to support it?' That was never the idea. It was not that costly to start a paper," Lew explains. "Secondly, I know that for a fact that if I bring in other people financially to support it, there would be arguments, there would be difficulties. It's very difficult to run a small paper with [other people]."[25]

Advertisements and Subscriptions

Advertisements filled both sections from the very beginning but, according to former staff members, only some advertisers paid for the space. The ads were mostly for local businesses and services. Lew called them community ads. "Some pharmacies put in an ad, $5 or $10 an issue," he says. "That was nothing. They were good supporters of the paper rather than a good revenue source."[26]

For a few years in the late 1970s, *East/West* had two advertising salesmen working on commission. "This was a period when there was a lot of interest in advertising in the Chinese community, especially in housing and real estate," says Richard Springer, whose many duties included selling ads and supervising other ad salesmen. The two salesmen generated a noticeable increase in ad revenue, thousands of dollars a week. "Both were very good," Springer remembers. "The revenue exploded."[27] More revenue allowed the paper to hire more staff and increase salaries. "For a few years we had good [ad] agents," Lew says.[28]

Paid subscriptions never yielded much revenue. Springer estimates that these subscriptions numbered about four thousand in the best years.[29] The annual subscription rate started at $3.50 and went to $15 in 1989, the last year of publication.

Overall circulation was more than four thousand because the newspaper sent out free promotional copies, even to cities outside of California, in an effort to generate more paid subscriptions. "We asked for a Phoenix telephone book and sent [*East/West*] to all the restaurants and looked for all the Wongs, Hongs, Dongs, etc., for promotional purposes," Lew recalls. "We would take one city at a time. It's really nothing to brag about because our newspaper had no significant street sales. It was mainly through mailing. You had to have a mailing because Chinese lived everywhere."[30]

Decline

For twelve years *East/West* had no competition. In 1979 *Asian Week* began publishing out of Chinatown, in English with an Asian American focus. It was founded by the late John Fang, formerly an editor with *Young China*, a Chinese newspaper linked to the KMT.

Asian Week competed with *East/West* for advertisements and hired away one of *East/West*'s successful ad salesmen.

This competition wasn't solely responsible for the gradual demise of *East/West*, however; *East/West* had always had trouble making ends meet.

East/West's financial woes were evident to staff members in the early 1980s. Lew wanted a change of leadership, so Peter Chau stepped in as publisher in 1982. Lew ceased daily oversight but remained involved.

Chau, who had immigrated from Hong Kong in 1968 and had worked in New York, moved to San Francisco in 1981 with an idea of starting a magazine for Chinese immigrants. He wrote a business plan, which he showed Lew and his wife. "They liked it and asked whether it could apply to *East/West*," Chau said. "Gordon and Helen wanted me to come on to oversee the business side of *East/West*."[31] Lew told Chau he would underwrite *East/West* for another $20,000 to $40,000—Lew doesn't recall the exact amount. "Beyond that, I have no money. That's my limit," he told Chau.[32]

Chau and editor Diane Yen-Mei Wong worked together to shore up *East/West*'s financial health. "Peter and I agreed that *East/West* had to broaden its base of readers in order for it to be financially viable so that it did not have to rely on Gordon's deep pockets. We needed to make it more relevant to a broader readership," Wong says.[33]

Wong's strategy to build readership—with Chau's approval—was to expand the coverage to pan-Asian and Asian American community issues, not just those of specific interest to Chinese Americans. Wong saw *East/West* as having a "sense of purpose to really educate the community about issues and rights of Asian Americans, not just Chinese Americans. It was more of an activist kind of role." That strategy, she felt, would "bring in more business and build up a customer base."[34] Ultimately, however, it didn't put *East/West* on more solid financial ground.

Lew's next move was to donate the newspaper to Chinese for Affirmative Action (CAA), a Chinatown-based civil rights organization established in the late 1960s. "I thought the newspaper should actually be run by the community if they think alike," Lew says.[35] CAA created a committee to oversee *East/West* and did not exercise any editorial or business control. In essence it created a new non-profit organization to run *East/West* in the late 1980s. A five-member board tried to revive the newspaper's fortunes, but on September 7, 1989, *East/West* ceased publication. The decision was based "entirely on financial grounds," its final editorial said. "When we tell people we are having financial difficulties, they don't believe us," Lew said. "They say politics did you folks in. That's not true at all."[36]

It is difficult to pinpoint more specific reasons for the demise of *East/West*. Peter Chau attributes *East/West*'s advertising difficulties to the fact that it was a bilingual newspaper, whereas the competing *Asian Week* was English only. "We were always fighting an uphill battle trying to get advertising," he explains. "The advertisers were complaining, 'Why are we paying for ads for people who aren't going to read my ad?' They feel that if they put their ad in the English section, Chinese readers won't read it, and vice versa. It was kind of like a no-win situation. It was not easy running this business for this reason."[37]

SIGNIFICANCE AND IMPACT

East/West defied conventional wisdom—some in Chinatown predicted it would die in six months—by surviving for twenty-two years and nine months. It also made its mark in Chinatown and the Chinese American community.

East/West bridged a gap: the paucity of news and views that Chinese Americans and other Asian Americans wanted and needed to feel more connected.

The paper also created its own niche as a voice and a significant forum open to many Chinese, Chinese American, and Asian American perspectives. It was an outlet for views that dissected and debated seminal issues within the Chinese American and Asian American communities, such as identity, history, politics, culture, immigration experiences, literature, the arts, and mass media treatment and portrayals. These topics were largely absent from the mainstream news media.

It also nurtured aspiring Chinese American and other Asian American journalists, giving young men and women opportunities to hone their latent journalistic, advocacy, and community-service skills.

East/West was strong in expressing a liberal civil rights position, speaking out for equality of opportunity and greater Chinese American participation in American political, social, and cultural life, and against discrimination and bigotry. While careful on the volatile China-Taiwan dispute, it was less cautious during the Chinese democracy crisis of 1989, editorially supporting the students and other ordinary Chinese who demanded more political freedom.

East/West also shined a light on government policies that affected Chinese Americans. By doing so, it made a "huge difference" in how these policies were created, according to L. Ling-chi Wang. For example, *East/West* wrote about and supported affirmative action in politics, employment, and business contracting. It also addressed deficiencies in health care policy for Chinese Americans. Wang believes this influenced the eventual retention of tuberculosis screenings for Chinese Americans when budget cuts threatened the clinics that did the screening. He also says that by covering the adverse effects on non–English-speaking legal residents and U.S. citizens of various government policies, such as welfare policy that discriminated against them, *East/West* helped remedy the problems.[38] *East/West* coverage and advocacy for a better census practice and policy for non–English-speaking residents and U.S. citizens helped improve how the census counts minority communities. The newspaper also covered and commented on proposed federal immigration law changes that would directly impact Chinese Americans and other Asian Americans.

San Francisco Chinese Americans had almost no political power to speak of in the 1960s. *East/West* paid a good deal of attention to emerging Chinese American political figures and urged the community to increase its voting and general political participation. *East/West* played a significant role in clarifying the importance of political participation to the community's interests. Decades later, Chinese Americans are much more active politically in San Francisco.

Because it operated when it did, *East/West* also helped forge the idea of a Chinese American identity separate from an identity related to China or Taiwan. Chinese American identity is complex and multifaceted, and *East/West* was a place for many different Chinese American voices to be heard. Writers expressed different views on a broad range of topics, such as identity, civil rights, politics, media portrayals, cultural arts, the Vietnam War, anti-Asian racism, and race relations.

Another beneficiary of *East/West* is the historical record. The issues the newspaper covered and commented on were organic to the community's awakening as a maturing participant in the American democracy. "*East/West* became a focus and a link among all of us concerned about the issues we were trying to cover," Judy Yung says.[39]

The newspaper also served non-profit organizations that cropped up in the wake of the Chinese American and Asian American empowerment movements of the 1960s and 1970s. It gave space to these organizations to advertise job openings and announce various programs and services. Affirmative action policies required public employers to advertise job openings, and *East/West* was also a venue for them to do so.

Many important issues cropped up in Chinese America and Asian America starting in the late 1960s. By writing about these issues, *East/West* helped educate Chinese Americans and other Asian Americans and inspired them to join the conversation and to take action to improve their conditions and status. Diane Yen-Mei Wong says:

> That is how I viewed the role of the newspaper—to bring attention to these issues. These are things of importance. Generally these are things not being covered by the mainstream in any detailed way. After we wrote about them, there may have been additional coverage about them by the mainstream. One of the greatest impacts *East/West* had was raising issues that mainstream media either don't recognize as issues or don't recognize the importance of them. We would have more contacts to provide more context and understand the history. We could provide more context for mainstream people to recognize why these issues are important to our community.[40]

Serena Chen says the newspaper served as a clearinghouse for San Francisco's mainstream newspapers—as a source on ideas, trends, and opinions in Chinatown and the Chinese American community. For example, *East/West* wrote about a scandal at one of Chinatown's most reputable organizations. After reading the story, a reporter for the *San Francisco Examiner* asked *East/West* for its sources of information, a request that Chen declined.

Chen summarizes the personal and community impacts *of East/West* as follows:

> It was an opportunity to take whatever skills and ability I had and apply them in a way that informed and hopefully motivated people to be more proactive in their community's life. I actually believe that if people had the information they need, they will behave and act accordingly. If people know what's happening and know other people are acting upon it, people will move forward. Apathy, ignorance by design, anti-intellectualism—all these things enable an abusive government to take over. The role of the journalist and communicator is to break through that. If you give people skills, they can use those skills to apply to their communities. That's how I felt about *East/West*.[41]

NOTES

1. Judy Yung, interview by author, June 19, 2008.
2. Ling-chi Wang, interview by author, June 5, 2008.
3. Judy Yung, interview by author, June 19, 2008. October 1 is the anniversary of the founding of the PRC.
4. Gordon Lew, interview by Richard Springer, 2003.
5. Ibid.
6. Ibid.
7. Gordon Lew, interview by author, June 25, 2008.
8. Gordon Lew, interview by Richard Springer, 2003.
9. Richard Springer, interview by author, April 30, 2008.
10. Ibid.
11. Gordon Lew, interview by Richard Springer, 2003.
12. Ben Fong-Torres, *The Rice Room: Growing Up Chinese American; From Number Two Son to Rock 'N' Roll* (New York: Hyperion, 1994), 190.
13. Serena Chen, interview by author, July 8, 2008.
14. Judy Yung, interview by author, June 19, 2008.
15. Richard Springer, interview by author, April 30, 2008.
16. Gordon Lew, interview by Richard Springer, 2003.
17. Ling-chi Wang, interview by author, June 5, 2008.
18. Mary Castagnozzi, interview by author, July 9, 2008.
19. Gordon Lew, interview by Richard Springer, 2003.
20. Ibid.
21. Richard Springer, interview by author, April 30, 2008.
22. Gordon Lew, interview by Richard Springer, 2003.
23. Him Mark Lai, interview by author, June 6, 2008.
24. Judy Yung, interview by author, June 19, 2008.
25. Gordon Lew, interview by Richard Springer, 2003.
26. Gordon Lew, interview by author, June 25, 2008.
27. Richard Springer, interview by author, April 30, 2008.
28. Gordon Lew, interview by author, June 25, 2008.
29. Richard Springer, interview by author, April 30, 2008.
30. Gordon Lew, interview by author, June 25, 2008.
31. Peter Chau, interview by author, July 2, 2008.
32. Gordon Lew, interview by author, June 25, 2008.
33. Diane Yen-Mei Wong, interview by author, June 20, 2008.
34. Ibid.
35. Gordon Lew, interview by author, June 25, 2008.
36. Ibid.
37. Peter Chau, interview by author, July 2, 2008.
38. Ling-chi Wang, interview by author, June 19, 2008.
39. Judy Yung, interview by author, June 19, 2008.
40. Diane Yen-Mei Wong, interview by author, June 20, 2008.
41. Serena Chen, interview by author, July 8, 2008.

A "Landmark"

History of Chinese Californians by Chinese Californians, 1969

Anna Naruta

It was in the wake of the massive and widespread student strikes of 1968—in the San Francisco Bay Area, the nation, Mexico City, Paris, and beyond—that Him Mark Lai, Philip P. Choy, and Thomas W. Chinn wrote *A History of the Chinese in California—A Syllabus*, the pioneering work that draws on intensive primary source research to set straight many of the enduring inaccuracies in the stories about California history.

Historian and architect Philip P. Choy is explicit about the work's origins within the environment of widespread and intense demand for correct historical and self-knowledge, in addition to and as part of work for social justice. "The streets of Newark were burning. People were rioting for change. The authorities were 'getting off easy' that Chinese Americans were not demanding more," Choy noted in a recent interview.[1]

Writing just prior to the student strikes, in a publication of the Chinese American Citizens Alliance's San Francisco Lodge, Miss Effie Chow listed issues of pressing concern to the well-being of San Francisco, and joined those who noted the educational improvements needed and the responsibility for "official" funding to be allocated to address the system's deficiencies:

> To combat all these problems we need improved and accelerated education.
> Just as the Cuban, Appalachian, Spanish and Negro people have already extra funds and support from the official structures of education, we should at this time, as a united Chinese community, seek recognition and special funds.[2]

With the 1968 Third World Strikes, students and community members articulated the increasing urgency of the need for accurate historical knowledge to replace incorrect generalities and legends. The Chinese Historical Society of America, established in San Francisco just five years earlier, began receiving "many inquiries from California school districts for the history of the Chinese in California . . . in response to recently-enacted California legislation requiring the teaching of minority group history, their culture and contributions, in the public schools." Complicating matters, a CHSA survey of "various schools and/or school districts"

showed they were undertaking ad hoc approaches in their attempts to develop material to meet needs. These "ranged from assignment of a teacher to research and produce the material to asking local Chinese to assist in assembling the information."[3]

When queried regarding interest in a CHSA-sponsored seminar for representatives of school districts, "The unanimous opinion of the educators, which represented urban and rural districts alike, was that such a seminar . . . was an absolute necessity."[4] The Chinese American Citizens Alliance donated use of its San Francisco Grand Lodge hall to accommodate the event, and by March, announcements of the "seminar for educators [were] being mailed to 900 school districts in the state."[5]

Photos in *East/West* show a packed hall of attendees, many of whom were members of the general public. Demand for *A History of the Chinese in California* was high and within three months, the first printing of "the syllabus . . . was completely sold out," necessitating further printings. Drawing extensively from and building on Him Mark Lai's articles in *East/West*, the rigorous attention to accurate scholarship and primary sources in *A History of the Chinese in California* has made it a reference work of unparalleled value to this day.

The society's own report on the seminar and the people who made it possible (pages 58–59) is complemented by L. Ling-chi Wang's report and criticism in *East/West* (pages 60–61). Of particular note is the young radical Ling-chi Wang's attempt to use the forum to elicit a public statement of CHSA's position on an urgent historic preservation issue important to the community, as well as to overall California history.

At stake was the planned demolition of "the oldest Chinese temple in S.F.": the Kong Chow Temple at 514 Pine Street. Ninety-six-year-old Mrs. Charlotte Chang had filed suit to prevent its demolition, noting that her father "originally donated the land for the temple to the Kong Chow Benevolent Association with the stipulation that the land would not be sold," but the family's legal documents substantiating the claim had been destroyed in the 1906 earth-

S. K. LAI, Philip Choy, Al Lim and H. K. Wong look over syllabus prepared by the Chinese Historical Society at seminar held at the Chinese American Citizens Alliance hall. (Kem Lee photo)

Researched and produced at the height of 1960s activism, the rigorous attention to accurate scholarship and primary sources has made 1969's *History of the Chinese in California* a reference work of unparalleled value to this day. (*East/West*, April 30, 1969, Philip P. Choy Collection, CHSA)

1969 Seminar attendees, by famed photographer and CHSA member Kem Lee. (*East/West*, April 30, 1969, Philip P. Choy Collection, CHSA)

quake and fire. The community was then urgently trying to get CHSA to take action, and at the seminar, Wang confronted members on a panel to no avail. Younger, more progressive members of CHSA attributed CHSA's inaction on the preservation issue to close business relations between one of the society's old-guard leaders and a party that would ben-efit from the real estate transaction and new development. Prior to the temple's demolition, Wayland Lee documented the temple with photos. CHSA younger-generation members Him Mark Lai and Philip P. Choy saved many unique manuscript records of the temple for preservation at CHSA, and continued to research and share its history.[6]

SEMINAR REPORT

On April 19, 1969, the Society sponsored a Seminar on the subject: "A History of the Chinese in California."

It was held at the Chinese American Citizens Alliance auditorium at 1044 Stockton Street, San Francisco, with Philip P. Choy, H. Mark Lai, and Thomas W. Chinn as co-chairmen.

BACKGROUND: Various California school district representatives had contacted the Society, requesting information on the history of the Chinese in California. Originally, the Society had individually replied to these inquiries. Then the Society felt that, as this history will be developed into classroom material, the basic history, together with such references as are in the Society's possession, should be made available to the California school districts as a whole; thus enabling educators to shape their classroom material with some assurrance that the basic history would be uniform throughout the state.

As a preliminary step, several school districts were invited to attend a special meeting held on February 1, 1969, to exchange ideas and make suggestions toward the programming of a seminar, its subject matter and depth. The meeting was attended by all those invited, and the program as discussed was heartily endorsed. Representation was from both rural and urban districts.

Following the meeting, the Society went to work to plan the Seminar. The following resource persons and an advisory committee devoted time preparing material, or participated in the Seminar:

Prof. Kenneth A. Abbott, Mrs. Barbara Adams, Mr. Charles C. Chan, Miss Rosemary Chan, Miss Frances Chin, Miss Mayme Chin, Mrs. Daisy W. Chinn, Mrs. Frances L. Chinn, Mr. Walter W. Chinn, Mrs. Sarah Choy, Mr. Daniel Chu, Mrs. Vyolet Chu, Miss Victoria Chun, Mr. Benton Dere, Miss Jean Dere, Mrs. Henrietta S. Fong, Mrs. Rosemary Fong, Mr. Gordan D. Gollan, Mrs. Gladys C. Hansen, Mrs. Priscilla Heinstein, Mr. William F. Heintz, Mr. Luke Hom, Mrs. Helen Hsu, Mrs. Helen Jang, Mr. Sing Jok Ju, Mr. William Jung, Mr. Alfred Kennedy, Mr. Lawton R. Kennedy, Mrs. Sally Kennedy, Mrs. Adrianne Kwong, Mrs. Laura Lai, Mr. S. K. Lai, Mr. Chingwah Lee, Mr. Lim P. Lee, Mr. Albert C. Lim, Mr. Paul H. Louie, Mr. Hobart M. Lovett, Mr. John F. Ma, Mr. Robert A. Nash, Mr. Yuk Ow, Miss Florence Owyang, Mr. Ernest Pattison, Mr. Robert C. Stevenson, Miss Doris Wong, Mr. H. K. Wong, Mr. James Wong, Miss Mary Wong, Mr. Francis Yee, Miss Frances Yen, Col. John Young, and Mrs. Alice F. Yu.

Three speakers appeared on the day's program: William F. Heintz, San Francisco author and economics historian; Thomas W. Chinn, historian, a founder and first president of the Society; and Chingwah Lee, noted Far Eastern Art and Culture consultant and a founder of the Society.

Panelists were Prof. Kenneth A. Abbott, Chingwah Lee, H. Mark Lai and Thomas W. Chinn. Moderator: Philip P. Choy.

Nearly 250 registrants attended, and the response of the registrants toward the seminar program was excellent. Many wanted additional seminars, and more than one in five bought additional copies of the syllabus. Immediately following the Seminar, bulk buyers of the syllabus were the San Francisco Public Library, 50 copies, and the San Francisco Unified School District, which ordered 68. Since then, many smaller orders have been filled, and at this writing, only a few dozen copies are still available at $5.50 per copy.

The significance of the Seminar and its purpose cannot be overlooked. In presenting the program, the Society made available to all interested persons and organizations, an opportunity to utilize the many years' research of the compilers, Thomas W. Chinn, editor, and H. Mark Lai and Philip P. Choy, associate editors.

The table of contents of the 90-page book:

Pre-Columbian Contacts—Fact or Myth?
Geographical Background
Language
Early Contacts with the West/ First
    Chinese in the New World
Chinese in the Americas in the 18th and
    Early 19th Centuries
Chinese Pioneers in California
Early Chinese in San Francisco

The listing "Mrs. Alice F. Yu" does indeed refer to Alice Fong Yu, the pioneering San Francisco educator and avid member of the Chinese Historical Society of America (*CHSA Bulletin* May and June 1969). See also Mildred Hamilton's profile of Alice Fong Yu, Bessie Wong Shum, Daisy Wong Chinn, Ann Lee Leong, and Ivy Lee Mah, "250 years of service to the Chinese [Square and Circle Club]" *San Francisco Examiner*, March 12, 1975, 22.

COMMEMORATIVE PLAQUES UNVEILED

On Sunday, May 4, the San Francisco Chinese community observed the centennial of the First Transcontinental Railroad in America, and at the same time paid tribute to the Chinese workers of the Central Pacific Railroad.

An audience of more than two hundred gathered at Society headquarters at 17 Adler Place, where an outdoor program was held with Albert C. Lim and Zeppelin Wong as Masters of Ceremonies. The program:

Greetings by President Philip P. Choy;

Messages and telegrams read by Zeppelin Wong and Francis Yee;

Introduction of honored guests, including most of the heads of the various family, district and fraternal associations of the Chinese community;

Remarks by Supervisor Peter Tamaras representing the Mayor of San Francisco, Joseph L. Alioto;

Presentation of Mayor's Proclamation by Supervisor Tamaras;

Remarks by Dennis Wong, President of the Chinese Six Companies;

Remarks by Tung-hua Chou, Consul General, Republic of China;

Remarks by Walter C. Frame, Chairman, Railroad Centennial Committee;

A Salute to Chinese Railroad Workers by Thomas W. Chinn, Executive Director;

Presentation of Railroad Painting by Col. and Mrs. John Young, representing Prof. Mui. Jue Tin;

Unveiling of Plaque by Mrs. Chinn Lee Shee Wing, 98-year-old daughter of Chinese '49er Lee Man Bien.

The Mayor's Proclamation reads:

FORUM

California Chinese seminar a landmark

By L. LING-CHI WANG

About 250 persons, mostly from different parts of northern California, attended the first all-day seminar on the "History of the Chinese in California," sponsored by the Chinese Historical Society of America at CACA auditorium on Apr. 19. The long overdue seminar, originally planned to assist over 1500 California school districts to develop classroom material for a grossly neglected and often erroneously depicted subject, included three lectures, slides, panel discussion, tour of Chinatown and a useful 81-page *Syllabus,* entitled, "A History of the Chinese in California." The unexpected lack of response and indifference on the part of school administrators (only 26 responded before the deadline) forced the Society to open the seminar to the interested public. In spite of that, the seminar was a tremendous success. This short article is intended to be both a report and review of this significant event in the history of Chinese in the U. S.

Philip P. Choy, president of the Society, delivered a brief opening address, stating the purpose of the seminar and deploring the widespread ignorance about Chinese in American society and perpetuation of the same old stereotype images of Chinese, even in the most up-to-date textbooks. Following his remarks, William F. Heintz, a S.F. free-lance writer and financial analyst, gave a fairly extensive and critical bibliographical review, based presumably on his forth-coming work, *The Chinese in California* (a 450-item annotated bibliography, co-edited by Mrs. Gladys Hansen of the S.F. Public Library). Heintz rightly cautioned the audience to read books dealing with Chinese, written between 1860-1890, critically, keeping in mind that the era was permeated with anti-Chinese sentiment and Christian missionary zeal. He cited a distastefully large number of blatantly racist quotations and phrases of hate to illustrate his point. However, he was right to attribute much of the prejudices and misunder-

standing now existing to that era. His review on recent publications was probably helpful to the generally ill-informed audience, as reflected in questions from the floor. This reviewer, however, failed to understand why books by S. W. Kung, G. Barth, Pei Chi Liu, S. Y. Wu, and Jun T. Sun were not mentioned. Important books in German and Chinese were also conspicuously missing. We hope that the forth-coming bibliography will bridge this gap.

★ ★ ★

The last lecture before lunch break was delivered by Thomas W. Chinn, the first president of the Society. Chinn discussed the contributions of Chinese in the U. S.— a subject extremely difficult to present in proper perspective. Avoiding the pitfalls of re-iterating the spectacular Chinese achievements by men such as Hiram Fong, Lee Tsung-dao, Yang Chen-ning, Dong Kingman, James Wong Howe, Ieoh Ming Pei, Gerald Tsai, etc., Chinn paid tribute to the thousands of

East/West, April 23, 1969, Philip P. Choy Collection, CHSA

Chinese laborers who opened the Western states to the East with the construction of the trans-continental railroad and who established many basic industries, such as fishing, mining, shoe, garment, agricultural, etc., that eventually turned California into one of the richest states in the U.S. Chinn also corrected the popular misconception that early Chinese immigrants did not intend to become a permanent part of the American population (the most recent example was expressed by G. Barth in 1964) by citing a resolution of the first known Chinese community meeting reported in the *Alta California* of Dec. 10, 1849, which called the U.S. "our adopted country." In the interest of unbiased scholarship, Chinn cited examples of men of courage and justice who came to the defense of Chinese during the anti-Chinese era.

The afternoon program opened with a unique multi-screen slide show by Mrs. Barbara Adams and Mrs. Adrienne Kwong. Simultaneously three screens showed art objects of ancient China, history of Chinese in the U.S. and present-day Chinatown. Those who are familiar with various slide collections of this type will not fail to recognize that this assemblage owes much to Alan Wong of YMCA and Epoch of Berkeley, even though credit was not given to them.

The third lecture by Chingwah Lee, a local art dealer, was supposed to be on Chinese temples in California. It was changed to "Footnotes on Chinese Religions." As far as this reviewer can ascertain, the talk bore no relation to the subject-matter of the seminar and at times bore the flavor of a talk to tourists. Within an hour, Lee covered Confucianism, Buddhism and Taoism in China and Shintoism of Japan, and he made only passing references to Chinese folk religions and Kwan Gon, one of the major deities in southern China. Lee made numerous claims and generalizations without giving documentary evidence. For example, the alleged relation between the Shang royal tomb and Sumerian royal burial was completely anachronistic and groundless. To avoid future repetition and to afford better control of subject matter, the Society should require all speakers to submit their papers in advance for screening.

A panel (Kenneth Abbott, Chingwah Lee, H. Mark Lai, Thomas Chinn with Philip Choy, as moderator) spent an hour answering questions from the participants of the seminar. Unfortunately the panel avoided answering political

and social questions even when they were obviously related to history. For example, this reviewer asked, "Is the Society engaged in rescuing important historical landmarks in California? If so, has the Society taken a stand on the Kong Chow Temple, the oldest Chinese temple in S.F., now destined to be demolished?" In my opinion, if the Society cannot and will not make a historical judgment on this significant landmark, how can it purport to perform this function for others? The panel discussion ended with many delegates expressing a desire to have more seminars of this kind in the future.

A tour of Chinatown followed the seminar. The tour included CACA, Chinese Six Companies, a family association, a Chinese newspaper and the home of the Historical Society. Surely, the Society will agree with this reviewer that the tour was too one-sided!

There is no question in this reviewer's mind that the seminar was an historical milestone and a tribute to the Society and its dedicated members. The Society should be congratulated for such an undertaking. The *Syllabus* ($5.00), in spite of some significant omissions, is an important contribution to our knowledge and future research. I join with other participants of the seminar to urge the Society to plan more seminars or conferences of this kind. I also urge the Society to open up channels of communication with Chinese college students in the Bay Area and to encourage young scholars and leaders to participate actively in all activities of the Society.

NOTES

1. Philip P. Choy interview by author, August 21, 2008, Chinese Historical Society of America Museum, 965 Clay Street, San Francisco.

2. Miss Effie Chow, "Dr. Robert E. Jenkins Reception," in Chinese American Citizens Alliance San Francisco Lodge, *Survey C.A.C.A.*, December 1967, Thomas W. Chinn Collection, CHSA, 2001.14.

3. *CHSA Bulletin*, February 1969.

4. Ibid.

5. *CHSA Bulletin*, March 1969; *East/West*, April 30, 1969; *Bulletin*, September 1969. One significant exception comes in the *History*'s mention of the history of San Jose's Chinatowns; see Connie Young Yu, *Chinatown, San Jose, USA* (San Jose, Calif.: History San José, 2001[1991]).

6. *CHSA Bulletin* May and June 1969; L. Ling-chi Wang, "California Chinese Seminar: A Landmark," *East/West*, April 23, 1969, English section, 8–9.

On the Kong Chow Temple, see "Suit Filed to Halt Temple Demolition," *East/West*, April 2, 1969. (A photo of Mrs. Charlotte Chang teaching immigrant women to sew at the YWCA in 1916 is in *Chinese America: History & Perspectives* [2008], 3.) One of the photos from Wayland Lee's photodocumentation of Kong Chow Temple prior to its demolition appears in Philip P. Choy's *The Architecture of San Francisco Chinatown* (San Francisco: Chinese Historical Society of America, 2008), 22. Philip P. Choy interview with Anna Naruta, August 21, 2008.

Some elements of the temple were salvaged and eventually installed in the modern building constructed in 1978 at Stockton and Clay Streets that currently houses the Kong Chow Temple and, on the ground floor, the U.S. Post Office. Since the demolition, no new construction has taken place at the temple's historic location (*Unshakable: Rebirth of S.F. Chinatown in 1906, Sing Tao Daily Commemorative Supplement*, April 15, 2006, 46).

Yellow Power 1968
Ruthanne Lum McCunn

Ruthanne Lum McCunn purchased this poster from San Francisco State College's campus bookstore in 1968. A graduate student training to teach in inner-city schools, Ruthanne was enrolled in a special program that held classes off campus in Sausalito. At the start of the Third World Student Strike, students and faculty in the program voted unanimously to halt methodology classes as a demonstration of solidarity with the strikers but to maintain student-teaching commitments.

Ruthanne and her husband, Don, were then living on the 1400 block of Sacramento Street in San Francisco. Unwittingly they had rented in a "whites-only" building. When Ruthanne's Chinese relatives from Hong Kong came to stay, the building's Irish manager accused her and Don of signing the lease "under false pretenses" and ordered them to leave. Refusing, they taped this poster on their apartment's frosted-glass front door so that until their lease expired, renters and visitors in the building's hallway could not avoid seeing "Yellow Power." Ironically the "whites-only" policy was that of the Chinese owner, who believed it would command higher rents. (Courtesy Ruthanne Lum McCunn)

A Wei Min Sister Remembers

Jeanie Dere

This article began as an entry in a blog started by a friend for Asian women who were active in the radical movement during the 1970s. I was invited to write down some of my memories of my involvement as a woman in the Asian American movement. I decided to do it because there is so little written about the Asian Community Center (ACC) and Wei Min She (Organization for the People), both important parts of the leftist movement in San Francisco Chinatown and the Bay Area during that time.

BEFORE THE ASIAN AMERICAN MOVEMENT

While my involvement with the Asian American movement began in 1968, I had been exposed to left-wing politics through my father, Wing Jung Dere, since I was young. My father came to the United States when he was eleven years old as a paper son of an uncle, so he was able to keep his real last name. On arriving in San Francisco, he met his paternal grandfather for the first time. He lived for almost a year in San Francisco Chinatown before he was sent back to China to complete his education. He came back to the United States when he was seventeen years old. In the 1940s and '50s he became involved with progressive Chinatown youth organizations, including Mun Ching (the Chinese American Democratic Youth League).

Because its members showed support for the establishment of the People's Republic of China in 1949, Mun Ching was among several organizations in the Chinese community targeted for persecution by the FBI during the Cold War and the McCarthy era.[1] To the U.S. government, the success of the revolution in China under Mao Zedong represented the spread of the Soviet communist bloc. Fearing communist influence on American society and institutions, the government initiated an anti-Communist crackdown that persecuted a wide range of people. The FBI went after not only members of the Communist Party but also other radicals and even progressives, ranging from labor leaders and unionized workers to Hollywood actors, directors, and scriptwriters.

For many Chinese living in the United States, the establishment of a "new China" represented liberation from for-

eign rule and hope for an end to the extreme poverty, oppression, and political corruption that had existed in China for decades, conditions that forced them to seek a living outside of China. The U.S. government saw things differently and looked on the Chinese community with suspicion, just as it had the Japanese community during World War II. Even sending money home to family in China, something done for decades, came to be seen as trading with the enemy, especially after China entered the Korean War. All the members of Mun Ching were harassed and questioned by the FBI, and eventually over half lost their citizenship.

The U.S. government carried out the anti-Communist investigation into the Chinese community for over two decades. The major way the government was able to attack the left and progressives was by investigating the use of false papers by many Chinese to emigrate to the United States. False claims of citizenship were often used to circumvent the discriminatory and racist Chinese Exclusion Act in effect from 1882 until 1943. After immigration records in San Francisco were destroyed by the 1906 earthquake and its aftermath, many Chinese living in the United States claimed to be U.S.-born citizens, making any children they said they had in China citizens also. As a result, thousands of Chinese came over as paper sons, including my grandfather in 1913 and my father in 1933. My father was among those politically targeted by the FBI and was harassed for many years by the government.

The Confession Program of 1956 put pressure on the whole community to "confess" about their immigration in exchange for immunity. An atmosphere of fear enveloped Chinatown. One person's confession inevitably incriminated many others.[2] When a cousin of my father "talked," this opened the door for the government to act.

My father was tried in court on three counts. Those alleging that he had "willfully and knowingly falsif[ied] and conceal[ed] material facts regarding his identity, parentage, nationality and right to enter and remain in the United States" and engaged in "conspiracy" were dismissed based on the statute of limitations. On the third count, "willfully and knowingly mak[ing] false and fraudulent representation in the naturalization proceedings of his wife," he was found guilty. He had his citizenship taken away and was threatened with deportation.

My father said losing his citizenship was all right because now he could really be "a citizen of the world." I was twelve years old and agreed that it sounded better to be a citizen of the world rather than of just one country. When I was older and became politically active myself, I understood his real meaning. He considered himself an internationalist and stood with the workers and oppressed people of the world struggling against oppression and imperialism. My father appealed the court's decision, however, claiming "that the prosecution was illegal and in violation of the due process clause in that he was picked out discriminatorily because of his suspected radical leanings."[3] In the end, my father was never deported. The United States couldn't send him to mainland China because it didn't recognize the government there, and it couldn't send him to the Republic of China on Taiwan because he was not from there.

Politics in Chinatown had been polarized over supporting Mao's communist revolution versus the corrupt government of the Kuomintang (KMT) ever since the late 1920s, when Chiang Kai-shek took control of the KMT. Chiang Kai-shek waged terrifying attacks on leftists, communists, unionized workers, and students, killing thousands of people indiscriminately.[4] After Mao and the Chinese Communist Party took power in China, the KMT, led by Chiang Kai-shek, fled to the island of Taiwan with the financial and military backing of the United States. The U.S. government refused to recognize the new government and continued to support the KMT as the legitimate government of China.

With the loss of mainland China the KMT desperately needed to maintain control of the Chinese living overseas, including in the United States. Therefore, when the Chinese Workers Mutual Aid Association in San Francisco organized a victory celebration eight days after the founding of the People's Republic of China on October 1, 1949, the KMT went on the offensive. It hired thugs to disrupt the meeting and intimidate the people. The next day it posted leaflets with a hit list containing fifteen names.[5] Later the KMT organized the Chinese Six Companies (a group of district associations) and other traditional Chinatown associations to form the Chinatown Anti-Communist League. These heavy-handed KMT tactics, along with the anti-Communist witch-hunt of the U.S. government, succeeded in suppressing the left-wing and progressive forces in Chinatown. So when the Asian American movement arose, things had been relatively quiet in Chinatown politically for almost two decades, with the KMT and the Chinese Six Companies in control.

The passage of the Hart-Celler Act of 1965 put an end to the national-origin quota system of the Immigration Nationality Act, which had favored immigration by people of European descent. The change opened the door to immigration from Asia. In the following years a new wave of Chinese immigrants entered the United States, many of them from Hong Kong and Taiwan. These immigrants came as whole families, bringing their children, intending to make this country their permanent home. For both the blue-collar workers and the non-English-speaking professionals, this meant living and working in the Chinatowns across the country, exacerbating the overcrowded conditions. San Francisco Chinatown had the highest TB rate in the country. Language barriers to getting an education led to social problems such as delinquency among youth. Parents worked long hours at low-paying jobs in restaurants and garment shops. These conditions would lead to renewed consciousness of the need for social change and action in Chinatown.

WOMEN'S OPPRESSION

What is women's oppression? Although it had a big impact on how I developed as a person, I was not conscious of it at the time. And when I first heard the term, I didn't think it applied to me. How was I oppressed as a woman? I believed I was free to be and do what I wanted.

In the early 1970s I went to some of the first International Women's Day (IWD) celebrations held in the Bay Area. IWD had its origins in the struggle of women textile and garment workers against poor working conditions and low wages in New York in the late 1800s. In 1909 American socialists declared an IWD, and the following year the Second International in Europe established it as a holiday. It was widely celebrated in the 1910s and 1920s but then declined until revived by the feminist movement of the 1960s. I celebrated IWD (March 8) because it was a holiday for oppressed people. I would also celebrate International Workers' Day, or May Day (May 1). But I did not fully grasp how important it was to take on the "women's question," a term we used in the 1970s when talking about women's oppression, fighting for equal rights for women, and women's liberation.

For me to see my own oppression as a woman took many more years and the influence of both my political activities and the literature coming out of Mao's China on the changes being made in women's lives in China under socialism. Women's oppression should have been one of the initial reasons for my becoming involved with the radical movement in the 1970s. Also, my own experience of women's oppression was behind the lack of confidence that prevented me from stepping forward to make even more of a difference during that period of widespread turmoil and activism.

I did not see myself as a leader and shied away from that role. One of the most vivid examples of this occurred during a trip to Vancouver, Canada, in 1971 to attend a women's conference that hosted women speakers from Vietnam. This was an important international conference to build opposition to the Vietnam War and expose the atrocities being committed by the U.S. military. A busload of women from the San Francisco Bay Area and other West Coast cities went to the conference. On its final day, the women voted for a representative to read a statement that would put forward their stand with the struggle of the Vietnamese people and against imperialism. I got the most votes because I was a member of the respected Wei Min She organization. But I was too timid to speak in front of an audience and declined, letting the runner-up take my place. A woman from I Wor Kuen, another Asian group, urged me to do it, since I would also represent the Asian attendees from the United States. But it was the runner-up, a Hispanic woman, who read the statement:

> The vicious imperialism which seeks to commit total genocide against the proud people of Indochina is the same imperialism which oppresses those of us here in North America by creating dehumanizing conditions in our Chinatowns, barrios, Black ghettoes and reservations. We struggle together to build a society which fosters cooperation, rather than competition; justice without exploitation or racism, with love and power to all people. To all of you we give our pledge that we will fulfill our duty, we will build and intensify our struggle to smash imperialism from within.

Needless to say, people from Wei Min She were not happy with me when I got back. Not being proud of my refusal to speak in front of an audience, I avoided speaking about my trip to Canada even though it was such an important event. The experience illustrates how oppression can suppress a person, preventing the full development of an individual's abilities to be a contributing member of a society or cause.

Women's oppression affected my life not only directly but also by influencing my mother's life. My mother, Shoy Mun, came to the United States in 1948 on a boat from China at the age of twenty-two, just married and pregnant with her first child. My father had enlisted in the U.S. Army Air Corps in 1942 to help fight Fascism, and after the war he had gone to China to get married under the War Brides Act. On arriving in China, my father had been introduced to two young women and had picked my mother to marry him. I asked my mother why she had married my father when it meant she had to leave her family and village and travel so far away. She said that everyone wanted to go to the United States where they had hopes for a better life. When a flood of Chinese American GIs went back to China to find brides, this was an opportunity that many single women didn't want to miss. Luckily my mother had a cousin living in my father's village, and a meeting was arranged. After marrying, she had three children in three years; I was the third. Here she was, with three babies and very little money, in a new country where she couldn't speak the language.

My father wasn't around much in those days. He went to school, first at City College and then at Healds College, on the GI Bill. In addition, he was working most nights as a janitor, washing dishes and cleaning up at restaurants to support the family. My grandfather had opposed the idea of his going to college, saying that American businesses would never hire a Chinese. But the Second World War had marked a change in the treatment of the Chinese in America. They were no longer confined to Chinatown for housing and employment. When my father was a boy, any Chinese who crossed Broadway to go out of Chinatown was likely to receive a beating from the whites or even the police.

When my father finally graduated from college he started working as an electrical engineer, first at Bechtel and later at other companies, and our financial situation became better. Fortunately my mother didn't get pregnant again for three years after I was born. She ended up having a total of six children. This was quite common in Chinatown back in the 1950s. People had big families then.

When my paternal grandmother came from China to live with us at the end of 1951, she put pressure on my mother to go out and work. My mother did work on and off at garment shops, but with children to look after, she was mostly a housewife during her first ten years in this country. My grandmother also worked in the garment industry, but she was gone seasonally to work on one of the many flower farms that once existed in the South Bay, pruning by hand the leaves of chrysanthemums and other flowers. After my mother attended night school to learn English and typing, she eventually found work as a keypuncher in downtown business offices until her retirement.

I faced two disadvantages from birth. First, I was born with a weak constitution, so I had poor health with frequent headaches most of my life. Second, I was born a girl into a Chinese family with traditional views on the value and role of women. Even though my father was politically progressive, both my parents placed more value on boys than on girls. This outlook was very common in my parents' generation, though less so than in the many generations before theirs who lived under feudalism in China. While my parents wanted me to have good grades in school, they didn't expect me to go to a four-year college like my brothers. What a painful shock it was to hear my father's response to my applying to San Francisco State College. "Why would you want to do that?" he asked. He thought that if I went to college, a two-year college would be good enough. Why waste the money? "All you will get is some office job and then get married."

I excused my father's response by being understanding of the financial pressure he was under with four sons to put through college. While he paid for everything in my first year at SF State, I paid much of my own way after that. I originally was going to major in math but switched to health science, which would be more relevant to work I was doing in the community. After I graduated I was accepted into a nursing program, but my mother very strongly objected to this, saying the work was heavy and dirty, so I had to give it up. I eventually completed a job-training program as a pharmacy technician.

My mother has never treated me very well because I was not a boy. I tried to explain this to my oldest brother a few times when we were adults, and he never believed me until one day he saw it for himself. My mother made soup for the family, and there were a number of bowls filled with soup on the table. I went over to get one and my mother said, "No, those are for your brothers; go get your own." My brother looked at me and I said, "See what I mean?" He understood then what I had been talking about. I was a second-class citizen in my own family. It was unfair to be treated this way, but when we brought this to my mother's attention, she refused to recognize that she was ever unfair. She claimed to love all her children the same.

By this time I understood that this view of women was due to the Confucian cultural outlook that my parents had grown up with in China. Things had become clearer for me after reading some literature coming out of China's Cultural Revolution in 1974 during an anti-Confucius campaign. Women's oppression is part of Chinese traditional culture. Women were considered subordinate to men, and women's role was to serve the men in the family. My mother was never able to break from this view, and it is sad for me to see how much her interests in life are limited to the family. Mao's China took on this oppression, liberating the women of China from this feudal outlook and even influencing the development of the women's movement in the United States. Unfortunately many of the gains for women in China, as well as those for workers and peasants, were reversed after Mao's death as succeeding leaders betrayed the revolution and embraced capitalism.

For the past thirty years slander and distortions have been rampant as leaders in China, pro-Western expatriate Chinese writers, and the Western media have denigrated Mao and the Cultural Revolution. In reality great achievements were made in China during the Mao era. While things were chaotic during the first two years of the Cultural Revolution and the Red Guards engaged in excessive violence, the Cultural Revolution was never intended to involve any physical violence at all. Once violence did break out, every attempt was made to control it, and finally the army was brought in to break it up.

What was good about the Cultural Revolution? You have to look at what it did for the workers and peasants who make up the vast majority of China's people, not the urban and social elite, with their exclusive education and privileges, who were horrified at being sent to live and work with peasants and workers. Mao saw great value in the educated elite and party leaders periodically living and working among the peasants and ordinary people. How can you serve the people if you don't go out to them and learn about their lives and what they think? Managers in factories should also take part in production periodically because there is something to be learned from working side by side with the workers. Mao had sent his own children and staff to work on farms in the countryside so they could experience and share in the hardships of the people. But some elites could only see this experience as a punishment and looked down on the peasants.

The Cultural Revolution allowed democracy to come into existence at all levels of society and improved the well-being of the people. Workers had a voice in running their own factories; peasants were allowed to enter colleges and to carry out scientific experiments; women took on new roles, including top leadership positions in the government; new form and content for art and literature were created; doctors were sent to the countryside; barefoot doctors were trained to bring health care to the peasants where there had been no doctors before; and much, much more. For a detailed account of how China handled the women's question, I highly recommend Claudie Broyelle's book *Women's Liberation in China.* It deals with how China tackled issues such as husbands and home life, children, participation in production, political struggles, special classes and programs to train women cadres so women could be leaders, and the Confucian ideology that continued to be held by both men and women.[6]

These events in China during the early 1970s had a huge influence on my political development and reinforced my class viewpoint. I loved the art and literature that came out of China during the Cultural Revolution, with workers and peasants as heroes.[7] I still have the collection of short stories and novels from the Mao era that I bought at Everybody's Bookstore and China Books.

I was very happy to read the recent book by Mobo Gao, *The Battle for China's Past: Mao and the Cultural Revolution,* which sets the record straight on what really happened in the 1960s and '70s in China. Gao documents with extensive research how writers like Jung Chung and Jon Halliday, who wrote *Mao: The Unknown Story,* and Li Zhisui, who wrote *The Private Life of Chairman Mao,* fabricated their accounts of Mao's life and of events in China to demonize Mao and distort history, claiming that there was massive destruction with millions killed during the Mao era. Gao then discusses the e-media in China that challenge the view of these expatriate writers as well as the official view of the Chinese government on Mao and the Cultural Revolution.[8] The e-media are playing an increasing role in China despite attempts at censorship by the Chinese government. On the Internet, people can say what they really think; debate various questions, including reevaluating the so-called Gang of Four and the Cultural Revolution; and discuss how they see the situation in China today. This newly rising voice will battle for the truth on China's recent history and for the future of the masses of people in China.

"I'M GOING TOO"

The 1960s was a time of social turmoil, both internationally and within the United States. Countries in Africa, Asia, the Middle East, and Latin America were fighting for freedom from colonialism. In the United States, people were marching and demonstrating for civil rights, the right of Blacks to vote, and an end to Jim Crow laws in the South. There was the

Free Speech movement on college campuses. There was the start of the Vietnam War and the antiwar movement. With the start of the Black Power movement, similar movements arose in the Latino, Native American, and Asian communities. Militant groups like the Black Panther Party and Brown Berets developed across the country. San Francisco State College (now University) was one of the hot spots for the Free Speech movement and the site of many demonstrations.

In 1968, I was eighteen years old. In my first semester at SF State, the first Third World Strike broke out.[9] Among the demands were that education should be relevant to the community; that college education should be made accessible for minorities and the poor; that colleges and education should not be geared to making profits for corporations and the military-industrial complex; and that there should be ethnic studies so minorities could know their own histories and learn how to be of service to their communities. The strike was my start in becoming active in San Francisco Chinatown and the Asian American movement. It was here that I walked my first picket line and signed up to tutor immigrant schoolchildren in Chinatown. But the leaders of the strike did not reach out to involve me further and I was too shy to approach them myself. My further involvement would come from another direction.

Beginning in junior high school, I was pretty much a book-reading recluse with dreams of becoming an astronomer or a research scientist like Marie Curie. My two older brothers were more socially active. They went to Boy Scouts and drum and bugle corps, joined a kung fu club in Chinatown, and played sports with friends. All my time was spent going to school, studying, and reading books from the library on a wide range of topics. But this was going to change. Around 1968 I heard my brothers talking about going to Leways, a pool hall for youth, where there were people talking about Mao Zedong and the Black Panther Party and reading from Mao's Little Red Book. This was where the Red Guard Party would form.[10] Later on, my brothers would bring one of the founders of the party, Alex Hing, to our home to meet our father. The party wanted someone to translate its leaflets into Chinese. My father agreed to help.

The Red Guard Party was modeled after the Black Panther Party. It recruited mainly street kids as members, following the example of the Black Panthers in looking to the section of society called the lumpen proletariat as being the most oppressed and most ready for revolution. My father was very progressive in his politics. He was against the war in Vietnam; he supported revolutionary China; and after the Black Panther Party formed in the Bay Area, he paid close attention to news of the Black Panthers on television and began bringing home copies of their newspaper. The Black Panthers were the first to popularize Mao Zedong and Mao's Little Red Book, actually titled *Quotations from Chairman Mao Tse-tung*. Quotes such as "Political power grows out of the barrel of a

gun" and "Serve the people" would become widely used as slogans by the New Left. So it was no surprise that my father would help translate for the Red Guard Party. He would later also translate material for ACC and *Wei Min Bao* newspaper. I was proud of him for his hard work. He would go to work all day, and when he came home he would stay up late to do the translations. He continued to translate even after he had a heart attack. My father's political views also made it easier for me later when I got politically active; they limited how much my parents could complain about how I was never home anymore or came home late.

When the Red Guards, like the Black Panthers, started a free breakfast program, I volunteered to help during the summer of 1969. The program was run out of one of the clubs on Broadway. Usually only one or two Red Guard members came to work on it, and I helped set up, cook the meals, and clean up afterward. But the program was short lived because the turnout was small, usually two or three children. In contrast, the Black Panthers would have a room packed full of people.

My long-term involvement in Chinatown as an activist would not be with the Red Guards but with a group of students from Berkeley who would set up ACC and Everybody's Bookstore at the end of 1969. Both my older brothers went to Berkeley and got pulled into action, like many others. Berkeley had a history of student activism. In the late '60s it really heated up with protests. There were teach-ins on the Vietnam War, antidraft actions, the Third World Strike, People's Park. In response the National Guard was sent in with tear gas and even fired shots into crowds.

The first time I saw some of these Berkeley students was at a huge antiwar protest in 1969 that marched from downtown San Francisco to Golden Gate Park. My brothers were going to the march with a friend. When I said, "I'm going too," they didn't object, and I went too. Although my family was against the war, this was the first time we had taken part in protest.

Opposing the war was the correct thing to do. The United States should never have gone into another country and bombed its people with napalm, antipersonnel bombs, and toxic chemicals like Agent Orange. It was unbearable to hear about the suffering of the Vietnamese people at the hands of the U.S. military. Many years later, I would read accounts of horrible birth defects resulting from the chemicals dropped on Vietnam. My father had bought a copy of Felix Greene's book *Vietnam! Vietnam! in Photographs and Text*, which uncovered what the war was truly about. There was no choice but to support the Vietnamese people's struggle for liberation.

The antiwar march was very exciting, with so many different people. We came across the Asian Contingent and marched with it. The Asians had their own banners and signs. They opposed the war from an Asian perspective, one I had never thought about before. They said the Vietnamese people were our brothers and sisters, that the war was genocide against Asian people, that the U.S. military called the Vietnamese "gooks" and viewed all Asians that way. I had strong views that all people were part of the same human race, but beginning with my meeting with the Asian Contingent, I learned that to fight discrimination directed at a whole group, you need to unite as a group to fight for justice and change.

I later found out that the Asian American Political Alliance that originated in Berkeley in 1968 was the first group to ever use the term "Asian American." Before that, we were Chinese American, Japanese American, or Filipino American. I was amazed that some of the marchers spoke Chinese; in fact, some spoke Sze Yup, as my family did at home, not Sam Yup (Cantonese). I had avoided speaking Sze Yup in public for many years, ever since I had seen how Cantonese speakers laughed and snickered at people who gave speeches in Sze Yup during events in Chinatown as I was growing up. Cantonese was spoken in the city while Sze Yup was from the countryside and looked down upon as crude. Later my Sze Yup would be very useful when I became active in the community. As the march approached Golden Gate Park, we saw some Black Panther Party members passing out pamphlets written by Mao Zedong and selling their newspaper. We stayed to hear speeches and finally had to leave since we had nothing to eat or drink.

SURROUNDED BY BANNED BOOKS

One day my oldest brother was talking about how he and a number of other students at Berkeley had chipped in $50 each to open a bookstore. I immediately said I wanted to go there to work. I loved to read and had always wanted to work in a bookstore or library. That was how I ended up going to a basement on Kearny Street, where I attended my first ACC meeting in December 1969. I was quite shocked when I was asked to give my opinion. I was still pretty reclusive and did not talk much. Besides, all the Berkeley students with the bookstore and ACC were men except for one woman, and when she graduated six months later, she left to go back home, leaving me the only woman in a group of about ten people. Other women occasionally came down to ACC but their work was in other areas, such as on campus, in Japantown, or with the Garment Coop located next door. The Garment Coop was started by some Berkeley students with a few garment workers around the same time as the bookstore and ACC.

The bookstore, named Everybody's Bookstore, had been set up by the end of December but would not open until January because a number of the students had to go home to visit their parents for the holidays. The bookstore was in a very small storefront, about the size of one room in a house, located in the International Hotel (I-Hotel) at 840 Kearny Street. In a few years it would expand greatly as the back

wall was removed to expose another huge room. Everybody's Bookstore had very few books in the beginning, some in English and some in Chinese, and a number of periodicals. Many of the pamphlets and books were from China.

The source of the books was probably China Books & Periodicals, which was the only importer of books, periodicals, posters, and records from China in the United States. It was located in the Mission district of San Francisco. When I was younger my brothers and I had gone to China Books with our father and a number of his old Mun Ching friends. It was brave of them to go to China Books because this would have been considered subversive and everyone in Mun Ching had been investigated by the FBI. My father had shown me words stamped on some of the books by U.S. Customs to indicate that the material was considered banned.

How was China Books able to import publications from China when a trade embargo had been put in place in 1951 under the Trading with the Enemy Act? The owner of China Books, Henry Noyes, explained this in his book *China Born: Adventures of a Maverick Bookman*.[11] The key was that no payments would actually be sent to China until the ban on the export of capital to China was lifted. The payments were held in escrow, in a U.S. bank account that was blocked by the U.S. Treasury. With this blocked account in existence, Henry Noyes was able to get a U.S. Treasury license allowing him to legally import publications from China under the First Amendment of the U.S. Constitution, which guarantees Americans the right to read, including books and magazines from the PRC.

The first time I went down the stairs to the basement on Kearny Street, people were watching revolutionary movies and newsreels. The free community film showings were the first program the Berkeley students had set up. The newsreels were documentary shorts on recent news and events such as developments with the Black Panther Party. A typical movie was *Battle of Algiers*, which depicted how the Algerian people organized to fight for liberation from the French. The film program was one of the ways to educate the people to become political and class-conscious so they could organize themselves as a force to change society. I would eventually learn to run the projector and help set up weekend movie showings. We often showed movies about revolution and the struggle for socialism in China. The films from China came from sources in Canada, since Canada had relations with China while the United States did not. I will never forget the first weekend we showed *East Is Red*, a musical drama of the Chinese revolution. We showed it fourteen times and it was packed for each showing. There was so much emotional response from the audience. Once during a scene of a woman forced to sell her daughter, a woman in the audience started sobbing loudly. It was too dark to see who it was, but we wondered if something similar had happened in her family.

ACC was officially formed a couple of months after we started having meetings. Its first location was the basement at 832 Kearny Street in the building next to the I-Hotel. Formerly the United Filipino Association Hall, it was a huge room with a small stage, a kitchen, and a diner that had a long counter with stools. We tried to chip in to buy food and cook there. Later we arranged to pay one of the men who came down regularly to buy the food and do the cooking. Anyone who wanted to eat dinner just needed to sign up and help pay for the food. Nine months later, our lease was suddenly terminated in response to pressure by the right-wing Chinatown establishment (the Six Companies and the KMT).

A location was desperately needed for ACC's ongoing programs, especially the film program and the food program, which distributed government supplemental food to three hundred women and young children every month. I had became the main person responsible for the food program, signing up women and their children, going to meetings with other community centers that were also distributing food, and working with the health educator at the public health center on Mason Street in Chinatown. Fortunately we had started working with a group of Hong Kong students named Red Door, which had recently rented one of the basements in the I-Hotel and had painted its door bright red. When we were evicted, we moved only a few doors away into this basement at 846 Kearny Street.

Fortunately there was a woman in the Hong Kong group, so I was no longer the only woman around, and the two of us eventually worked closely together on many projects. The Hong Kong students could read and write Chinese, making it easier for us to put out a bilingual newsletter, and things moved forward rapidly in our work in Chinatown. Staffing for ACC and the bookstore was all voluntary because there was no money to pay for staff. Soon both the bookstore and the ACC programs would attract many more student and community volunteers, and the number of men and women would become more balanced. When staffing the bookstore I met the man who would later teach a group of us at ACC how to practice Yang-style tai chi chuan. I would always be thankful for this because it has been my main form of exercise.

My second brother didn't get involved in ACC. He worked to save the I-Hotel for a while and often hung around with three Filipino I-Hotel supporters.[12] Many students had started to come to the I-Hotel to support the tenants in their fight against eviction. At that time the students and other supporters were making repairs to a section of the hotel where a suspicious fire had started, killing three of the tenants on March 16, 1969. Many people suspected that the fire was linked to the attempts by the owner, Milton Meyer & Company, to evict the tenants. Milton Meyer was planning on tearing down the hotel and building a garage in its place. The I-Hotel fight would become a very important one during the 1970s for the Bay Area and a rallying cry for low-income housing.

"WHAT WE SEE, WHAT WE WANT, WHAT WE BELIEVE"

At ACC we held many meetings to discuss the center's aims and purpose. Many groups in those days had a platform and program. The Black Panther Party had its Ten-Point Program. We wanted something of our own. After discussing the issues that plagued Chinatown, such as the highest TB rate in the country, crowded living conditions, garment sweatshops, and restaurants with low-paying jobs and long working hours, we came up with "What We See, What We Want, What We Believe."[13] This platform and program would be printed on the back page of every issue of the *Asian Community Newsletter*, which came out every month from June 1970 until the newspaper *Wei Min Bao* was started in October 1971. It read as follows:

WHAT WE SEE
We see the breakdown of our community and families.
We see our people suffering from malnutrition, tuberculosis, and high suicide rates.
We see the destruction of our cultural pride.
We see our elders forgotten and alone.
We see our Mothers and Fathers forced into meaningless jobs to make a living.
We see American society preventing us from fulfilling our needs.

WHAT WE WANT
We want adequate housing, medical care, employment, and education.

WHAT WE BELIEVE
To solve our community problems, all Asian people must work together.
Our people must be educated to move collectively for direct action.
We will employ any effective means that our people see necessary.

I learned a lot about radical politics in these meetings. One issue the Berkeley students raised was how to work together. We were going to work collectively. Everyone would have input on decisions. We also decided that we were going to base ACC on the working class or proletariat, not the lumpen proletariat (street people) as the Black Panthers and the Red Guard Party had done. Our work was to educate the community that there was a need to organize for change and that they were the ones who must step forward to act. Through this kind of work I became aware that groups had different political lines. People who had similar lines would be able to come together and do work, whereas people with different lines would not. Some of the youth and students attracted by the community work going on along Kearny Street chose to join the Red Guard Party, for example, instead of ACC. The original group of students who formed ACC were all American-born but were able to join with a group of Hong Kong–born students shortly afterward because they had similar views.

In the early days many of the regulars who came down to ACC as a drop-in center were elderly men. But later people of all ages would come down, including grade-school children. Due to exclusion laws against the Chinese, many of the early immigrants could not bring their wives or family members to the United States. The men grew old alone, working here and sending money home to families in China. At ACC they could relax and hang out, drink tea, socialize with friends, read the newspaper, flip through *China Pictorials* and other magazines from China, and have a place to stay besides the park or the tiny room they rented in a flophouse or hotel. Some supported Mao and China for political reasons, others out of pride in seeing their home country strong.

The political atmosphere was tense because of the KMT and its Anti-Communist League. I hear that some of the old men said they would help defend the community center if the KMT decided to attack. The KMT did not bother us much after the eviction from our first location. But a few months after we moved there were police raids on ACC, Leways/the Red Guards, and Asian Legal Services, all tenants at the I-Hotel. On February 5, 1971, the police entered with loaded shotguns to search the premises of these organizations, claiming that they were looking for someone. The groups held a press conference a few days later to protest the police harassment. I wasn't there when the raids happened, but I heard that the old men told the police they should get out and leave the center alone.

The old men did not respect the KMT or the Six Companies. They called them *faahn tung*, or "rice bucket," which is a slang term for "idiot" in Cantonese. Most people in Chinatown viewed the Chinese establishment as representing the rich who did little for the community.

ACC became a real home for many of these old men. In the beginning I used to do some cleaning up at the center, sweeping the stairs and other areas and cleaning the toilets. Some of the old men objected to my doing this work and took over doing it themselves. They also took over the task of making the tea when we opened at eleven in the morning and making sure the supply lasted until closing time at ten at night.

Soon we learned that some of these old men had a long history of struggle themselves. A few had been involved with workers' struggles from the 1920s to the '40s, and some had once been members of the Communist Party. They had participated in some very militant workers' organizations, including the Chinatown Unemployment Council, during the Depression, and they had stood up to the right-wing KMT, which had tried to infiltrate and disrupt the growing workers' movement at that time. Olden Lee, for example, was active in the 1934 San Francisco general strike and was arrested and imprisoned for ninety days as a result. Olden Lee and a few others had also belonged to the Chinese Workers Mutual Aid Association (1937–54), which at one point had four to five hundred members, many of whom worked seasonally in the Alaskan salmon canneries. They also broke through decades of racism toward the Chinese to work with the American labor movement, including the Cannery Workers Union, the International Longshore and Warehouse Union, and the Communist Party, USA.[14] We saw them as advanced workers who helped us in our organizing work, but they most likely saw themselves as longtime organizers and Marxist-Leninists trying to influence us and lead us in our work.

Following the Third World Strike on college campuses, ethnic studies programs were set up in a number of colleges and universities across the country, including UC Berkeley and SF State. The students from Berkeley who started ACC were also involved with the Asian American Studies program at Berkeley. They had ACC set up as a field office for the program, and office equipment and supplies were brought to ACC for our shared use. The most important piece of equipment we obtained was a printing press, which enabled us to print out newsletters and flyers. In the first few years of the program students were brought to the field office for lectures and encouraged to become involved with work in the community, such as with the I-Hotel, Chinatown, or Japantown. But use of ACC as the field office declined as the ACC Berkeley students graduated and became less involved with the department.

While I spent much of my time at ACC during the early 1970s, I still attended the meetings at SF State to discuss the very beginnings of its Chinese American Studies program. People identified me as someone from ACC. George Woo was becoming an important leader in the Chinese American Studies program and was very vocal in community meetings in Chinatown. I joined a team of women to discuss and plan the first Asian American women's class at SF State with Pat Sumi as the instructor. Involvement with the community was also an important component of Asian American Studies at SF State but this aspect decreased in later years, with the department becoming more academic in orientation.

We started many other "serve the people" programs at ACC. The Summer Youth Program provided classes and field trips for school-age children. I volunteered with this program for the four years when it was run out of ACC. We put out the monthly *Family Newsletter* beginning in May 1972 specifically for women and children in the community. During ACC's first year, we set up community health screenings for TB and glaucoma with staff from the Public Health Department and the Northern California Society for the Prevention of Blindness, respectively, coming down to do the testing. Later we helped organize health fairs with other Chinatown organizations at Portsmouth Square, where many people from the community hung out every day. These activities inspired students majoring in medical fields to later set up the free Asian Community Health Clinic at the Ping Yuen Housing Project on Stockton Street. We also took on housing issues, such as improving conditions at the Ping Yuen and other housing units in Chinatown; fighting rent hikes and evictions, as at San Fran Hotel; and the I-Hotel struggle. We supported workers' struggles at restaurants, garment shops, and electronics factories. We worked with the U.S.-China Peoples Friendship Association to build people-to-people friendship and put on exhibits and programs to teach people about socialism in China. Later, as more people began to come down to ACC, they would start new activities such as a singing group, English-language classes, and tai chi chuan classes. Children from the summer program would come down to play ping-pong or just hang out with us.

In January 1971 Wei Min She was formed as an anti-imperialist organization to lead the work politically for ACC, Everybody's Bookstore, and the Chinatown Garment Cooperative. Plans were made for a newspaper, and *Wei Min Bao* began coming out monthly starting in October 1971. Articles were written on all of the issues we took on, as well as on the mass movements of the people in the community, events related to China, the Vietnam War, and labor issues. We participated in as well as wrote about meetings and demonstrations in the community for housing, child care, education, and school busing. On many weekends Wei Min She members went out to the busiest street corners in Chinatown to sell the newspaper, sometimes using bullhorns to do political agitation. We also went door to door to sell *Wei Min Bao* and talk to the people at the Ping Yuen Housing Project, hotel rooming houses, and apartment buildings throughout Chinatown. We became a real presence in the community.

There were so many areas of work—labor, health, housing, student work, the newspaper, and the bookstore, among others—that special work groups had to be set up at various times. We also set up study groups to carry out political education for ourselves and for the volunteers who were interested in working more closely with us. We studied the writings of Mao Zedong and applied much of his thinking to our work. We studied the current conditions in the world, in the United States, and in Chinatown. We tried to apply criticism and self-criticism as we summed up our work. We went out to the masses to investigate their situation and get their opinions. In the summer of 1971, historian Him Mark Lai gave a series of six lectures on Chinese in America for the activists in ACC. We studied the writings of Marx, Engels, and Lenin, as well as books on the revolution in China, such as Edgar Snow's *Red Star over China*. We read the writings of Malcolm X, Che Guevara, Frantz Fanon, and many others in search of the direction forward for revolutionary change.

We also set up classes to study "the women's question" and "the national question." In the 1970s the term "national question" was often used when talking about the struggle against racism and the fight for democratic rights. The struggle of Blacks in America, for example, was frequently referred to as the black liberation movement as they compared it to the liberation struggle against colonialism in third world countries. So it was common for activists in the 1970s to say they were involved in "the struggle against national oppression" and refer to the importance of "building multinational unity" in the fight against racism. On the women's question,

we initially had study groups with the women and the girlfriends of the men who came down to ACC. Later we had study sessions for all Wei Min She members so that the men would also be urged to take on different aspects of women's oppression. There were some complaints from the women about how the men treated them, especially on how the men spoke "at them" rather than "to them," and this was one of the issues taken on in discussions.

In 1974 we became involved with two very significant workers' struggles in Chinatown. One was the Jung Sai (Great Chinese American Sewing Company) garment workers' strike, the other the Lee Mah electronics workers' attempt to unionize. The workers in these two factories faced similar oppressive conditions that forced them to fight back against the bosses. Wei Min She got involved not only with supporting these workers on the picket line but also with trying to link up their struggles with the working-class movement and the struggle against the whole capitalist system. Our work with the Jung Sai and Lee Mah workers led them to join together to put on a workers' festival. At the Chinese Cultural Center on the evening of August 24, 1974, they performed skits and sang songs about their situation and their struggle. Over six hundred people attended the spirited event. In the weeks leading up to it much work had been done in Chinatown to build support for the workers through the distribution of hundreds of flyers, agitation on street corners, and a car caravan that paraded throughout Chinatown charging up the atmosphere. "Support the Jung Sai and Lee Mah workers!" "Workers united will never be defeated!" "Unity is strength!"

KEARNY STREET AND THE I-HOTEL STRUGGLE

The block of Kearny Street between Jackson and Washington Streets was all that was left of Manilatown, reduced from a community of ten blocks to just the I-Hotel, a barbershop, Mabuhay Restaurant, and the pool hall across the street. Of primary importance was the fight against eviction of the residents of the I-Hotel. This drew many supporters, especially students and Filipino groups, such as Union of Democratic Filipinos (KDP). Also drawn to the hotel were many Asian organizations that rented storefronts or basements there. From the late 1960s into the '70s, these groups included Chinatown Draft Help, Asian Legal Services, the Chinatown Garment Cooperative, the Red Guard Party, I Wor Kuen, the Chinese Progressive Association, and the Kearny Street Workshop (an organization set up to promote artistic expression in the community). Looking back, I wish there had been more interaction and unity among all these groups.

I remember how excited I was when I first heard that there was an organization coming from New York City. It was called I Wor Kuen, which translates into "Harmonious

Righteous Fist" and was taken from a name used for Chinese fighters in the Boxer Rebellion.[15] There were a large number of women in the group's leadership. I thought we would be able to work together as we had with the students from Hong Kong. Instead, after some initial meetings between a few of the members of Wei Min She and I Wor Kuen, it was decided that there were serious political differences between the two organizations. We were not going to work together. I was very disappointed when I heard this. I wanted to know why, but what was discussed in those meetings was never made public. By this time Wei Min She had grown too big and had too much going on to work as a collective. It had had to evolve into a more complex organization with a steering committee made up of representatives from the various work areas.

Wei Min She had also gotten involved with another organization, the Revolutionary Union (RU). RU had its roots in Students for a Democratic Society and was mainly made up of radicalized whites. A member of RU, an Asian woman, had joined Wei Min She and would come to have a major influence on its political development. As a whole RU members were a few years older and had more experience, and they had gained our respect through their involvement with working-class struggles, including in the factories and in the fields with migrant farmworkers. However, their main objective was building a vanguard party of the proletariat. They had published a series of pamphlets called Red Papers and engaged others in discussing them as part of the process of building a new communist party in this country, a revolutionary party that would uphold Marxism-Leninism and "Mao Tse-Tung Thought."

During the 1970s many other radical groups in the United States were also involved with forming Marxist-type parties. Most people in the New Left had some basic understanding that the Communist Party, USA, which continued to support and maintain ties with the Soviet Union, no longer represented the interests of the working class. In international polemics led by Mao Zedong from the mid-1950s into the 1960s, struggle was waged over the path that the Soviet Union was taking under Khrushchev. Mao argued that the Soviet Union was no longer socialist but had become revisionist, having restored capitalism—not capitalism with a free market and competing capitalists, as in the West, but "state capitalism" with the Communist Party as the new capitalist class. It was this change that brought Mao to an understanding of the need for the Cultural Revolution in China and the need to fight capitalist roaders within the Chinese Communist Party. So, many of the organizations on the left saw a need for a new party of the working class in this country.

In the process of party building, differences in line would define how these groups would relate to one another. Sectarianism is a term that many people have used to describe the events going on in the leftist movement at the time, events that led to much division in the movement and to splits within organizations.

Wei Min She and I Wor Kuen's relationship was a reflection of all this. Some of our differences would eventually come out in open polemics. In September 1974 Wei Min She published a twenty-page polemic on its differences with I Wor Kuen over celebrating May Day that year. This pamphlet gave some concrete examples of the differences in line. The two groups held separate activities and programs, especially around the yearly events of IWD, International Workers' Day, and the October 1 celebrations.

We even had differences over the Jung Sai garment workers. I Wor Kuen opposed linking up the Jung Sai and Lee Mah workers' struggles, wanting to keep the Jung Sai workers within the confines of a union-led strike. On the other hand, Wei Min She not only saw similarities in the working conditions and daily lives of the Jung Sai garment workers and the Lee Mah electronics workers but also worked to bring them together to put on a cultural program and to build broad community support for both struggles.

In practice, Wei Min She and I Wor Kuen were rivals because we were doing almost identical work. Both groups had "serve the people" programs and worked with the same population, mainly the immigrants living in and around Chinatown. In addition, we were next-door neighbors, located in adjacent basements of the I-Hotel. It seems strange now that at a time when we were all filled with the desire to fight U.S. imperialism, we failed to bridge or put aside some of our differences to unite on broader terms.

Wei Min She became increasingly involved with RU in building a revolutionary workers' movement and discussing the question of forming a party of the working class. We were very excited over the idea of a "multinational working-class party based on Marxism-Leninism and Mao Tse-Tung Thought." We had heard that a group of Black workers, the Black Workers Congress, was involved in serious discussions with RU on the East Coast. In fact, two members of the Black Workers Congress came to meet with members of Wei Min She's steering committee, encouraging our organization to join in forming a party. I was told years later that this meeting was a crucial factor in Wei Min She's decision to participate. In 1975 the new party was formed, the Revolutionary Communist Party (RCP).[16]

Almost immediately Wei Min She was dissolved as an organization. This came as a shock to me, especially after it became clear that not everyone from Wei Min She was going to be admitted into RU's new party. Some of us were left out, especially the people most involved with the "serve the people" programs. All of these except the film program had been eliminated during the last year of Wei Min She's existence. RU members argued that it was a waste to put so much time and energy into these programs because they were "reformist" social service work, not revolutionary work. Focus shifted to working-class struggles such as supporting the

Jung Sai and Lee Mah workers and fighting for housing in the community, struggles that would help to build a workers' movement. Within months after formation of the RCP a large number of Wei Min She members were sent to do political work in other cities across the country, some as far away as Chicago, Detroit, and New York City. So Wei Min She's membership was dispersed. While ACC continued to exist, many of its programs were gone.

After being a part of an organization for five years, I felt I was left in limbo. Looking back, I think that dissolving Wei Min She was a mistake that RU/RCP made due to an incorrect line on what was needed for the struggle of minorities in the United States as well as what it takes to make revolution. While forming a party of the proletariat is critical for revolution, there is still need for other types of grassroots organizations among the people. People come up against the system through many different arenas in society. There were and will be Asians, as well as members of all other minorities in a racist America, coming forward as activists over issues of racism, discrimination, and the fight for democratic rights. An anti-imperialist Asian organization like Wei Min She would have been able to bring political understanding to these struggles, clarifying that class division is the basis of this oppression and that class struggle is what is needed to end it. Work of this type would contribute greatly to building a revolutionary movement in this country. Wei Min She could have existed side by side with the RCP.

For over two decades the absence of cutting-edge leftist politics has left a political void in Chinatown and other Bay Area Asian communities. But there are always signs of Asian youth wanting to take things on, and in recent years these youth have been a more visible presence, opposing the Iraq War, fighting for immigrant rights, opposing cuts in education, etc.

I Wor Kuen would later also be involved with forming a party. Shortly after arriving in San Francisco it merged with the Red Guard Party (retaining the I Wor Kuen name). It put out a Twelve-Point Platform and Program. I Wor Kuen also continued to be active in New York City, which made it a national organization.[17] In San Francisco it started the Chinese Progressive Association in the basement of the I-Hotel a few doors from ACC and set up its own "serve the people" programs. The Chinese Progressive Association still exists today. In 1978 I Wor Kuen merged with the Chicano-based August 29th Movement and became a party, the League of Revolutionary Struggle (Marxist-Leninist). Due to the difficulties of doing revolutionary work in the 1980s with no massive upsurges in struggle, the League of Revolutionary Struggle became involved in mainstream electoral politics and joined Jesse Jackson's Rainbow Coalition. It abandoned revolution and Marxism-Leninism and disbanded as an organization in 1990.

I continued to go down to ACC, where the work was now under the leadership of the RCP. I had finished school and started working in a hospital. In 1976 someone from the RCP asked if I would quit my job and get work in the garment industry. This industry was fairly large in San Francisco at that time and had mainly immigrant and Black workers. I was to seek out some of the more class-conscious workers in the factories and help translate for the Chinese workers at the meetings of the International Ladies' Garment Workers' Union. The union paid little attention to the immigrants who made up the majority of the garment workforce, holding its meetings only in English.

Unfortunately I was not able to work fast enough to hold a job in the larger garment shops, which all laid me off after a few weeks at most. I finally settled into working in the garment shops in Chinatown. These could be found on many of the streets and alleys, and you could hear the roar of the machines when you walked by their doors. In the larger shops sewing-machine operators specialized in sewing only one part of the garment (sleeves, or collars, or pockets). In Chinatown the boss gave each worker a bundle of one dozen cut-up pieces and a completed sample of the garment, and the worker pieced the whole garment together. Pay was on a piecework basis, often at a rate of around $4 to $6 per dozen, sometimes more if the garment was more complex. With the pay so low, the workers in most Chinatown sweatshops had to work long hours. I worked almost two years in the garment industry before moving on to a job with the San Francisco School District. Today the garment shops are gone, with most garment production in this country having moved to overseas sweatshops where the clothing manufacturers can make even bigger profits.

The fight at the I-Hotel intensified when Four Seas Investment Corporation, an Asian overseas investment group, bought the hotel in 1973. Many demonstrations against eviction were held in the following years, sometimes with thousands of people gathering to support the tenants and the demand for low-cost housing. On the night of the I-Hotel eviction in August 1977, thousands of people from many communities and many organizations were mobilized to form a human blockade to prevent it. All through that evening we stood with determination. Then the police came in wearing their tactical gear, some mounted on horses, and started beating us with their batons to move us out of the way. I was grateful to one Asian brother who stepped in to protect another woman and me from some of the blows, taking more blows himself. We were bruised and sore for days afterward. Many of us were there all night. I couldn't believe that we had lost, and I wished that there had been more resistance that night.

With the eviction we lost our base. ACC and Everybody's Bookstore relocated in Chinatown, renting a small building in the alley between Clay and Washington Streets right across from Portsmouth Square. The bookstore was on the ground level and ACC was on the second floor, which consisted of a number of small rooms. This setup did not work well for ACC. There wasn't even a way to show movies in such a space. ACC eventually folded and the bookstore became Revolution Books, the bookstore of the RCP.

An additional factor behind ACC's demise was Mao Zedong's death in 1976, which led to a reversal of the revolution in China and the restoration of capitalism under Deng Xiaoping. The RCP upheld Mao and the revolutionary leaders labeled as the Gang of Four, denouncing Deng Xiaoping and the other new leaders in China as capitalist and revisionist. I agreed with their view, but it was not popular with many of the people in Chinatown whose main reason for supporting China was nationalism, not the politics of socialism or revolution. Some, however, including my father, agreed that China was becoming revisionist, so we still had some support in the community. It was heartbreaking to see the accomplishments of socialism in China being dismantled over the years, communes broken up, health care services eliminated, educational opportunities taken away from the workers and peasants and given back to the sons and daughters of the urban elite, and the division between rich and poor widened. Gone was one of the greatest social movements in human history to narrow the gap between urban and rural, industry and agriculture, mental and manual labor.

SOME OF THE BEST TIMES OF MY LIFE

However, during the years on Kearny Street, we did so many things. Those ACC years were some of the best times of my life, rich with experience and people. I learned to do things I had never dreamed of doing before, such as leading group meetings and discussions. I stopped being timid and became a community activist, selling newspapers and passing out flyers on the streets of Chinatown, talking to people about issues and struggles. I relished the many discussions on Marxist theory and charting the way forward to socialism, and I dreamed of moving society even farther, to a society without classes or Communism. I formed lifelong bonds with many of the other activists, bonds based on a commitment to fight for revolution and transform the world as well as ourselves. In the basement of ACC we were able to re-create to some degree the kinds of relationships and attitudes seen in socialist China, as opposed to the dog-eat-dog competitive social relationships promoted by capitalism. Socialist China inspired us to see a vision of what could be possible once the oppressed classes seized power and ruptured the old social relationships of the oppressors. Our "serve the people" programs provided people with a glimpse of a society where people collectively took care of each other's needs. People in Chinatown had begun to come down to ACC to look for support when they wanted to fight against oppression, whether poor working conditions or rent hikes and evictions.

In addition, we did not want to just keep things on this level of struggle for temporary gains, but brought up the need for real change. In everything we did we stressed the need for the people to become involved themselves and to take an active role. We formed a workers' committee where workers who had come forward on one issue could then take up broader political issues in society. Unfortunately things did not quite turn out the way we expected with the formation of the RCP.

The RCP is one of the few groups from the 1970s that still exist today, but it is very different from what it started out to be over thirty years ago when it based itself among the working class. In 1981 the RCP came out with its New Programme. Dumping its previous work with the working class, it made its newspaper the heart of its work under the slogan "Create Public Opinion, Seize Power." This marked the beginning of a change in line that would lead the party to become increasingly divorced from involvement with the struggles of workers and other oppressed people. By the mid-1980s, as the RCP withdrew any remaining forces, leftist politics would have no presence in Chinatown at all. I helped sell the RCP's newspaper throughout the Bay Area and helped staff Revolution Books in Berkeley. The RCP also put out the slogan "Revolution in the '80s—go for it!" When it became increasingly clear that revolution was not going to happen anytime in the 1980s, I kept waiting for the RCP to announce a new analysis of the world situation, reevaluate the possibilities of revolution, or even retract the slogan. It never did. It gave no explanation and no summation of its wrong assessment of the objective situation.[18] This was one of many factors that led me to end my relationship with the RCP in 1990.

It was not easy for me to take this step. It felt as if I was abandoning the revolutionary cause. There was no alternative organization that I could work with because the leftist movement was in a slump. Many of the other people from Wei Min She who had been members or supporters of the RCP had also stopped working with the party, some by the early or mid-1980s. Many people left with very bitter feelings, saying they felt they had been "used" and "treated with disrespect," and a few even said they had experienced racism from the party's leadership while in New York. Where was the respect due to fellow comrades? The group that had influenced us to join with the RU in party building, the Black Workers Congress, either never actually joined the party or left in its very early stages over differences on the national question. Can a communist party call itself revolutionary in the United States without having significant numbers of Blacks and other minorities as members? The experiences of former Wei Min She members with the party have yet to be summed up.

I no longer have ties to an organization. But I have continued to pay attention to the political situation in the world and to participate in various demonstrations that come up. I have also continued to look for news coming out of China of workers or peasants taking on the new exploitative conditions in that country. An old Wei Min She member recently sent me email about a new online magazine, *China Left Review*, which had many excellent articles, including one on peasant protest over land privatization. Peasants were rebelling over "their collective farmland, forests, and grassland commons sold to private investors, companies, and those connected to local leaders."[19] The magazine also included an article on the Tibet situation.

I've been married for the last sixteen years, having met my husband in an Oakland hospital where we both had jobs. At the time I was already close to forty and believed that I would be single for the rest of my life, so it was a surprise for me to find myself a husband. I am in a mixed marriage since my husband is Black. Early in the 1990s I began taking classes on Chinese medicine and acupressure and obtained a certificate as an acupressure therapist. Not wanting to leave my job, which provides health insurance, I decided to volunteer to make use of what I had learned. I have volunteered at the Quan Yin Healing Arts Center, the HIV Center in Oakland, and the Charlotte Maxwell Complementary Clinic, which provides acupuncture, herbs, massage, and other alternative therapies for low-income women with cancer.

So here we are: the United States has once again invaded another country. The invasion of Iraq was based on government lies and deceptions, and this country is again involved in a war it cannot win. The British polling agency Oxford Research Bureau reports that 1.3 million of Iraq's people have died because of the war, 2 million have been displaced inside Iraq, and 2.5 million have become refugees in other countries.[20] A new economic crisis looms for the United States, financial institutions face bankruptcy, the mortgage crisis and home foreclosures have left people homeless, food and gas prices are rising, and there is talk of recession. Internationally, rising prices have led to food shortages and riots in some third world countries.

I look forward to the new generation coming up to fight this system. You see them at the antiwar demonstrations that have been taking place since the invasion of Iraq five years ago. Then there were the May Day demonstrations of 2008, which included the International Longshore and Warehouse Union's shutdown of all twenty-nine West Coast ports for eight hours to protest the Iraq War. This was a very significant action for a union to take, with dockworkers staging a one-day strike for political reasons ("No peace, no work") and not economic gain. Unfortunately, the mainstream media did not give it much coverage. In addition, the May Day immigrant rights demonstrations and march in the Mission district of San Francisco included high-school and college students speaking out for amnesty and an end to the Immigration and Customs Enforcement raids against undocumented immigrants at their jobs and homes.[21] One high-school girl spoke of how difficult it was to pay attention in the classroom as she lived in fear that her parents could be taken away for deportation at any time. Looking at the world now, there is much work to be done to end the oppressive system of imperialism.

Wei Min Bao front-page coverage of restaurant workers picketing for fair wages, April/May 1972. (All photo images are from *Wei Min Bao* [*Wei Min Chinese Community News*], a monthly published by Wei Min She. Author's collection.)

WHAT IS WEI MIN SHE ?   1974

Wei Min She is an Asian American anti-imperialist organization in the S.F.
Bay Area. Our name means "organization for the people." Our organization is
committed to building an anti-imperialist, multi-national, revolutionary mass
movement in this country. Our strategy is to build a united front movement of
all who can be united against the system of imperialism, led by the working class.

The system of imperialism is controlled by the small class of capitalists
who own the majority of the world's wealth, while everyone else must work to live.
We see the system of imperialism as the root cause of oppression of workers,
national minorities, students, and women. While it exploits workers and national
minorities at home, imperialism oppresses and exploits the people of the world.
Since the end of WWII, the U.S. has become the most powerful power in the world.
Its tentacles have reached out and seized political and economic control of the
underdeveloped nations of Asia, Africa, Latin America and the Middle East.

In the last couple of years, we have seen U.S. imperialism on the decline.
The rise of national liberation movements in the underdeveloped and oppressed
nations have been kicking U.S. imperialism out of their countries. Vietnam and
other countries in Southeast Asia, Africa, the Middle East, and Latin America
have cut off the ability of U.S. companies to make superprofits. In other parts
of the world, the political and economic strength of the U.S. is being challenged
by other capitalist nations in Europe and Japan. Competition with another imperiali
power, the Soviet Union, has also weakened the U.S. position.

Because of the rising struggles and economic and resistance abroad, the
U.S. has found itself in a vise. U.S. imperialists find that they cannot maintain
their rate of profits. They are turning to the working class at home to insure
the profits they lost abroad. Nationwide, the living standards of the people
are being attacked in a thousand different ways. People are being confronted
with work speedups, mass layoffs, elimination of protective work laws, cutbacks
in social services, increased police terror in Third World communities, energy
freezes and food shortages.

Immigrant and minority workers are being attacked even harder. Because of
the economic crisis, the companies are coming out with all sorts of propaganda
to prevent unity in the class. The recent wave of anti-alien propaganda in the
news and the massive deportations of Mexicans in California are bringing back
reminders from the past. In the 1890's, when the capitalists no longer needed
the labor of Chinese and when the workers' movement was on the rise due to the
depression, the employers put the blame for the economic crisis on the large
influx of Chinese workers into the country. Hence, a misguided workers' movement
began to develop around the slogan, "The Chinese Must Go!" instead of "The
System Must Go!" When the Chinese were kicked out or forced into hiding in the
Chinatowns throughout the West, unemployment was not solved and economic depressions
continued on.

Today, immigrant workers are kept unorganized and used as cheap pools of labor.
They have little job protection and work the longest hours at the lowest pay. The
present crisis only intensifies their exploitation even further.

However, this does not mean that working people are not resisting. These
attacks on the people's living standards have been met with a militant and ever
growing anti-imperialst movement. People everywhere are fighting back. Together
with the peoples of the world, the American people are uniting across national
lines to begin building the struggle against imperialism.

The anti-war movement, the struggles for childcare, and the increasing numbers
of strikes and walkouts are powerful testimonies to this development. Asian
American and other Third World people are fighting for our democratic rights and
against national oppression. The Lee Mah and Jung Sai organizing drives in the
S.F. Chinese Community, the struggle for equal employment in N.Y. Chinatown and
the fight for Ethnic Studies at U.C. Berkeley are a few examples. As Third World
people, we must fight both oppression as minorities and exploitation as working

"What Is Wei Min She?" (1974 statement)

ople. Not only must the struggle be taken to the Asian communities, it must
so be linked-up with the overall struggle of the multinational working class
inst the system.

The development of the mass movement into one is key to building the United
nt Against Imperialism. Through this united front, we can rally various
tors of the American people against this system which must exploit in order
survive.

In building this united front, Wei Min She is involved with these areas of
k: 1) Building Labor Struggles--building the movement of Asian workers
to link up with the larger working class movement to be able to lead
the fight against imperialism. We have had practical experience in
building support for the Farah strikers, Farmworkers, Nam Yuen
Restaurant Busboys walkout, Asia Garden Restaurant workers dispute,
S.F. Gold garment factory organizing drive, and now, Jung Sai and
Lee Mah.

2) Student Organizing--fighting for ethnic studies and building the
anti-imperialist student movement through various forms of student
organizations.

3) Fighting For Democratic Rights--building a movement in the community
around the issues of health, housing, education, equal employment etc

4) Building the Friendship of the Peoples of U.S. and the People's of
China--through film programs on China, forums, and U.S.-China People'
friendship events such as the 1974 Friendship Fair and October 1st
Celebration.

5) Building the Struggle Against the Oppression of Women --forums, supp
struggles of working women on the job, building the fight for childca
and participation in initiating events such as International Women's
Day.

FOOD SUPPLEMENTS

America is a very wealthy country. But here in our community, there are hundreds of families that do not get enough food. To take some of the pressures off, the government releases some of its surplus food stocks and makes it available to organizations who are willing to distribute it to the people. Because food is a basic need, Wei Min She has distributed the food since the program began 18 months ago. The program releases surplus food (food bought by the government to keep the farm prices high) to parents of children under the age of six and to pregnant or new mothers who qualify under the poverty guidelines set up by the government. For the past three months, bureaucratic red tape and inefficiency on the part of the high-up administrators had tied up the food program. Many of the people on the program need the food desperately. Wei Min She intends to put pressure on those responsible for the foul-ups and make the food surplus available again as soon as possible to the people on the program.

Food distribution by Wei Min She (Organization for the People), *Wei Min Bao*, October 1970 (first issue). The food program was started in April 1970 at ACC, then located at 832 Kearny Street. When the center was evicted in October 1970, it moved to 842 Kearny Street. The program distributed supplemental food to three hundred women and children.

Working together and cooperating with each other is strongly encouraged. Learning can be fun as these young brothers and sisters explore subjects such as math, science, art, and Chinese American history.

The yellow scarfs with the Chinese character "min" printed on them in red ink was an art project done with the help of the Kearny Street Workshop for the children to wear during field trips.

Field trips are an important aspect of the program. Visiting places such as the Lawrence Hall of Science and the International Hotel add to their education. Here the children are planting seeds at the Japanesetown Community Garden.

Wei Min She's Summer Youth Program, an eight-week program for children eight to ten years old. (*Wei Min Bao*, August/September 1972)

THE MONTHLY DINNERS AND SUNDAY BRUNCHES
ARE COOKED AND SERVED BY THE TENANTS.

The International Hotel (*Wei Min Bao*, February 1972)

大眾書店
EVERYBODY'S BOOKSTORE
840 KEARNY STREET
SAN FRANCISCO, CALIFORNIA
94108

HOURS: DAILY, 10:30 AM UNTIL 9:00 PM

As an on-going project of Wei Min She, Everybody's Bookstore has been made possible because of community support. Everybody's Bookstore is non-profit and self-sufficient. We have no paid staff as all labor is voluntary. Any money we make is re-invested into the bookstore to expand the inventory. However, we hope to earn enough in the future so that we can support other "serve the people" programs, such as maintaining the Asian Community Center. Through this way we can put the people's money into good use.

Everybody's Bookstore was opened to make literature and art from the People's Republic of China more a-vailable to the Chinese community of San Francisco. Our selection of low-cost books from Hong Kong, which includes translations from English works, has been very popular. Our English books are listed and arranged under different topics such as China, Asian Americans, minority struggles in the United States, the Third World, labor history, and community organization and educational change. Our address is 840 Kearny Street. Our phone number is 781-4989. We are o-pen from 10:30 AM until 9:00 PM.

Feature on Everybody's Bookstore (*Wei Min Bao*, October 1971)

The CHINATOWN CO-operative

The Chinatown Cooperative garment factory--humming machines, laughing, talking voices. At first it looks like the other garment factories in Chinatown. But where's the boss? Why is there free talk, workers speaking their minds, saying what they think of the manufacturers and work?

At the Chinatown Cooperative there is no boss. The Co-op is run and controlled by its workers. Together the workers decide what work they will do, time they will put in, and discuss the financial situation of the Co-op. When the manufacturers come in with contract work, the workers negotiate with them for the prices. They plan their own lines of clothes and arrange for the cutters and materials themselves. What brought these Chinese and Filipino women together to start their own business? Why did they pick this way of operation?

GOOD ALTERNATIVE

To the women of the Co-op, the factory is their alternative to the exploitative work conditions that face garment workers in other factories. It means a step to self-pride, control over their work, the right to reap the benefits of their labor, and eliminating the middle man or contractor who decides the pay and work conditions of the workers.

Feature on Chinatown Cooperative Garment Factory (*Wei Min Bao*, October 1971)

Lu Yu-lan (center), a woman member of the Ninth Central Committee, chats with young commune members.

Chinese women have been enjoying equal rights with men in the political, economic and cultural fields and in domestic life for the first time in history since the founding of the People's Republic of China in 1949.

With greatly raised social and political status, they participate in running state affairs.

With the development of socialist revolution and construction, Chinese women are making ever greater contributions in various fields. Almost all job opportunities are open to women, with due regard to their health. China has women scientists, prospectors, drivers and fliers. In Peking, women account for 40 per cent of the cadres and staff members in the scientific and technological fields, 38 per cent of the teachers of secondary schools, 19 per cent of the lecturers and professors, and 35 per cent of the senior doctors.

Chairman Mao teaches: "Times have changed, and today men and women are equal. Whatever men comrades can accomplish, women comrades can too."

A Tibetan woman tractor driver.

Excerpts from Hung Ying, "Women in China on Equal Footing with Men," *China Features* (reprinted in *Wei Min Bao*, March/April 1973). *China Features* was an English-language periodical from China.

OCTOBER 1ST CELEBRATION 1972

Over 500 people came to the rally at Portsmouth Square.

花園角中五百多名群衆歡慶新中國國慶。

Food and refreshments were enjoyed by many at the ACC.

十月一日下午，大家到干尼街八五〇號及亞洲人民聯合中心參
加茶會，吃點心。

October 1 celebration of the 1949 founding of the People's Republic of China: rally in Portsmouth Square, refreshments at ACC (*Wei Min Bao*, October 1972)

KEARNY STREET WORKSHOP

Since mid-October, a storefront near the corner of Kearny and Jackson Streets has been the scene of great activity. Within the confines of the former East Asian Art Gallery, men and women paint, do graphics, sew, and a number of other things. This is the newly created KEARNY STREET WORK-SHOP. It was finally opened to the public after two months of pre-para-tion.

When asked what the purpose of the workshop was, one of the members said it was to have a place to develop an art which reflects the experiences of Asian Americans in America , from which to spread art forms which re-flects the values and feelings that working class Chinese Americans and other Asians can identify as their own and can appreciate. Present Amer-ican art, taught and exhibited in American schools and museums are de-fined by the values and experiences of the white middle class.It does not help Chinese Americans of high school and college age gain any self -aware-ness of being Asian here.

The group urges that all come to learn and develop together. Further information can be obtained by going to the Workshop at 852 Kearny Street and check it out; or call the Neigh-borhood Arts Program at 558-2335.

Feature on the opening of the Kearny Street Workshop (*Wei Min Bao*, December 1972)

ON THE KMT AGENTS' DISRUPTION OF S.J. CHINA NIGHT

China Night--a cultural event held on April 7 and sponsored by various groups in the San Jose area including the U.S.-China Friendship Association, the Chinese Culture Club, and the Associated Students of San Jose State University--was a success in building friendship between the Chinese and the American people.

However, the event was marred by one incident which was vigorously resolved. Fifteen Kuomintang (the political party of Chiang Kai-shek) goons were successfully beaten away by progressive overseas Chinese and Chinese American youth as they attempted to disrupt the performance.

The theme of this performance, attended by a full house of 1,200 people from all nationalities, was "Friendship Between the American and the Chinese People." Since the theme was friendship and was designed to introduce Chinese culture, concessions were made allowing pro-Kuomintang students a literature table, singing performances, and a circus stunt act. However, even these concessions did not satisfy the desperate Kuomintang.

When a progressive overseas Chinese youth group went on stage to sing three songs from the New China, 15 Kuomintang goons stormed the stage area and displayed the Kuomintang flag. They were not students but agents sent here from Taiwan to intimidate progressive Chinese in America. Armed with pipes, these huge attackers were immediately repelled by progressive youths from the audience. Although one progressive Chinese youth was knocked unconscious by a metal pipe, the Kuomintang thugs were so badly beaten that the police had to come in to save them. Unfortunately, the police were uncooperative and refused to arrest these thugs . One of them who was detained by the police was immediately released when he displayed diplomatic identification.

Front page (detail) of *Wei Min Bao*, March/April 1973: "On the KMT Agents' Disruption of S.J. China Night." China Night was a cultural event produced mainly by area overseas Chinese students. They allowed pro-KMT students to participate, but when some songs from China were performed, fifteen KMT agents (nonstudents) disrupted the program by storming the stage carrying pipes. They were repelled and the program ended successfully.

This is from a health fair that was held in Portsmouth Square in Chinatown in 1971 or 1972.

The button on the left is from the Jung Sai Garment workers' strike and the button on the right is from Lee Mah electronic workers' attempt to unionize their factory. Both struggles broke out in 1974.

These are three buttons put out in support labor struggles in the 1970s, electronic workers, farmworkers and garment workers.

This a a Leway button, Leway Inc. was formed by American born Chinese youth who were getting into trouble with the police on the streets of Chinatown. They raised money and bought a pool hall forming a non-profit organization called Leway or "Legitimate Ways" in 1967 to tackle their social problems.

This is a button of Jiang Qing, Mao's wife, who was arrested as part of the so called Gang of Four for trying to uphold Mao's revolutionary path. Much of the slander directed at her stems from gender discrimination. She led the cultural work during the Chinese Cultural Revolution with works like: "The White Hair Girl" and "The Red Detachment of Women" - ballets "Breaking with Old Ideas" - a movie being some of my favorites.

This button was made for the memorial meeting for Mao Zedong after his death in 1976. Hundreds of people attended the memorial meeting, packing the auditorium at Marina Jr. High School on September 19, 1976.

This May Day 2008 button is from the International Longshore and Warehouse Union. The Union organized a one-day shut down of all of the ports on the West coast in protest of the Iraq War. There was a march to the Justin Herman Plaza for a rally. Other May Day activities included marches and rallies in the S.F. Mission district for immigrant rights. This was one of the best May Day in my life.

Political buttons from community activism in San Francisco Chinatown and the Bay Area (author's collection) (continued on next page)

These four buttons are from the International Hotel struggle that lasted from October 1968 until August 1977.

The Chinese character for "min" means people and was the logo for Wei Min She after it was formed in January 1971.

This was a button put out in celebration of October 1st, on the founding of the People's Republic of China in 1949 in the early 1970s.

These two buttons were from the Tiao Yu Tai Movement of 1971. In 1968, sub-sea oil fields were discovered near eight Chinese fishing islands called Tiao Yu Tai. When Japan tried to claim these islands, protest erupted in Hong Kong and among thousands of overseas students including in the United States. A number of demonstrations were held in the San Francisco Bay Area and Chinatown. It created a big stir in the Chinese community.

An International Women's Day button from the early 1970s.

第一自　第五十一期　第十六卷　太平洋週報　一九六一年十二月廿一日

半年，二元二毫五仙
每年，四元五毫正
地址　企李街七五一
電話天勤二一六七四八

一九六一年
十二月廿一日
第十六卷第五十一期
每份　一毫

報週洋平太
THE CHINESE PACIFIC WEEKLY

VOL. 16 NO 51

751 CLAY STREET, SAN FRANCISCO 8, CALIFORNIA　　DECEMBER 21, 1961

THE CHINESE PACIFIC WEEKLY

Published every week of the year by THE CHINESE PACIFIC PUBLISHING COMPANY, 751 Clay Street, San Francisco 8, California
Second-class postage paid at San Francisco, Calif. under the Act of March 3, 1879.
SUBSCRIPTION RATES: : Per Copy $ .10　Half year 2.25　One year 4.50

物築建埠華的香古色古與廈新之居所司公船輪統總
The International Building

謝榮忠要出境或處徒刑五年

聯邦法官烏倫堡，上星期五日（十二月十五）判謝榮忠入獄五年，但假如他在六十日內出境，則不必入獄。

關於報導失實

本報於十一月三十日，在本頁發表『史榮責華埠』一文，說謝增基對於移民總局長史榮曾指責華僑社會許多人無疑的會使華僑社會許多人發生疑惑』。所謂極不正確，相信是指蔡增基先生的報告。

本埠移民分局，於十二月十一日，發表新聞，第一段說『太平洋週報最近發表一篇關於華人坦白計劃的文字，其中有些極不正確，這無疑的會使華僑社會許多人發生疑惑』。所謂極不正確，相信是指蔡增基先生的報告。

△同情心

移民分局的新聞稿第二段說：『我們一再說明坦白計劃的機會，是符合人道及有体諒之心。我們可以向你保證，他已經說過，他對於過去華人坦白政策的願望，就是所有華人，早一天有利於華僑社會。反之，我們對於這一段，很喜歡花勞說明他的立場。

△野心領袖

新聞稿的最後一段說：『那些有意代表華僑社會發言，又獲得代表他們發言，對於移民分局又有眞誠的關懷的人士，至於那些存着個人的野心，我們無意於協助他們進行。不過，我們很願意在華人福利方面協助他們，設法尋求公平的辦法來替華埠人。

我們隨時準備協助，解決所有的難題。每一個華人代表，將獲得本局有禮貌及同情的待遇』。移民分局的人對我們，也不是指編者而言。

△算作了結
我們又探悉，移民分局分發這些新聞稿，

△同情心

本報編者說，這一段和太平洋週報無關，本報編者說，也不是指編者而言。

新總局長新聞稿第三段說：『在（太平洋週報）同一篇的文字裏，說新移民總局長，為局員所熱稔。花勞先生在移民局裏，他是符合台人道去華人坦白政策的，將繼續下去。他對於過及華人之身份坦白，成功，則早一天有利於華僑社會。』我們

到移民局坦白所有華人，應該相信，移民局對於個別的案件，將以同情憐憫之心處理。我們將協助所有合格的華人獲取身份的調整』。

這一段似和太平洋週報沒有關係，我們素來鼓勵僑胞坦白，不會說過移民局處理坦白案件時沒有同情心。

Schedule for ACC's film program (*Wei Min Bao*, May 1972). The film program showed movies about socialist China, liberation struggles of third world countries, and struggles of workers and the fight against racism in America.

Masthead of the bilingual monthly *Family Newsletter* (April 1974), with flyer announcing talk on education in China by Chinese teachers who had visited the PRC.

NOTES

1. The other groups included the Chinese Mutual Aid Association in San Francisco and two from New York City, the Chinese Hand Laundry Alliance and *China Daily News*. For more on Mun Ching (Min Ching), see Him Mark Lai, "A Historical Survey of Organizations of the Left among the Chinese in America," *Bulletin of Concerned Asian Scholars* 4, no. 3 (Fall 1972), and Him Mark Lai, "To Bring Forth a New China, to Build a Better America: The Chinese Marxist Left in America to the 1960's," *Chinese America: History & Perspectives* 6 (1992) (hereafter cited as "Him Mark Lai's essays on the left"). Also see the documentary film by Amy Chen, *Chinatown Files*.

2. For more on the Cold War, the McCarthy era, and the Confession Program's effect on the Chinese community, see, e.g., Iris Chang, *The Chinese in America*, chap. 14, "A Mass Inquisition," or Peter Kwong, *Chinese America*, chap. 15, "Cold War and the Chinese American Community."

3. *Dear Wing Jung v. U.S.*, 312 F.2d 73 (9th Cir. 1962).

4. Chiang Kai-shek's atrocities, corruption, and close ties to the Shanghai underworld are documented in Sterling Seagrave, *The Soong Dynasty* (New York: Harper & Row, 1985).

5. See Victor G. Nee and Brett de Bary Nee, *Longtime Californ': A Documentary Study of an American Chinatown* (Stanford, Calif.: Stanford University Press, 1972), for an interesting interview with a participant in this October 9 event and details of what took place. Him Mark Lai, "To Bring Forth a New China," includes the hit list in a note.

6. Claudie Broyelle, *Women's Liberation in China* (Atlantic Highlands, N.J.: Humanities Press, 1977).

7. Lincoln Cushing and Ann Tompkins, *Chinese Posters: Art from the Great Proletarian Cultural Revolution* (San Francisco: Chronicle Books, 2007), vividly shows workers, peasants, and women in their new roles under socialism in Mao's China as the heroes who will transform society. The spirit of internationalism of the period is also well represented.

8. Mobo Gao, *The Battle for China's Past: Mao and the Cultural Revolution* (London: Pluto Press, 2008).

9. For collected material on the strike, see *www.library.sfsu.edu/about/collections/strike/index.html*.

10. To read more about Leways and the Red Guard Party, see Fred Ho, *Legacy to Liberation: Politics and Culture of Revolutionary Asian Pacific America* (Brooklyn, N.Y.: Big Red Media, 2000), which includes an interview with Alex Hing. Former I Wor Kuen members have also set up an Asian American movement e-zine at *www.aamovement.net/* with a history of these organizations.

11. See Noyes, "China Books and Periodicals: Extracts from the Autobiography *China Born*," this volume, page 37.

12. For essays by people involved with the I-Hotel struggle, see *Asian Americans: The Movement and the Moment*, ed. Steve Louie and Glenn Omatsu (Los Angeles: UCLA Asian American Studies Center Press, 2001).

13. This platform and program appeared in an article on ACC in *RODAN, Northern California Asian American Community News* 1, no. 5 (November 1970), reprinted in UCLA Asian American Studies Center, *Roots: An Asian American Reader* (Los Angeles: UCLA Asian American Studies Center, 1971).

14. Him Mark Lai's essays on the left mention Olden Lee as a participant in the Chinese Workers Mutual Aid Association. Olden Lee is also mentioned in Josephine Fowler, *Japanese and Chinese Immigrant Activists: Organizing in American and International Communist Movements, 1919–1933* (New Brunswick, N.J.: Rutgers University Press, 2007).

15. For more background on I Wor Kuen, see *Asian American Movement Ezine* at *www.aamovement.net/*. Also see Ho, *Legacy to Liberation*, which includes an essay on I Wor Kuen and reprints its Twelve-Point Platform and Program.

16. See Ho, *Legacy to Liberation*, for essays by two Wei Min She members who continued to work with the RCP.

17. For more on the merger of the Red Guard Party and I Wor Kuen, see Ho, *Legacy to Liberation*. Also see Sadie Lum, "Asian American Women and Revolution: A Personal View," in *Chinese American Voices: From the Gold Rush to the Present*, ed. Judy Yung, Gordon H. Chang, and Him Mark Lai (Berkeley and Los Angeles: University of California Press, 2006).

18. For criticism of the RCP's line and discussion of why it became isolated, see "Nine Letters to Our Comrades," *www.mikeely.wordpress.com*. Mike Ely was formerly the editor of the newspaper of the RCP.

19. *China Left Review* 1 (May 2008), *www.chinaleftreview.org*. The article on land privatization is Luke Erickson, "Land from the Tiller: The Push for Rural Land Privatization in China."

20. For more information on the consequences of the Iraq war, see *www.ivaw.org*.

21. Two newspapers had good articles on the May Day activities of 2008: the *San Francisco Bay Guardian*, May 7–13, 2008, p. 10, and the *San Francisco BayView National Black Newspaper*, May 7, 2008, p. 1.

Third World Liberation Comes to San Francisco State and UC Berkeley

Harvey Dong

Harvey Dong's "A Bookstore for Everybody" also appears in this volume, page 122.

INTRODUCTION

Forty years have passed since the Third World Liberation Front (TWLF) strikes for ethnic studies. When San Francisco State College (SFSC) students went on strike for a third world studies curriculum, students such as myself at the University of California, Berkeley (UCB), were moved to call on our classmates to support them. We believed then that the best way to express our solidarity was to fight for the very same demands and principles at UC Berkeley. That way another front would be opened that would diminish the repression of the SF State strikers. The strikes left their mark on both campuses and especially changed how history was being taught.

The Third World Liberation Strikes that occurred in 1968–69 at SFSC and UCB had profound effects on the history of Chinese in America. First, the strikes won civil rights changes in higher education—the institution of ethnic studies curricula and programs. This new approach enabled the study of Chinese American history in a comparative context that was focused on looking at racial discrimination and the struggle for equality. Second, the strike movements caused a significant shift in the mind-set of many Chinese American college-aged youth in the San Francisco Bay Area. The post–World War II path toward acculturation into mainstream society from the urban Chinatowns was replaced by another calling. Instead of working only for professional self-advancement, many Chinese American college students turned their attention toward fighting institutionalized racism on their campuses and oppression within the Chinese American community. Not only was the study of American history revolutionized, the struggle for ethnic studies became part of a revolutionary movement.

International events in the late sixties provided an important backdrop for the rise of Asian American activism. Revolutions in the third world, the rise of Black Power protests, and institutional racism in the educational system, which took the form of erasure of Asian Americans in history and society, led many Asian American activists to become more resolved in their involvement. There was strong identification with the struggles for independence in former colonies in Asia, Africa, and Latin America; internal colonialism was a dominant paradigm for activists who saw themselves as part of an oppressed third world within the United States (namely, Asian Americans, African Americans, Chicanos, Latino Americans, and Native Americans). This context helped them look beyond their individual ethnicities and see themselves as Asian Americans who were part of the third world.

The vehicles for their activism were the TWLF organizations that led strikes for ethnic studies programs at SFSC and UCB. The SFSC TWLF Strike began on November 6, 1968, and the UCB TWLF Strike followed seventy-seven days later on January 22, 1969. Student activists from the two campuses were in communication as early as spring quarter of 1968, when the Asian American Political Alliance (AAPA) organized an issues forum on the UCB campus. Over ninety attendees listened to representatives from the Black Panther Party and the Chicano movement, as well as San Francisco Chinatown activists from Intercollegiate Chinese for Social Action (ICSA).[1] Presentations introduced topics on black identity, Asian American identity, and the concept of third world unity. The Panther representative expressed appreciation that Asian Americans were beginning to move along radical political lines. This forum would be the first in a series of meetings that facilitated AAPA's political vision of solidarity with other racialized minorities.[2]

YELLOW SYMPOSIUM

These types of meetings were preludes to a major Asian American political activism conference at the UC Berkeley campus. On January 11, 1969, the AAPA, the Chinese Students Club (CSC), and the Nisei Students Club (NSC) sponsored a symposium titled "The Asian Experience in America/ Yellow Identity," also known as the "Yellow Symposium." Widely attended by Asian American (Chinese, Japanese, and Filipino) college students from throughout California, the symposium helped chart the direction for future Asian American activism. Asian American identity, Asian American

Studies, community service, Asian student movements, and support for the Third World Liberation Strike at SFSC were focal points of the conference. Speakers included professors from Stanford, UC Berkeley, and UC Davis. Topics included the history of Chinese and Japanese in America, presented by Stanford Lyman (Stanford University); the Asian policy of the United States, presented by Paul Takagi (UC Berkeley); and Asians in the "melting pot," presented by Isao Fujimoto (UC Davis).[3]

One unscheduled speaker who had impact was George Woo, representing ICSA and the SFSC TWLF. Woo critiqued the idea of developing an Asian American identity devoid of community responsibility. He called upon the student audience to show their commitment to activism by passing a conference resolution in support of the SFSC TWLF Strike. Arguing that identity without action was only a form of "mental masturbation," Woo challenged students to look into the real conditions that people in the communities faced and called for a reversal of the traditional brain drain of educated youth from the community.[4]

According to conference organizer Bryant Fong, who was a member of UCB CSC and AAPA, "the issues were support for the strike going on at San Francisco State and the conditions going on in Chinatown itself. In Chinatown the conditions at that time were ripe for change. There was a lot going on. It was ripe for rebellion . . . a lot of youth were in motion. ICSA brought out things differently about what was going on. They were working with the gangs in Chinatown. They were working with Leways and Youth Council."[5]

A minority of conference goers had reservations about supporting the SF State strike. This reluctance was related to disagreement with the idea that Asian Americans were oppressed and suffered racial discrimination. While supporting the teaching of Asian American history courses, they argued that these courses should be taught within the traditional departments and not in separate Asian American programs. The majority of conference attendees felt that this approach was too gradual and fraught with uncertainties. Largely influenced by the radicalism of the Black Power movement, the conference moved in the direction of self-determination. "Self" meant the community and "determination" meant political decision-making power. Applied to the TWLF demands for ethnic studies, self-determination meant not just having a few courses under a mainstream department but power and control over an entire school of ethnic studies or third world college for the benefit of the community.

The Yellow Symposium eventually passed a resolution in full support of the SF State TWLF Strike, the demand for Asian American Studies, and the establishment of third world colleges on other campuses. The resolution was an important juncture for Asian American college students who were becoming more socially aware and no longer wished to seek improvement through individual advancement, which never worked well for the community.[6]

The next day, Sunday, January 12, a statewide AAPA meeting was held to plan strategy and extend the discussion of the Yellow Symposium to build the movement on a broader basis. To the surprise of AAPA organizers, the gathering became an organizational meeting for the establishment of a loose-knit network of AAPA chapters nationally. There were representatives from thirteen campuses in locations including San Francisco, San Mateo, Los Angeles, Berkeley, San Jose, Sacramento, New York, and Hawaii. Discussions focused on common projects, such as defining the content of Asian American Studies and facilitating community work in communities such as Japantown, Chinatown, and Manilatown. Berkeley AAPA took on the responsibility of channeling information to the various chapters. This working meeting furthered support for the SFSC TWLF as well as encouraging similar movement on other campuses.[7]

SIMILARITY IN DEMANDS

It was not an accident that student demands were similar on both sides of the San Francisco Bay. The students demanded educational relevance that would meet the needs of their communities. This would be achieved through the establishment of ethnic studies programs that would include departments of Asian American Studies, African American Studies, Chicano Studies, and Native American Studies. Curricula were to be "community-based" and students were to participate in fieldwork in the relevant communities, such as Chinatown, Manilatown, or Japantown.

The SFSC TWLF students made the following demands:

1. That a School of Ethnic Studies for the ethnic groups involved in the Third World be set up with the students in each particular ethnic organization having the authority and control of the hiring and retention of any faculty member, director, and administrator, as well as the curriculum in a specific area of study.
2. That 50 faculty positions be appropriated to the School of Ethnic Studies, 20 would be for the Black Studies Program.
3. That in the Spring semester, the College fulfill its commitment to the non-white students by admitting those that apply.
4. That in the Fall of 1969, all applications of non-white students be accepted.
5. That George Murray and any other faculty person chosen by non-white people as their teacher be retained in their position.[8]

The UCB TWLF students made the following demands:

1. That funds be allocated for the implementations of the Third World College.
   a. Department of Asian Studies controlled by Asian people.
   b. Department of Black Studies as proposed by the AASU.
   c. Department of Chicano Studies.
   d. Department of Native American Studies.
2. Third World People in positions and power. Recruitment of more Third World faculty in every department and discipline and proportionate employment of Third World

people at all levels from Regents, Chancellors, Vice-Chancellors, faculty, administrative personnel, clerical, custodial, security services personnel, and all other auxiliary positions and contractual vending services throughout the University system.

Specific demands for immediate implementation:

a. Hiring of Third World Financial Counselors (Special Services).

b. Third World Chancellors in the University system.

c. Third World people put in the Placement Center as counselors.

d. Third World Deans in the L and S Departments.

e. Third World people in the Admissions Office.

3. Specific demands for immediate implementation:

a. Admission, financial aid and academic assistance to any Third World student with potential to learn and contribute as assessed by Third World people.

b. 30 Work Study positions for the Chinatown and Manilatown projects, and 10 EOP counselors, including full-time Asian Coordinator.

c. Expansion of Work Study program jobs to the AASU East campus Berkeley High School Project, to include at least 30 positions.

d. That the Center for Chicano Studies be given permanent status with funds to implement its programs.

4. Third World Control over Third World Programs. That every University program financed federally or otherwise that involves the Third World communities (Chicano, Black, Asian) must have Third World people in control at the decision making level from funding to program implementation.

5. That no disciplinary action will be administered in any way to any student, workers, teachers, or administrators during and after the strike as a consequence of their participation in the strike.[9]

The students sought complete program autonomy with third world people in positions of power over decision making in all areas, including curriculum, admissions, promotions, research, and hiring. In its third world college proposal, the UCB TWLF argued that the primary reason for all this was to produce students with the knowledge, expertise, understanding, commitment, and desire to identify and present solutions to problems in their respective communities. The strikers believed this could only be done by the establishment of an autonomous school of ethnic studies at SFSC and an autonomous college of third world studies at UCB with complete control over course curriculum, admissions, and hiring.

It would be an understatement to say that the demand for establishment of ethnic or third world studies faced enormous opposition. College and university administrators were unwilling to accede to the idea of community-based programs that involved students in decision making. Governor Ronald Reagan had taken a hard-line position against the student movements in general to rally conservatives behind him for a future presidential nomination bid. He supported repressive measures against the SFSC TWLF Strike and eventually declared martial law during the UCB TWLF Strike.

The TWLF proposals were essentially a call to recast the foundations of the education system. They were also a challenge to the state's 1960 Master Plan for Higher Education, which called for an "objective" system of testing in the secondary and higher educational systems. Students were tracked at an early age by intelligence tests to determine their fitness for continuing on to either a two-year junior college or a four-year university. This tracking system proved detrimental to educational advances in minority communities because of the lack of good teachers and resources. Additionally, standardized testing provided advantages to students from white middle- and upper-class backgrounds and disadvantages to students of color and poorer working-class students. The strikers addressed the fact that this was institutionalized racism and that third world minorities were underrepresented on campuses such as SFSC and UCB.[10]

ICSA AND AAPA

Chinese Americans who participated in the TWLF movements were members or affiliates of ICSA at SFSC and AAPA at UCB. While students on both campuses held similar goals, their areas of focus differed. ICSA worked within the San Francisco Chinatown ethnic community, AAPA in a more dispersed panethnic setting.

According to Karen Umemoto, ICSA began in October 1967 and focused the bulk of its work on poverty-related issues within the Chinatown community. In July 1968 ICSA opened a basement office in Chinatown at 737 Clay Street. Its work included teen tutorial projects, youth advocacy, and participation in marches calling attention to socioeconomic problems within the Chinatown community. Militancy stemmed from having to deal with the conservative Chinese Six Companies establishment, which viewed ICSA as a group of young upstarts threatening its claim to be the sole representative of all Chinese in America. Its initial community base provided ICSA with the foundation for its demands.[11]

Many ICSA members, rooted in the San Francisco Chinatown community, sought an education with an urgent community focus. In one strike bulletin, ICSA members expressed reasons for participation in the strike:

Chinatown is a *ghetto* in San Francisco, there are approximately 50,000 Chinese of whom the vast majority live in Chinatown. It is an area of old buildings, narrow streets & alleys, and the effluvia of a great many people packed into a very small space. At present, more than 5,000 new Chinese immigrants stream into this overpopulated ghetto each year, an area already blessed with a birthrate that is rising, and will rise more. Tuberculosis is endemic, rents are high and constantly rising, city services are inadequate to provide reasonable sanitation, and space is at such a premium as to resemble the Malthusian ratio at its most extreme. There are no adequate courses in any department or school at S.F. State that even begin to deal with the problems of the Chinese people in their exclusionary and racist environment.[12]

Because San Francisco State College was primarily a commuter school with many students from the local ethnic communities, organization along Asian American panethnic lines did not become as well established as at UC Berkeley. Filipino American students who participated in the SFSC TWLF Strike were members of Philippine Americans for Collegiate Endeavor (PACE), founded in 1967. PACE focused on educational opportunities for low-income Filipino American youth. It also saw third world solidarity as the way to create a new humanism to collectively control the destinies of third world people.[13] Japanese American students in the strike participated in an SFSC AAPA chapter that was an affiliate of the Berkeley AAPA chapter.

At UC Berkeley, AAPA used the "Asian American" concept as a vehicle for its political activism and self-determination. A major factor in bringing Asians together along panethnic lines was the belief that they shared a historical experience of racism and exclusion. Because Asian Americans made up less than 1 percent of a total U.S. population of two hundred million, Asian American solidarity became a political necessity. Historical and pragmatic reasons emerged for Asian Americans to remove the negative "oriental" label and to come together under a new name.[14]

AAPA consisted of Chinese, Filipino, and Japanese Americans, many of them previously involved in the Civil Rights, Black Power, antiwar, and farmworkers' union movements. The majority of members were second-generation native-born Americans, though there were a few foreign-born members from Hong Kong. Some were from urban Asian American communities such as San Francisco Chinatown; others had grown up in smaller cities or rural areas throughout California. In common was their general family experience of immigration exclusion and institutionalized racism. The Vietnam War, the Black Power movement, and conditions in the Asian American community provided the background for the transformation of many of these students into political activists. Leaders from campus social clubs such as the CSC (American born), the Chinese Students Association (foreign born), and the NSC (second generation) became AAPA leaders.

AAPA founder Victoria Wong, a second-generation Chinese American from the Salinas area, spoke about coming to political consciousness:

> The first time you awaken is when you become politically aware. The second awakening is when you see all these Asian people talking the same way you are. This was the other part of my life which I always felt but could not yet identify . . . why I felt a little bit different [being the only Asian] going to Black Panther Support Committee meetings. That's why the Yellow Symposium was important . . . the very concept of political power for Asian Americans was not really expressed before. We were always treated like new immigrants even though some of us were actually fourth and fifth generation.[15]

At a unique point in history, AAPA was able to bridge the divides among various Asian ethnic communities. Homeland enmities, language and cultural differences, and geographic isolation have long separated these groupings.

Regionalism was a norm, which AAPA activists consciously attempted to change with campaigns calling for a common Asian American interest. There were both cultural and pragmatic bases for this new panethnic solidarity. Culturally many of the AAPA activists were English-speaking post–World War II baby boomers who had grown up in the same integrated neighborhoods. Many of them were 1.5-generation or second-generation youth. Unlike their immigrant parents, they often associated with other Asian Americans to protect themselves within mainstream society. AAPA's ascendance was a continuation of this social trend in radical political terms.

In its October 1969 newspaper AAPA outlined its quick transformation since its founding in May 1968:

> Since May, 1968, AAPA has grown from a small group of students and community workers to a powerhouse for Asian thought and action. AAPA is now a member of the Third World Liberation Front, Asian Association, and Asian Coalition. Some past activities of Berkeley AAPA include: Free Huey Rallies at the Oakland Courthouse, Chinatown Forums, McCarran Act lobbies, MASC Boycott, Third World Liberation Front Strike, development of Asian Studies, and liaison with and development of other AAPA's throughout the state.

Under the heading "Understanding AAPA," this issue further outlined the changes in political consciousness among Asian American college students:

> The Asian American Political Alliance is people. It is a people's alliance to effect social and political change. We believe that the American society is historically racist and one which has systematically employed social discrimination and economic imperialism, both domestically and internationally, exploiting all non-white people in the process of building up their affluent society.

> The goal of AAPA is political education and advancement of the movement among Asian people, so that they may make all decisions that affect their own lives in a society that never asks people to do so.[16]

Whether organizing from a single- or panethnic viewpoint, Asian American students on both sides of the San Francisco Bay saw that their major strength lay in gathering support from their own communities, from fellow Asian American students on campus, from other third world students, and from the majority white student population. The single-ethnic focus of ICSA and its base of operations in San Francisco Chinatown placed it in the position of being the alternative to the Chinatown establishment. The panethnic focus of AAPA enabled it to go more broadly throughout the student population and the different Asian American ethnic communities for support.

THIRD WORLD LIBERATION FRONT AT SAN FRANCISCO STATE

Before their strike began, many Berkeley TWLF members gained protest experience by attending SF State TWLF Strike activities across the bay. The SF State Strike was a major impetus and model for the Berkeley TWLF. The model was essentially to use direct mass actions to shut down the campus, with the goal of forcing the administration to come to terms with the strikers. In the aftermath of the assassination of Dr. Martin Luther King and the ensuing urban rebellions across America, TWLF strikers took a confrontational approach to disrupt the normal functioning of the campus.

At SFSC, the confrontational strategies were responses to a buildup of unproductive negotiations, broken agreements, and increased police repression. Legal channels had run thin and more extreme measures had become the dominant form of interchange and communication between the college administration and students seeking social justice. Negotiations between the Black Students Union (BSU) and the administration over racism on the campus had dragged on unsuccessfully for three years. The BSU was incensed over the low enrollment of black students. In November 1967 it was also incensed with the alleged racist overtone in the *Daily Gator* student newspaper. This resulted in the newspaper offices being trashed and its editor beaten. Four BSU members, including graduate student and Black Panther Party member George Murray, were arrested and suspended.[17]

Murray's association with the Black Panthers resulted in a hearsay *San Francisco Chronicle* article stating that he had called on black and brown students to carry guns to protect themselves from "racist administrators." The reporter was not present at the moment of his alleged statement. Still, the article drew the quick ire of the college trustees and the mayor's office. This resulted in Murray's being suspended as a graduate student and instructor for thirty days in October 1968.[18]

Murray's suspension and the deadlock in negotiations over the formation of a Black Studies department led to further polarization between the BSU and the administration. This in turn led to the formation of the TWLF at SF State. The TWLF comprised six campus minority student organizations: the BSU, the Latin American Students Organization (LASO), the Mexican American Student Confederation (MASC), ICSA, PACE, and AAPA. Although the BSU instigated the formation of the TWLF, its structure allowed for equality in group representation and decision making. A twelve-member central committee comprised two delegates from each organization. If there was disagreement, member groups were free not to participate in TWLF activities.[19]

The relationship between the TWLF and white students at SF State was based upon the principle of "self-determination of third world peoples." In practice, this meant that whites played a supporting role that was negligible in terms of political decision making and strategy. Strategy and decisions were in the final hands of the TWLF organizations. White student supporters had been the majority in many of the picket lines at SF State. They also made up a majority of those arrested, including the four hundred arrested on January 23, 1969.[20]

CONDITIONS RIPE FOR PROTESTS AT UC

Conditions on the campuses were ripe for organized protests. A 1966 race and ethnic survey conducted on the UC Berkeley campus showed a poor track record on minority enrollment. Blacks, Chicanos, and Native Americans combined made up 1.4 percent of the student body. Of 26,000 total students, only 226 were African American (.87 percent), 76 Chicano (.29 percent), and 61 Native American (.23 percent). By comparison, blacks, Chicanos, and Native Americans made up approximately 19 percent of the population of California. Statistics in 1970 showed an increase of 4.7 percentage points in the representation of these three groups at UCB, for a total of 6.2 percent. Released numbers included 1,020 African Americans (3.9 percent), 381 Chicanos (1.4 percent), 166 Latinos (0.6 percent), 89 Native Americans (0.3 percent), 2,543 Asian Americans (9.7 percent), and 15,813 whites (60.1 percent).[21] Minority faculty appointments remained sparse. As late as 1980, only 1.8 percent of the faculty was African American. There were only two African American women with tenured or tenure-track status.

Although Asian Americans fared a little better than other minorities at the time of the strike, making up around 7 percent of the student population, this figure was challenged as misleading. Before the strike, a report sponsored by the cabinets of the CSC and the NSC acknowledged that Asian Americans appeared overly represented. Out of a campus total of 27,000 students, 2,000 were Asian American, though Asian Americans made up less than 3.5 percent of the state population (671,000 out of 19,171,000). Both clubs, however, made four points related to these numbers. First, most of the students were from upper- and middle-class families, while access to higher education was still limited for those from poor urban and rural areas. Second, the Filipino American population remained barely represented. Third, although Asian Studies existed, its focus was on international studies. Fourth, the Asians in faculty and administrative positions remained at the lower end of the employment scale. Asian Americans were not present in executive positions.[22]

FORMATION OF TWLF AT UC

Like the SFSC TWLF, the UCB TWLF emerged when African American students initiated demands and approached the other third world groups for reinforcements. Each group had previously approached the university separately and received a separate response. Lack of progress for several of the groups in negotiating their individual minority-based studies programs had led activists to see the need for a TWLF coalition. In the view of the participants, third world solidarity was not an ideal but a necessity whose rationale would develop in process.[23]

Previously the African American Students Union (AASU) had conducted nine months of negotiations with the university administration for the establishment of African American Studies. The AASU proposal was first submitted to the chancellor in April 1968. In November the chancellor asked AASU representatives to revise the proposal three times. It was then referred to the College of Letters and Science (L&S) for review. L&S referred the proposal to the Executive Committee of the college, which met and revised it, making numerous deletions that had important effects on the program's community orientation and fieldwork and on student participation in its implementation. By December African American students and professors had been excluded from all meetings and decision-making positions. AASU members and Andrew Billingsley (an African American professor whose position was Assistant to the Chancellor for Establishment of Black Studies) were barred from the Executive Committee meeting when these deletions were made. The university administration responded to the original twenty-two-page proposal submitted by students and professors with a one-page rejection.[24]

On January 15, 1969, a watered-down Black Studies proposal was finally approved by L&S but was rejected soundly by the AASU. It was seen as an affront to the principle of self-determination, a continuation of white elites dictating the needs of racial minorities. According to AASU spokesperson Don Davis, "we submitted a program which was well conceived, air tight, and free from any basic flaws. We're not interested in anything less than what we proposed. We've made that clear again and again. . . . No matter what the [L&S version] said, it was wrong because we did not have power to determine our own destinies."[25]

Meanwhile, MASC had been undergoing similar experiences. MASC had been involved in a table-grape boycott in support of a statewide United Farm Workers (UFW) strike. Involving thousands of Mexican and Filipino migrant farmworkers, the strike was one of the largest organizing drives in the Central Valley of California. At the UC Berkeley campus, strike support work meant the boycott of table grapes and the demand that UC campuses stop all purchases. The campus boycott movement involved a five-month dispute between the university and the Chicano student activists.[26]

By August 1968 MASC had reached an agreement with lower-level University Housing and Food Services officials to remove table grapes from dormitories and campus food facilities. Both Vice Chancellor O. W. Campbell and Business Manager Scott Wilson of Housing and Food Services gave verbal approval for the immediate removal of table grapes.[27]

On October 1 anti-UFW elements in the state government, including Governor Ronald Reagan, Agricultural Secretary Earl Coke, and Superintendent of Public Instruction Max Rafferty, issued strong statements of condemnation of the UFW strike. Shortly thereafter, on October 11, UC President Charles Hitch issued a statement of neutrality on the UFW strike. He directed the purchasing departments of all nine campuses not to refuse to purchase any food as a policy decision. This situation set the stage for a half-hour meeting on October 14 between MASC representatives and President Hitch. After thirty minutes of deadlocked discussion, President Hitch left the meeting. Eleven MASC representatives were then arrested for unlawful assembly and trespassing.[28]

Three days later, on October 17, President Hitch partially agreed to the establishment of a Center for Mexican American Studies and the appointment of a Chicano assistant to the president. By fall one course in Chicano history was taught at UC Berkeley, while the center actively recruited Chicanos around the state. Hitch had also given another verbal agreement to remove table grapes from the UC system.[29]

MASC representatives considered these gains important steps toward something larger. Still, the gains were minuscule. The new center had a budget of only $25,000. Final decision-making power, as in the African American Studies program, still rested with a small white elite. MASC representative Manuel Delgado wrote, "The University gave them [Chicanos], as a result of long negotiations and of the arrested eleven Chicanos, an assistant to the President whose contract stipulates that he can do no more than suggest."[30]

In the spring of 1968 AAPA had begun negotiations with the university for the establishment of an Asian American Studies curriculum. The end result was the establishment of one course, Asian Studies 100X: The Asian Experience in America, during the winter quarter of 1969. It was taught under the sponsorship of Professor Franz Schurmann from the History Department and Professor Paul Takagi from the Criminology Department. Six graduate students conducted the actual teaching of the course, which had an overflow attendance of four hundred students.

The course was envisioned to be the genesis for a larger Asian American Studies program. Weekly topics incorporated international, third world, and community frameworks. The curriculum included the historical backgrounds of colonialism in China, Japan, the Philippines, and Korea; Asian American history, with specific topics on Asian American labor history; current analysis of modern China and the Vietnam War; and present-day Asian American community issues.[31]

In the first week of lectures AAPA called an after-class meeting for individuals interested in discussing the feasibility of a student strike for a third world college at UC Berkeley. Twenty students from the class participated in the discussion. AAPA argued for joining with the AASU and MASC, whose individual negotiations with the administration for Black and Chicano Studies programs had reached critical impasses. AAPA members argued that their experiences showed that negotiations for Asian American Studies would be equally difficult. The discussions eventually moved from broad generalizations about supporting a third world strike to the mechanics of organizing one.[32]

According to Steve Wong, one of the students who stayed at the meeting and later participated in the strike, "I took that class because of the influence of the Civil Rights movement and antiwar movement. It was a natural progression. By then I felt there shouldn't be so many national boundaries between people. The Asian concept, I felt, was much broader than the each-to-his-own-ethnic-group idea. I saw myself as a world citizen. Taking a course like Asian Studies 100X was the way to do it."[33]

The semester before, Wong had been active in the San Francisco Chinatown YWCA tutorial project. Having grown up poor in Sacramento, he saw tutoring as an important component of social activism and a way to make the world better socially. He saw striking for a third world college as a way to make the world better by changing the balance of power politically.[34]

FALL 1968

In the fall quarter of 1968 at UCB, the AASU had begun to approach the Asian American and Chicano organizations about the possibility of forming a TWLF to present common demands for a third world college. Responses varied according to the individual progress of each group's own negotiations with the university. MASC representatives had fundamental questions about equal representation and power. Also, MASC had recently won a minor victory, the establishment of the Center for Mexican American Studies. According to Manuel Delgado, however, "we understood that there was a larger struggle for freedom, privilege and respect for third world people that we had to be a part of. We could not let our specific gains divide us."[35]

Native American Students United (NASU), the fourth organization to become part of the TWLF, was the smallest group, with five members. NASU was still in its formative stages and was attempting to locate the few Native Americans present at the campus. It was not until the beginning of January 1969 that NASU formally became a part of the TWLF. Most of its members were subjects of a governmental relocation program to assimilate Native Americans into mainstream America.[36]

Solidarity among the third world groups was not a given. The pull for solidarity was influenced by revolutionary movements throughout the world that began to connect their causes; by the Black Panther Party, whose platform called for multiracial unity; and by the SF State TWLF activists, who had already developed third world solidarity as a major point of unity. First and foremost, the grievances of the students and the severely inadequate response from the administration warranted public sympathy and support from fellow students and staff. Once protest activity around student demands ensued, public controversy over the strike issues led to the refinement of the students' political rationale.

Third world anticolonialism, Black Power, and Marxism were ideas that the activists developed to formulate a counter-hegemonic ideology among their ranks.[37]

White students and organizations met separately each week as the TWLF Support Committee, whose task was to solicit support and inform the broader student population about the issues of the strike. In many respects, these meetings became the main forum for carrying out policies of the TWLF. Although decision-making powers were subordinated to the TWLF Central Committee, the Support Committee debated how to conduct strike support. Its meetings were attended by a broad spectrum of the radical left, including Students for a Democratic Society, Independent Socialist Club, Young Socialist Alliance, and nonaffiliated individuals.

REPRESSION AND BROADENING OF SUPPORT

Breakdown in negotiations led each TWLF to call a strike at its campus. At SFSC strikers combined picketing with entering classrooms to call on other students for support. The SF Police Tactical Unit was called onto the campus multiple times. On the seventh day of the strike the unit engaged in a confrontation with two thousand strikers. The police clubbed students and at one point drew their weapons. Students and faculty demanded that SFSC President Robert Smith close down the campus, which he did, for an indefinite period.

Smith was under enormous pressure from those above him (a conservative, Republican-dominated board of trustees; state college system chancellor Glenn S. Dumke; Superintendent of Public Instruction Max Rafferty; and Governor Ronald Reagan) to keep the campus open at all costs. On November 25 Smith organized a BSU/TWLF-approved convocation to discuss the issues of the strike while the trustees met in Los Angeles to discuss the crisis. The convocation ended abruptly the next day when striking students received letters of suspension. Smith resigned, citing inability to resolve issues amid the various political pressures. Immediately the trustees named S. I. Hayakawa as the new president of SFSC.[38]

Under Hayakawa confrontations between strikers and police intensified. On December 2 Hayakawa instigated a riot when he personally attempted to force open the campus. With the backing of 650 police, Hayakawa climbed onto the strike sound truck, ripped out its wires, shoved students away, and tossed into the air blue armbands, which were being passed out to students who were against the strike. The armbands were emblazoned with the letter H, which meant support for Hayakawa. Anti-Hayakawa students rallied and marched to police-occupied classrooms, where confrontations occurred between thousands of strikers and police. More confrontational incidents occurred throughout December. In January support built for the TWLF as three hundred professors struck for their own union demands as well as TWLF demands. Other campus unions joined in support, with clerical, commons, and library workers honoring the picket lines. Teamsters Union drivers refused to cross picket lines, and deliveries to the campus came to a halt.

IMPORTANT STRIKE JUNCTURES AT UC BERKELEY

The experience of the SFSC TWLF was transferred to Berkeley, where students were up against a similar institutional structure. Instead of the board of trustees, the UC student strikers had to deal with the Reagan-appointed UC regents, who were just as adamant about opposing student demands. Similar repressive measures were used to stem student protest. The university was concerned about its image of being too repressive toward minority students. At the same time, there was pressure from Governor Reagan, who felt that the university administration should take a hard line. Eager to win votes, Reagan took every opportunity to express his opposition to student protest.[39]

On January 22 the first task for the TWLF was to station informational picket lines in front of various entries to the university. Initial student responses were nondescript and dependent upon how spirited the chanting and singing on the picket lines was. Protestors borrowed chants from the Southern Civil Rights and Black Power movements with slight variations, such as changing "Black Power" to "third world power." Manuel Delgado recalled, "First we chanted, 'say it loud, I'm black and I'm proud. . . and then we alternated with I'm brown and I'm proud, followed with I'm red and I'm proud, followed with I'm yellow and I'm proud, and I'm white and I'm proud. We even added I'm bourgeoisie and I'm proud. We all laughed."[40]

That night a fire destroyed Wheeler Auditorium. A shocked TWLF Central Committee quickly issued a public statement disavowing any connection with the fire. UCB Chancellor Roger Heyns implied that the strike precipitated acts of violence; however, fire bureau laboratory tests failed to show evidence of arson. Through the duration of the strike, the campus administration and the press brought up charges of TWLF-sponsored violence and property damage to discredit the legitimacy of the strikers' demands.[41]

Support from the campuswide American Federation of Teachers, Local 1570 (Teaching Assistants), occurred incrementally. Initially Local 1570 called for a work stoppage between January 22 and January 27 in support of the strike. On January 27 a strike vote was taken, and support for the strike was narrowly defeated. On February 13 the police completely surrounded a Local 1570 picket line in support of the TWLF Strike and arrested thirty-six people, even though the line moved and allowed people through. The arrests created further momentum to support the strike. On February

18 Local 1570 voted to strike in support of the TWLF Strike and union organizing rights.[42]

On January 30 the UCB administration announced that disciplinary action would be taken against "identified students who violated campus regulations." In response the Associated Students of the University of California (ASUC) Senate, the governing student body, passed a resolution condemning "disruptive and violent tactics" and urged students and faculty to pressure the administration to implement a department of Afro-American Studies. The resolution also supported the administration's efforts to consider the possible advantages of instituting a college of ethnic studies.

Academic faculty support was inconsistent and became dependent upon the increase in confrontations between police and strikers. On January 27 the overwhelming majority of third world faculty and administrators signed a public statement giving support to the strike. On February 5 the Academic Senate was reluctant to fully support resolutions favoring the principle of an autonomous college of ethnic studies organized by third world faculty and students. The resolution was tabled for a month. It was not until March 4 that the Academic Senate endorsed the establishment of an interim Ethnic Studies Department responsible only to the chancellor, with third world people allowed to formulate the curriculum.[43]

After a short period of informational picketing the TWLF gave notice that unless demands were met, Sather Gate would be blocked. On February 4, 1969, the escalation of tactics entailed the sealing of Sather Gate Bridge, a major cross-campus thoroughfare, with shoulder-to-shoulder stationary picketers blocking off the bridge.[44]

The TWLF's intention was to symbolically disrupt traffic flow in order to call attention to the demands and principles of the strike. Debates occurred immediately between striking and nonstriking students over the issue of freedom of access, although the existence of alternative access routes suggested this was a moot point. Though the TWLF intended the action to be largely symbolic, police overreaction further polarized the situation. Undercover police officers attacked the stationary line, attempting to arrest student protestors. Forty campus police and Alameda County sheriffs entered a pitched confrontation with demonstrators. The events culminated in fifteen arrests and twenty injuries.[45]

In the face of overwhelming police presence, on February 5 the TWLF held a serpentine-formation protest march around campus. Instead of holding ground in the traditional manner of sit-ins, the mobile, snake-shaped picket line allowed flexibility in the face of police attack and enabled outreach to students beginning to sympathize with their fellow students. The disruptive effect was no longer contained within the traditional central campus rallying area but became more dispersed and difficult to contain.[46]

Even during the peaceful informational picket period, police misconduct was a heated issue. On January 29 AASU/

TWLF member Cordell Abercrombie was arrested and allegedly beaten. As a strike captain and chant leader with a bullhorn, Abercrombie had played a vocal role in maintaining strike line organization. According to TWLF spokesman Fernando Garcia, Abercrombie was arrested in the evening as he was walking across campus. Garcia stated that Abercrombie was neither charged nor told of his constitutional rights when taken into custody. He was allegedly held and beaten in the Sproul Administration Building by six police officers.

On February 13 police moved to break up a moving picket line of one thousand strikers on Sproul Plaza. Police attempted to clear picketers walking on the administration building steps, where several TWLF leaders persisted in remaining. Arrests were made, which resulted in physical confrontation between police and protestors. Six university employees reported they had witnessed plainclothes Alameda County sheriffs beating arrested demonstrators in detention. The witnesses wrote an open letter to the *Daily Californian* to expose the violence.[47] A February 13 editorial in the *Daily Californian* called upon students to oppose the police terror and support the demands of the TWLF. It also pointed out that the teaching assistants' union, on strike because of police terror, might be fired for striking. The editorial asserted, "The blood-stained beasts stalk the campus. The police have suspended the constitution and are making arrests at will, and without provocation. They then proceed to rarified forms of torture."[48]

Law enforcement used the strategy of isolating the leadership from the rank and file. Speakers at rallies and strike captains were identified in police or media photographs and targeted for arrest. Sometimes this was comical: because Asian Americans "all looked alike," one would be arrested because he looked like another who had made a public statement to the media.[49]

BALANCE BETWEEN DIRECT ACTIONS AND NEGOTIATIONS

Negotiations between the TWLF representatives and the chancellor's office mirrored the intensity of protest activity on the strike lines. Sometimes strike activities caused cancellation of negotiation sessions. One session was cancelled when a confrontation took place within window eyesight of both the TWLF negotiation team and Chancellor Roger Heyns. The daily strike activities and mounting support resolutions by professors, teaching assistants, and community organizations constituted an important backdrop to the negotiations. Student response to campus repression rallied more widespread support. Both students and professors, who at first had marginally supported the strike, became drawn in as the atmosphere of martial law on campus limited them from doing campus business as usual.

The following events encapsulated the swings between strike activities and institutional response:

February 4: UCB. Twenty arrested and twenty were injured when plainclothes officers attempted to arrest strikers. Police declared strike support activity in Sproul Plaza an "illegal assembly" and ordered people to disperse.

February 5: UCB. Administration canceled noon rallies because of the possibility of violence—a clear case of prior restraint.

UCB. Governor Ronald Reagan declared a "state of extreme emergency" on the campus and surrounding areas to enable more California Highway Patrol to enter campus.

February 8: UCB. Chancellor's Office and TWLF Progress Committee reached a tentative agreement on implementing committee (2 students and 2 faculty from each group), but the agreement was then repudiated. Chancellor claimed that TWLF repudiated agreement; TWLF faculty claimed that Heyns said "key faculty" would not approve it.

February 10 UCB. Subcommittee of Dean Knight's Committee on Ethnic Studies (headed by East Asian Studies Professor George DeVos) recommended that Third World faculty draw up the proposals for the creation of a College of Third World Studies. TWLF criticized the report for excluding students and for forwarding the proposals to regular administrative and faculty channels, where TW faculty would be only ex-officio (non-voting) members.

February 19. UCB. Negotiations between TWLF and Chancellor Roger Heyns broke down on the powers of implementing committee. Chancellor claimed that the TWLF demand would "[compromise] the integrity of campus academic review procedures" and if the TWLF would not accept his proposal, "we will, of course, seek other ways and other students and faculty members who are willing."

February 26, Heyns broke off negotiations because of "violence" of the strikers. This occurred at the time of the brutal arrest of MASC member Manuel Delgado. After he was arrested, Ysidro Macias was clubbed on the back of his head and arrested. He was unconscious for several hours. This incident resulted in student confrontation with police, who used clubs and teargas

February 27: UCB. First use of National Guard on campus. Police used teargas to drive students off campus. This represented intense pressure from Governor Reagan's office to intervene in campus negotiations.[50]

By the end of February there was apprehension among AAPA members that the strike might be getting out of hand. Clashes with police were becoming intense, with a large police presence and the introduction of CS tear gas dropped by helicopter. By February 22 the university had announced that 127 individuals had been arrested. Arrested students were immediately placed on interim suspension and barred from strike participation. There was fear that the eventual declaration of martial law by Governor Reagan would make negotiations for third world college demands exceedingly difficult. At a press conference, the governor argued for martial law. He stated that the police had run out of tear gas and that the National Guard would be present to replenish the depleted supply and to provide support to law enforcement.[51]

On the evening of Thursday, February 20, an emergency AAPA meeting was conducted to discuss how to handle the confrontations with police. There was debate late into the night. Positions were polarized. The "soft-liners" felt that the violence had gotten out of hand. The strike was being taken over by "crazy white radicals" and was no longer controlled by third world people. They feared that the ongoing negotiation between the TWLF and the chancellor's office would be replaced by military martial law. The "hard-liners" felt that there was a need to intensify the protests and that the only basis for negotiations was the mass pressure on strike lines. One argued that it was a question not just of fighting for a third world college but of defeating a power structure that was responsible for the slaughter in Vietnam.[52]

The resulting vote was twenty to "cool it" and seven to continue on the same militant path. The other TWLF leaders were contacted, and on the following day TWLF monitors went among the crowds of students and high-school youth and gave the directive that no violence should occur. Three thousand strikers and protestors rallied outside the February 22 regents' meeting attended by Governor Reagan. This was one of the largest support rallies and one of the more peaceful. According to one local newspaper, strike leaders and monitors went into the crowds asking them to "be cool, no rock-throwing and don't give Reagan an excuse to call out the guard."[53]

According to the *Berkeley Daily Gazette*, this was also the largest show of organized law enforcement presence in Berkeley history. Over twenty law enforcement agencies formed a mutual-aid force of six hundred police and highway patrol officers. Over three hundred riot police were in visible view of the protest, and three hundred more were stationed in nearby parking garages. Fifty armed National Guardsmen were present with equipment vehicles and an army helicopter. One thousand more National Guard soldiers were encamped on a military facility in nearby Alameda .[54]

The cooling-off tactic did prove that the TWLF was sincere about negotiating for a settlement. At the same time, strikers felt that little had been resolved other than the need for more pressure. The regents voted to suspend students when there was "reasonable cause to believe" they had violated campus rules. Negotiations with the chancellor continued but remained inconclusive. As violence and arrests continued—including the arrest of strike leaders and the use of tear gas—the chancellor broke off meetings. Finally, Governor Reagan officially ordered the National Guard onto the campus, effectively making it an armed camp.[55]

On March 4 the Academic Senate voted 550 to 4 in support of the formation of an interim Ethnic Studies Department responsible only to the chancellor. The Senate allowed for third world student participation in the formulation of course curriculum and promised that the department's structure would be "of sufficient flexibility to permit evolution into a college." The chancellor announced that the depart-

ment would "immediately offer four-year programs leading to a B.A. degree in history, culture, and contemporary experience of ethnic minority groups, especially Black Americans, Mexican Americans, Asian Americans, and Native Americans." Study of each of the four groups would constitute a division within the interim department.[56]

President Hitch announced final approval of the formation of this department, to begin instruction in fall quarter 1969. In response, the TWLF announced the immediate suspension of all strike activities, with the stipulation that the strike could be reactivated at any moment if negotiations over the third world college demands reached any impasse.[57]

Meanwhile, at SF State, President Hayakawa stated his opinion that granting ethnic studies was the only way to move past three semesters of student strife. He acknowledged that third world student frustrations stemmed from being excluded from academic opportunities. At the same time, he drew a distinction between students who participated because they wanted inclusion and other students who participated because of New Left ideologies. He supported the former but asserted that there was nothing he could do for the latter.[58] The assumption here was that third world students were willing to work for reforms whereas many of the white students were members of leftist organizations whose goals did not include reforms.

The TWLF Strike at San Francisco State College was somewhat more successful than that at Berkeley. The first school of ethnic studies in the nation was established and was eventually able to confer degrees in ethnic studies, American Indian Studies, Asian American Studies, Black Studies, and La Raza Studies. UC Berkeley, on the other hand, received budget allocations for a single Department of Ethnic Studies with subdivisions in Asian American, African American, Chicano, and Native American Studies. There was disagreement among Berkeley TWLF strikers over how far an interim Ethnic Studies Department could develop and consternation over the fact that future generations of students might not be able to continue pressing the university for the original goal of a third world college. In many respects, the ending of the strike was more a stalemate than a final settlement.

CONCLUSION

The TWLF Strikes became an important training ground for many future community activists. The daily strike activities, the conflicts with the administrations, and the many alliances created became important learning tools for the future. The strike settlements were uplifting for the third world student movement, previously without institutional power and now in partial institutional control. Student energies turned to building programs previously seen as pipe dreams and to legitimizing Asian American and ethnic studies.

The challenge was how to develop the programs while maintaining the original goals and purposes of educational relevance and community orientation. The balancing act at times leaned toward bridging the campus and community, but more often the focus was on legitimization on campus at the expense of the community. There are still many campuses today where students are fighting for the establishment of Asian American Studies and ethnic studies programs. And colleges that have these programs still face ongoing battles against program marginalization and budget cuts.

Unquestionably the establishment of ethnic studies programs has been one of the chief legacies of the TWLF Strikes. Similar programs have grown nationally in over 250 universities, colleges, and high schools. Both UC Berkeley and SF State University now provide undergraduate and graduate degree programs in ethnic studies. Still, the most important but often forgotten legacy of the strikes was the building of solidarity among the different racial and ethnic groups that truly wished to change the educational environment. This solidarity found value in future struggles such as the International Hotel antieviction movement and the Alcatraz Island Native American movement, when many former TWLF participants were involved in struggles within their own ethnic communities but were linked in cooperation.

NOTES

1. Bryant Fong, interview by author, 2001.
2. Ibid. In 1968, Yuji Ichioka and Emma Gee initiated a small Asian American caucus within the Peace and Freedom Party in the Berkeley/East Bay area. Ichioka was a history graduate student at UC Berkeley. Both Ichioka and Gee were involved in the Civil Rights movement in the American South. The caucus became the forerunner to the AAPA, the first self-named group that called itself "Asian American," a term that Ichioka proposed.
3. *AAPA Newspaper* 6, no. 2 (January 1969); Bryant Fong, interview by author, 2001.
4. Bryant Fong, interview by author, 2001.
5. Ibid. Leways was a Chinatown street youth self-help organization that ran a soda fountain and pool hall on Jackson Street and was dedicated to community service and change. Youth Council funded employment training as the youth arm of the federal Office of Economic Opportunity poverty program. It concentrated on the swelling Chinatown youth population during this period.
6. Ibid.
7. The only documentation of the Yellow Symposium and statewide AAPA meeting was "Area Movements—AAPA," *AAPA Newspaper* 6, no. 2 (January 1969).
8. SF State Strike Committee, *On Strike: Shut It Down* (1968), 3. George Murray was an English Department lecturer who was dismissed for his participation in the Black Panther Party.
9. "TWLF UCB Strike Demands," *Solidarity Newsletter* (1969), 3.
10. Research Organizing Cooperative, *Strike at Frisco State: The Story Behind It* (San Francisco: 1968), 2–8.
11. SFSC Strike Committee, *On Strike* (1968), 6.
12. ICSA, *SF State Strike Bulletin*, 1968.
13. "Statement of the Philippine-American Collegiate Endeavor: Philosophy and Goals." PACE, SF State College, mimeograph (1967).
14. This would change remarkably during the next decade due to the effects of the 1965 Immigration Act and the ensuing refugee migration in 1975 with the fall of Saigon. New conditions again challenged the basis for Asian American panethnic unity as the Asian American population balance shifted toward larger numbers of foreign-born Asian immigrants.
15. Victoria Wong, interview by author, 2001.
16. "Understanding AAPA," *AAPA Newspaper* 6.5, no. 7 (1970), 4–5.
17. W. H. Orrick Jr., *Shut It Down! A College in Crisis: San Francisco State College, October 1968–April 1969* (San Francisco, National Commission on the Causes and Prevention of Violence, 1969), 22.
18. Ibid., 34–35.
19. Ibid., 100–101. The egalitarian decision-making aspects of the TWLF at SF State were forwarded to TWLF-Berkeley during the formative stages of the Berkeley organization. Strike leader Richard Aoki emphasized this point in a 1995 Ethnic Studies 41 course panel at UC Berkeley.
20. Class attendance during the strike was 20 percent, according to the American Federation of Teachers, or 68 percent, according to the college administration. Ibid. The relegation of whites to a supporting role in the TWLF finds its genealogy in a 1964 strategizing session of the Student Nonviolent Coordinating Committee (SNCC), a major civil rights organization, that resulted in the exit of all white members. White membership in SNCC was viewed as an encumbrance to building grassroots black leadership. Blacks were to develop the Black Power movement and whites to organize against racism in their own white communities. See Clayborne Carson, *In Struggle: SNCC and the Black Awakening of the 1960s* (Cambridge, Mass.: Harvard University Press, 1995), 144.
21. The earlier figures are from an essay by Matthew Dennis in the Free Speech movement book *The Third World Liberation Front Strike of 1969* (unpublished). The 19 percent figure for African American, Chicano, and Native American California populations is found in 1970 census materials in State of California Department of Finance archives, *dof.ca.gov/html/demograp/race7090.xls*. There was no Chicano census category; the Hispanic category combined the majority Chicano population with Latinos. The 1970 student demographic materials are from UC Berkeley archives. Office of Student Research, UC Berkeley, *Enrollments from Fall 1970 to Fall 1985* (2001).
22. NSC and CSC, *Fact Sheet by Nisei Students Club and Chinese Students Club of UC Berkeley* (Berkeley: unpublished, 1968).
23. Berkeley Third World Liberation Front, *Strike 1969* (Berkeley: unpublished, 1969) (hereafter cited as TWLF, *Strike 1969*).
24. Ibid.
25. L&S essentially did not want to allow African American faculty and students control over the department or its admission of freshman students. M. Dennis, "Unpublished Report," in *Ethnic Studies 41 Course Reader*, UC Berkeley (1995). See also Steve Duscha, "Third World Votes—Strike Wednesday," *Daily Californian*, January 20, 1969.
26. TWLF, *Strike 1969*.
27. Ibid.
28. Ibid.
29. Manuel Delgado, presentation at conference entitled "The Third World Strike: Historical Lessons. Crossing Over: A Strategy Session and 30 Year Commemoration of the UC Berkeley Third World Strike" (Berkeley: unpublished, 1999) (hereafter cited as "Historical Lessons").

30. Manuel Delgado, *TWLF Strike Status* (Berkeley: unpublished, 1969).
31. Bryant Fong, interview by author, 2001.
32. Ibid.
33. Steve Wong, interview by author, San Francisco, 2001.
34. Ibid.
35. Delgado at "Historical Lessons."
36. L. Boyer at "Historical Lessons."
37. From a pure social-science viewpoint, the TWLF can be depicted as a utilitarian instrument, a temporary coalition formed so each group can gather its share. Once progress is made, the coalition is demobilized and each racial group continues in its own space. While this may have been true in the beginning stages of the struggle, the political consciousness of the activists, influenced by context and by their participation, needs to be an important part of the analysis.
38. SFSC Strike Committee, *On Strike!* (1968), 49–51. S. I. Hayakawa served as president of SFSC from 1968 to 1973. A conservative Japanese American and Republican Party member, he later was elected to the U.S. Senate and served from 1976 to 1983. Hayakawa's perspectives were consistently in line with those of Ronald Reagan, who was California governor from 1966 to 1974 and U.S. president from 1980 to 1988.
39. M. Kitchell, *Berkeley in the 60's* (Berkeley: Kitchell Films, 1990).
40. Delgado at "Historical Lessons."
41. TWLF, *Strike 1969.*
42. Ibid.
43. Ibid.
44. J. Bartl, "Strike Violence Grows, Police Invade Campus," *Daily Californian*, February 5, 1969, 1.
45. Ibid.
46. Ibid.
47. R. Dillion, "Sproul Beatings Reported," *Daily Californian*, February 19, 1969; Michael Hall, "Jim Nabors Beaten, Arrested in Confrontation at Sproul Plaza; ACLU Threatens Lawsuit," ibid. According to a statement by the TWLF, on February 13, 1969, statements signed by twelve university employees and independently by others recounted indiscriminate severe beatings by police in the basement of Sproul Hall. TWLF, *Strike 1969.*
48. Editorial, "The Horror," *Daily Californian*, February 13, 1969, 1.
49. Richard Aoki, interview by author, 2001.
50. TWLF, *Strike 1969.* According to the *Berkeley Daily Gazette*, on February 20, over a thousand National Guard were on standby at the Berkeley Marina and in Alameda. "How Long Will the Guard Remain?" *Berkeley Daily Gazette*, February 22, 1969, 1.
51. G. Cant, "Police Mass on Campus," *Berkeley Daily Gazette*, February 22, 1969, 1.
52. Arnold Li, interview by author, San Francisco, 2001.
53. Cant, "Police Mass on Campus."
54. Ibid.
55. L. Ling-chi Wang, *Chronology of Ethnic Studies at U.C. Berkeley* (Berkeley: unpublished, 1997).
56. Ibid.
57. TWLF, *Strike 1969.*
58. Orrick, *Shut It Down!* 172.

Taking to the Streets
Scenes from 1968–72
Anna Naruta

People tried a variety of approaches to working for change and social justice in the 1960s and 1970s. These images show a few scenes from public actions taking place in California between 1968 and 1972.

May 4th anniversary
Red Guards seize rally at Portsmouth Square

by Ken Wong

The flag of Red China flew over Portsmouth Square Sunday. For real. The Red Guards, patterned after the Black Panthers, dominated the May 4th rally.

The Peking flag and the guards' uniform, PLA's caps and Cuban guerilla's field jackets with red arm bands, shook up visitors at the plaza.

The rally was to commemorate the 50th anniversary of the May 4th Movement of 1919 in Peking where students demonstrated to lead a nation-wide strike that awakened old China being bamboozeld by unfair foreign treaties.

MAO'S PORTRAIT

The day's original program was sponsored by the Bay Area Asian Students Coalition. But it was changed without notice. The platform was decorated with a portrait of Chairman Mao Tze-tung and a flag of the People's Republic of China.

Chinese Consulate General Chou Tung-hua was a scheduled speaker along with attorney Gordon Lau and youth worker Franklin Fung Chow. However, none of them spoke and later issued statements disavowing any affiliations with the Red Guards.

Counsel General Chou, interviewed on television, commented, "They do not know enough of Communism to realize what they are doing."

Following a skit depicting the May 4th movement by the college students, Red Guard leaders Pat Kajiwara and Alex Hing, between exhortations of "Power to the People," told the crowd that the Guards serve the people in the Asian community.

ECHOES PANTHERS

"The Black Panthers is the most revolutionary group in the country and we are patterned after them," Hing said.

The 11 demands enunciated at the rally echoed the Panthers' demands that include, "Pigs off," arming with guns for protection against the police and demanding the release of all Asians in city, state and federal prisons because they did not have fair trials.

Another demand was for freedom. "We want the freedom to make our own destiny. Chiang Kaishek is ruling us through the Six Companies."

On Guard

A GIRL RED GUARD exhorts crowd to save the Chinese Playground from becoming a garage at May 4 rally in Portsmouth Square. (Kem Lee photo)

Two projects were being undertaken by the Guards. One was seeking signatures for a petition to save the playground from being turned into a garage. The other was breakfast for needy school children and the churches were denounced for not helping.

BUSTED

Police harassment was told by Red Guard Sheldon Lee who was busted last Thursday by members of the newly-formed 150-man crime prevention unit. Lee, along with three other guards, was booked for concealed weapons when a hunting knife was found in their auto at the corner of Lombard and Fillmore streets.

According to Lee, copies of Mao's little red books found on them were ripped by the arresting officers.

Most of the old-timers at the plaza were playing their usual game of Chinese chess and paid no attention to the speeches and two rock bands that alternated sets.

The music was still going strong at 5 p.m. while the crowd which came at noon for the rally began to break up.

"On Guard": San Francisco's Portsmouth Square hosted a rally commemorating the fiftieth anniversary of the May Fourth Movement of 1919, when, in Beijing, "students demonstrated to lead a nation-wide strike" to protest unfair foreign treaties. In this Kem Lee photo of the Red Guard takeover of the rally, "a girl Red Guard exhorts [the] crowd to save the Chinese Playground from becoming a garage." (*East/West*, May 7, 1969; Philip P. Choy Collection, CHSA)

EAST WEST

報西東

THE CHINESE - AMERICAN JOURNAL • PUBLISHED EVERY WEDNESDAY • VOLUME 3, NUMBER 19 • MAY 7, 1969 • 10 CENTS

中華民國五十八（一九六九）年五月七日・第三卷第十九期・中英文週報・逢星期三出版・每份一毫・全年五元

Red Guards seize rally at Portsmouth Square

華埠紅衛兵 公開集會活動

抗議集中營案

RED GUARDS sell "Quotations From Chairman Mao" to crowd attending May 4 rally at Portsmouth Square. (Kem Lee photo)

華埠街頭 報復事件

華埠人語

Second Class Postage Paid at San Francisco, California

EAST/WEST
758 Commercial Street
San Francisco, Calif. 94108
Phone: 781-6480.

GARBED IN CUBAN and Chinese revolutionaries uniform, a Red Guard stands at ease as May 4 movement of 1919 tableaux is enacted on stage. (Kem Lee photo)

The Red Guards: Modeled on the Black Panther Party, the Red Guards also established and operated a free breakfast program for children. Above: "Little Red Books. Red Guards sell 'Quotations from Chairman Mao' to crowd attending May 4 rally at Portsmouth Square."

Below: "Garbed in Cuban and Chinese revolutionaries uniform, a Red Guard stands at ease as May 4 movement of 1919 tableaux is enacted on stage." (Kem Lee photographs, East/West, May 7, 1969, front page; Philip P. Choy Collection, CHSA)

"Yellow Peril Supports Black Power": Protesting the arrest and imprisonment of Black Panther Party leader Huey Newton, steps of Alameda County Courthouse, 1225 Fallon Street, Oakland, California, on opening day of the trial, July 15, 1968. (Photograph by Roz Payne, *www.newsreel.us*, reproduced courtesy of the photographer; photo also in collection of the International Center of Photography, New York)

100 Asian-Americans in anti-Ky march

A hundred Asian-Americans under the banner of the Asian- Americans for Peace join the demonstration against visit of South Vietnam's Vice President Nguyen Cao Ky and his wife in front of the Ambassador Hotel in Los Angeles.

Anthropology undergraduate forms group to study Isle Chinese history

By DOUGLAS WOO
(Honolulu Advertiser)

Honolulu
To Clyde D.G. Wong, 22, one way to solve the problems of our society is to enliven and reevaluate values of the cul-

Museology is the science of museum organization and management.

"We'll try to present a relevant and meaningful presentation through visual aids, recordings, artifacts and demonstrations on how the artifacts were used.

"There are approximately

Wong, a 1965 Hilo High School graduate, became interested in anthropology three years ago while looking over Chinese antiques. The antiques revealed to him a particular life style of a certain historic period.

Background

The Hawaii Chinese History Center had its first organizational meeting last month.

"We'll be trying to answer why the Chinese people immigrated to Hawaii, how they got here, and how they can go on working productively in society trying to make things more livable.

Protesting the Vietnam War: "A hundred Asian-Americans under the banner of the Asian Americans for Peace join the demonstration against visit of South Vietnam's Vice President Nguyen Cao Ky and his wife in front of the Ambassador Hotel in Los Angeles." (*East/West*, December 9, 1970; Philip P. Choy Collection, CHSA)

BACK COVER

ANNOUNCEMENT FROM THE FEDERAL BUREAU OF INVESTIGATION OF THE UNITED STATES

Now that you have settled in America, you are not only entitled to enjoy the various blessings of America's free political system, but in addition will be able to shoulder the responsibilities of protecting these free traditions.

Since you have personally experienced the suffering and bondage which is perpetrated by tyrannical communist rule, you must by now certainly be able to realize in a profound way how valuable freedom is and how terrifying and detestable communism is.

Communists frequently engage in secret activities within America's borders and plot to destroy the free traditions of America, and while our bureau is on constant alert and pays close attention to these matters, from now on you too may join in our defense against communism. We hope you will note the following:

1. If while in America you become aware of communists or Maoist spies who are engaged in intelligence work or destructive and subversive activities you are urgently requested to telephone the local branch of the FBI at once. (The telephone number will be clearly listed in the first two or three pages of the regular telephone directory of any city.)

2. You are requested to make your report based on hard facts known to you; do not become confused by hearsay.

3. It will suffice for you simply to report what you know; do not carry out your own investigations. You must realize that investigation is a specialized and sophisticated profession, and if ordinary people attempt it they not only risk their own safety but also risk startling the snake from his hiding place.

Should you have anything to communicate, please inform the local branch of this bureau immediately. Local branch telephone: 742-5533.

> —(*J. Edgar*) *Hoover*
> *Director, United States Federal Bureau of Investigation*

[leaflets posted on the walls of every large American Chinatown during winter 1971-72]

"To shoulder the responsibilities of protecting these free traditions": The special issue editors for this 1972 issue of *Bulletin of Concerned Asian Scholars* printed the Chinese text (with English translation) of this leaflet, copies of which, they reported, were "posted on the walls of every large American Chinatown during winter 1971–72." In it, FBI Director J. Edgar Hoover directed readers to phone the FBI to inform it of any suspected Communist activities.

Reminding readers of another era when people of Chinese descent were targeted as a group, treated with suspicion, and subjected to infringement of basic civil rights, the editors chose to print on the cover the image of one of the registration certificates that an 1892

U.S. law required every person of Chinese descent to carry. (*Bulletin of Concerned Asian Scholars* 4, no. 3 [1972], ed. Victor and Brett Nee, Connie Young Yu, and Shawn Hsu Wong; Connie Young Yu Collection, 2006.62.2, CHSA)

Outcry about the domestic spying activities conducted as part of J. Edgar Hoover's Cointelpro program of the 1950s–1970s led to reaffirmation that domestic surveillance is forbidden unless there is reasonable suspicion of criminal activity, or probable cause. (David Cunningham, *There's Something Happening Here: The New Left, the Klan and FBI Counterintelligence*, Berkeley and Los Angeles: University of California Press, 2004)

美國聯邦調查局ＦＢＩ通告

諸君今既定居美國，不惟得享受美國自由政制下種種幸福而已，將更能負起保衛其自由傳統之責任也。

共產專制政治所加諸人民之桎梏與痛苦，君等固嘗切膚受之，故今日必能深切體會自由之可貴，與乎共產主義之可畏可恨。

美國境內，共產黨徒經常從事秘密活動，圖謀破壞美國之傳統自由，本局固經常警戒，予以密切注意，而諸君今後正可以參預此防共工作也。請注意下列數事為幸：

（一）君等在美如有知悉共產黨徒及毛派間諜從事情報，破壞及傾覆活動者，務請隨時用電話通知當地ＦＢＩ分局（其電話號碼皆明載於各該城市通常電話號碼簿首二三頁）

（二）諸君務請根據所知事實報訊，切勿為道聽途說所惑擾。

（三）諸君但就所知而報訊足矣，切勿自己從事偵查。須知偵查係專門精細職務，常人而為之，自身固然冒險，且有打草驚蛇之虞

如有通訊，請即通知本局當地分局。　分局電話：

美國聯邦調查局局長賀華

Students at San Francisco's Galileo High School march in 1970 to make the family-oriented Chinese New Year's Day a school holiday: Photographer Leland Wong notes, "That protest was a very spontaneous protest, a reaction to the denial of having the Lunar New Year holiday off after a petition drive the previous year and a cancellation of a Lunar New Year assembly by the principal. . . . though [during the protest] many issues were brought up concerning Chinese American students." *East/West* reported 250 students marching on Van Ness Avenue. (Leland Wong photograph, reproduced courtesy of the photographer, *East/West*, March 11, 1970; Philip P. Choy Collection, CHSA)

Art and Living Revolution
Gary Woo and *AION* Magazine
Yolanda Garfias Woo

Many young activists in the 1960s and '70s found themselves questioning what often felt like nearly every assumption they'd been taught. From there, their task was to reinvent everything about their lives, from political action to artistic expression.[1] Simultaneously, many activists for social justice found that the work of dedicated artists had an important role in representing and cultivating the fullness of people's experiences and aspirations, as well as in communication. In 1970, activists preparing to publish a new literary journal, AION, sought the collaboration of Gary Woo (1925–2006), then one of the San Francisco Bay Area's "preeminent Asian American abstract painters."[2]

Gary was an artist who preferred to work alone, without the influence of trends or group thinking. It is therefore a compliment to the great enthusiasm and fervor of both Janice Mirikitani and Francis Oka that he made an exception. I'm not exactly sure how we met them, but they came to visit us one day, full of ideas for this new magazine they were putting together. Normally Gary would have gently turned down their offer for him to take part, but their sincerity was genuine, and I think the injustices Gary had also suffered as an immigrant and an artist made their goals ring true for him. He wanted to help and so agreed to do the magazine's cover and a few pieces of calligraphy to get them started.

I still remember long evenings with them sprawled out on our living-room floor, looking at prospective covers and paintings, drinking tea, and asking Gary his thoughts on all kinds of things! Finally the first issue was published and everyone was satisfied that it had a good beginning. I loved Gary's cover and so did they.

They began working on the second issue and once again asked Gary to participate. He had some work he said they could use for that issue; however, he told them that this would be the last time. I remember him saying that it was too time consuming and he wanted to continue painting on his own road rather than become a graphic artist for a magazine. It was hard. We liked them and knew they were disappointed but understood. We wished them much success. Shortly afterward, we heard that Francis had been killed in a motorcycle accident, and we never heard from Janice again.

NOTES

1. This sense of a need to examine and reinvent everything is articulated by activists in *Chicano! History of the Mexican American Civil Rights Movement* (Los Angeles, Calif.: National Latino Communications Center, 1996), as well as elsewhere.
2. Gordon H. Chang, Mark Dean Johnson, Paul J. Karlstrom, eds., *Asian American Art: A History, 1850–1970* (Stanford: Stanford University Press, 2008), 459.

FOOD FOR ALL HIS DEAD / BY FRANK CHIN

"Jus' forty-fie year 'go, Doctah Sun Yat-sen free China from da Manchus. Dat's why all us Chinee, alla ovah da woil are celebrate Octob' tan or da Doubloo Tan ...!"

The shouted voice came through the open bathroom window. The shouting and music was still loud after rising through the night's dry air; white moths jumped on the air, danced through the window over the voice, and lighted quickly on the wet sink, newly reddened from his father's attack. Johnny's arms were around his father's belly, holding the man upright against the edge of the sink to keep the man's mouth high enough to spit lung blood into the drain.

The man's belly shrank and filled against Johnny's arms as the man breathed and spat, breathed and spat, the belly shrinking and filling. The breaths and bodies against each other shook with horrible rhythms that could not be numbed out of Johnny's mind. "Pride," Johnny thought, "Pa's pride for his reputation for doing things ... except dying. He's not proud of dying, so it's a secret between father and son ..." At the beginning of the man's death, then he had been Johnny's father, still commanding and large, saying, "Help me. I'm dying; don't tell," and removing his jacket and walking to the bathroom. Then came the grin—pressed lips twisted up into the cheeks—hiding the gathering blood and drool. Johnny had cried then, knowing his father would die. But now the man seemed to have been always dying and Johnny always waiting, waiting with what he felt was a coward's loyalty to the dying, for he helped the man hide his bleeding and was sick himself, knowing he was not waiting for the man to die but waiting for the time after death when he could relax.

"... free from da yoke of Manchu slab'ry, in'epen'ence, no moah queue on da head! Da's wha'fo' dis big a parade! An' here, in San Francisco, alla us Chinee—'mellican 're pwowd! ..."

It's all gone ... I can't spit any more. Get my shirt, boy. I'm going to make a speech tonight...." The man slipped from the arms of the boy and sat on the toilet lid and closed his mouth. His bare chest shone as if washed with dirty cooking oil and looked as if he should have been chilled, not sweating, among the cold porcelain and tile of the bathroom.

To the sound of herded drums and cymbals, Johnny wiped the sweat from his father's soft body and dressed him without speaking. He was full of the heat of wanting to cry for his father but would not.

His father was heavier outside the house.

They staggered each other across the alleyway to the edge of Portsmouth Square. They stood together at the top of the slight hill, their feet just off the concrete onto the melted fishbone grass, and could see the brightly lit reviewing stand, and they saw over the heads of the crowd, the dark crowd of people standing in puddles of each

Calligraphy by Gary Woo opens the publication of Frank Chin's "Food for All His Dead," *Contact*, 1962. (Reproduction of work by Gary Woo courtesy Yolanda Garfias Woo)

A I O N

STAFF

Editor......................................Janice Mirikitani
Co-Editor...................................Francis Oka
Production Coordinator......................Jane Tabata
Staff Photographer.........................Jerry Pong
Business Manager...........................Neil Gotanda

ADVISORY COMMITTEE

Rev. Lloyd K. Wake
Masayo Suzuki
Neil Gotanda

LAYOUT

Leland S. Meyerzove
Bob Rita

GRAPHIC ADVISOR

Gary Woo

(Reproduction of work by Gary Woo in AION 1, no. 1 [1970]. Courtesy Yolanda Garfias Woo.) (*Continues on next four pages*)

AION

CONTENTS

DEDICATED TO:

General Elwell S. Otis
Eisako Sato
Ku Klux Klan
William Randolph Hearst
John Wayne
Chiang Kai Shek
FDR
Steve Canyon
Ferdinand Marcos
Emperor Ming
"Fat Jap" Agnew
S. I. Hayakawa
Commodore Perry
Native Sons and Daughters of the Golden West
Madame Chenault
Admiral Dewey
R. Mill-house Nixon
Chevron Island Girl
Theodore Roosevelt
Captain Fury & his Howling Commandoes
V. S. Mc Clatchy
Frederick Townsend Ward
Chung Hee Park
Dean Rusk
Admiral Yamamoto
Charlie Chan
Earl Warren
General DeWitt
The Six Companies
Madame Nhu
Captain America
Nguyen Van Thieu

and all others who made this magazine
necessary.

ALL POWER TO THE PEOPLE

EDITORIAL

The dominant white society in America, by perpetuating its racist values, has insidiously created a cycle of self-hate between and within ethic groups.

As Asian Americans, we have been conditioned by stereotypes imposed upon us by the white middle class and have internalized the consequent insecurity and confusion. Dependency upon these values and standards has caused an absence of self-knowledge and its complementary fear and paralysis.

Our continued complacency within this racist society will bring about our cultural destruction. We must join the international movement to end the explotation of all Third World peoples and work to create our own revolutionary culture in this country.

We hope that AION will provide a forum for Asian American self-definition and expression on issues revelant to problems and needs of our communities.

-The AION Staff-

SPECIAL THANKS TO Gordon Lau; Donna Nomura Dobkin; George Leong; Colin Watanabe; Rev. A. Cecil Williams; Jeff Chan; Janet Hedani; Jan Herman; Nick Harvey; Tony Ubalde; John Lee; Diana Yoshida; Wendy Yoshimura; Quon Shih Shung; Pat Salivar; Isao Fujimoto; Mitsu Yashima; Shigeyoshi Murao; Penny Nakatsu; Irene Miyagawa; Arnold Kawano; Eld-ridge Foundation; Epworth Foundation.

SNOW ON THE RIVER

On a thousand hills all bird life is cut off.

On ten thousand paths there is no trace of human footsteps;

In a lonely boat the old man with the bamboo hat and cape

Sits by himself fishing the river in the winter snow.

Poet : Liu Tsung Yuan

T'ang 618 A.D.

Translated by Gary Woo

Gary Woo

UNITY

A Bookstore for Everybody

Harvey Dong

PHOTOS BY STEVE LOUIE

Harvey Dong's "Third World Liberation Comes to San Francisco State and UC Berkeley" also appears in this volume, page 95.

After the Third World Strike, students sought to expand the ideals of the movement into the community. The International Hotel issue became a uniting point, with students and community residents working together to save the hotel and Manilatown. The new resistance opened further channels of involvement, and one extension of this new cooperation was the collaborative effort to start Everybody's Bookstore (EB) to serve the community. This bookstore far exceeded the originators' expectations. Little did those initially discussing its worthiness realize the long-term contributions it would make.

The following are personal recollections of how Everybody's Bookstore came into existence. Many thanks and acknowledgements to Steve Wong, its manager, for his input into this article and for his many years of envisioning, developing, maintaining, and anchoring the first Asian American bookstore in America. Many thanks also to the rest of the bookstore staff, who put in countless hours building shelves, cataloguing titles, working behind the counter, assisting customers, and believing in the ideal of establishing a source of knowledge for the Asian American community.

Everybody's Bookstore opened on January 1, 1970. Located at 840 Kearny Street in the International Hotel building in San Francisco Manilatown-Chinatown, it became established as the major source for books about the Asian American community and became an integral part of the progressive movement. However, very little is known today about its ten-year existence and the mark it left on its community.

Most of the bookstore's founders were members of the UC Berkeley Asian American Political Alliance (AAPA), an organization involved in the Third World Liberation Front (TWLF) strike for ethnic studies programs at UC Berkeley.[1] AAPA and the TWLF grew out of the Civil Rights and Black Power movements. After the strike there was discussion within AAPA about where to continue the struggle. The TWLF strike literature focused on establishing third world/ethnic studies courses that were educationally relevant and on promoting progressive change in oppressed third world communities such as San Francisco Chinatown and Manilatown.

Even during the strike AAPA members were attending rallies in support of the International Hotel tenants in Manilatown. Some 130 Filipino and Chinese tenants, mostly elderly bachelors, were involved in a bitter eviction dispute with Walter Shorenstein and his Milton Meyer & Company. The tenants were able to win a three-year lease, but the owners maintained that the building was unsafe and should be condemned. On the eve of the lease signing, a mysterious fire destroyed a section of the hotel and three tenants died. The owners placed the repair burden on the tenants. In the fall semester of 1969 the newly established Asian American Studies program began sending students to help bring the building up to code. In addition to hammering and painting, these volunteers organized social functions. The majority of the students were not from Manilatown or Chinatown but had family roots there. Those who had grown up in the neighborhood were receiving a college education that encouraged them to step away from the community. The movement was bringing them back.

AAPA members were looking toward longer-term involvement that would establish further roots in the community. Point One of the Black Panther Party's Ten-Point Program became an important starting point for discussion. It demanded an education that taught oppressed peoples their true history and their role in radically transforming society. After a late-night discussion at one Hong Kong student's apartment in Berkeley, the idea of establishing a bookstore in the San Francisco Chinatown-Manilatown community as an instrument of community education came into being. The thinking was that a bookstore could establish day-to-day contact with the community and become an information center where Asian American literature and other books would be available.

Ten people each contributed $50 to establish the bookstore. Because of the young activists' involvement in supporting the International Hotel tenants, tenant leader and manager Joe Diones accepted their request to rent an empty eight-by-ten-foot storefront for $50 per month. Diones, a retired longshoreman, had worked with International Longshore and Warehouse Union (ILWU) Local 10 and its president, Harry Bridges. Diones used his labor union organizing know-how to organize the tenants. While negotiations continued with Milton Meyer & Company, Diones was in charge of collecting rents from the upstairs residents and for finding commercial tenants who could pay rent and stay the course during a protracted antieviction fight. A number of commercial tenants had already decided to leave, so it made sense for Diones to lease to tenants such as EB.

Between the 1920s and 1942 the bookstore site had been a laundry owned, operated, and inhabited by the Japanese American grandparents of a bookstore volunteer. In 1942 the family had been ordered to vacate the premises and report to the War Relocation Center. Three decades later this store would be an important distribution point for books about what happened to the 110,000 Japanese Americans sent off to concentration camps. When the bookstore opened, the volunteer's mother returned to visit her birthplace.

The bookstore was next door to Tino's Barbershop, a local hangout for many Manongs (elderly Filipino men). At the end of a hallway between the bookstore and Tino's was a smokeshop–billiard room. After a year the smokeshop moved out, and Inprintmatic Printing leased the space for a short period. Adjacent to the bookstore at 832 Kearny Street was the Victory Building, a smaller single-room-occupancy building that housed about forty mostly elderly Chinese residents on the second and third floors. The street level was leased to the Mandalay Café, a Filipino-owned bar and restaurant. Every evening the jukebox at the Mandalay played Hawaiian music, and couples danced until closing. In the basement of the Victory Building was a large meeting hall that housed the United Filipino Association (UFA). The hall had a small office, a kitchen, and a large meeting area that could accommodate approximately one hundred people. The UFA was a community organization representing the mostly elderly residents of Manilatown. As the recognized voice of Manilatown, the UFA negotiated and signed the 1969 lease extension on behalf of the International Hotel tenants.

In 1970 the UFA moved its offices and began holding its meetings in the International Hotel lobby. The former UFA location at 832 Kearny Street was sublet to UC Berkeley's Asian American Studies program as its field office. Soon, however, UC Berkeley ended its operations there, AAPA disbanded, and a core of former AAPA members and community people renamed the location the Asian Community Center (ACC). ACC, also a collective of students, former students, and newly recruited community members, started a series of "serve the people" programs. These included a weekly film series (attended mostly by elderly Chinatown residents); an educational summer day camp for Chinatown elementary-school children; distribution of surplus food to the needy; TB screenings; and a Chinatown Cooperative Garment Factory. The center also became a drop-in location for garment, restaurant, and electronics workers, mostly Chinese

1972. Everybody's Bookstore storefront with adjacent shops: Leways, Tino's Barbershop, and Inprintmatic. Inprintmatic moved into the smokeshop space in 1971 and stayed for one year. In 1972 Everybody's Bookstore expanded into the vacated space. By 1972 Leways, a youth self-help organization, had moved from its Jackson Street location to Kearny Street after suffering police raids and right-wing attacks. The plywood boards on the windows of Leways were typical of the times, representing attempts to prevent vandalism by the various forces that disagreed with the organization's political activities. Also note the signage with two banners, "International Hotel" and "Low Cost Housing is a Right." The Chinese characters on the Everybody's Bookstore sign, Da Zhong Shu Dian (Dai Chung Shu Dien), include a *min* character with a circle around it that means "the people." This was the organizational symbol for Wei Min She, which determined the policies of the bookstore. (Steve Louie photograph)

immigrants, to discuss how to organize against sweatshop conditions and other work-related injustices.[2]

The response to the newcomers on Kearny Street was overwhelmingly positive. The elderly Chinese and Filipino men welcomed the younger generation's participation. When ACC opened, elderly Chinese men who sat daily in Portsmouth Square were invited to use it as a drop-in living room. Street youth were also welcome to come in to talk about community issues and were encouraged to volunteer in the "serve the people" activities. Kearny Street became a much safer community as the coldness of surviving alone was replaced with the warmth of cooperation. When the bookstore (also operated by ACC) opened, street crime decreased, largely because of the rise in social awareness that on this block, people looked out for one another.

The name "Everybody's Bookstore" was intended to be both neutral and welcoming and to bring in large numbers of people. It was also compatible with progressive movement terminology such as "people" and "masses." The choice was to reach out to the "average" person who might be curious about Asian American topics, revolutionary politics, and social change but not necessarily committed to them. The movement was engaged in debate over how to present itself favorably to the communities in which it worked. The English name "Everybody's Bookstore" held a politically wide connotation; its Chinese translation, "Da Zhong Shudian," meant the "bookstore of the masses."

The bookstore doors opened on January 1, 1970. According to Steve Wong, its first supplier was China Books and Periodicals, located in the San Francisco Mission district. Trips there usually meant filling up and bringing back three boxes of books, mostly titles about revolutionary China. The manager of China Books, Chris Noyes, recommended opening an account at Book People, a local book distribution cooperative in Oakland. Another general retail book account was opened with L&S Book Distribution in Daly City.

The emergence of Asian American Studies nationwide created a demand for reprints of older works of Asian American history and literature as well as for new writings by Asian Americans. EB could not have emerged at a better time. In the beginning, the bookstore relied heavily on selling textbooks to Asian American Studies classes at UC Berkeley and SF State College. Not many titles were easily obtainable. Titles such as *America Is in the Heart* by Carlos Bulosan were out of print and sold in a photocopied reader format. Jade Snow Wong's *Fifth Chinese Daughter* could only be procured directly from the writer's art studio on Polk Street in San Francisco. EB helped reintroduce the works of San Francisco Bay Area author Toshio Mori, who wrote *Yokohama, California* in 1942. Regular stock items included *Filipino Immigration* by Bruno Lasker and *Chinese Immigration* by Mary Roberts Coolidge, which were part of the American Immigration Collection Series republished by the Arno Press and the *New York Times* and were only available at EB. Also available were all the movement newspapers, including *Black Panther Party News*, *Palante*, *Getting Together*, *Gidra*, the *Guardian*, *New Dawn*, and *Wei Min, Chinese Community News*.

EB expanded its reach by creating a store catalogue including a range of titles on Asian American Studies, China, Japan, and martial arts. The catalogue was essentially a list of titles with a fill-in form at the bottom. Still, it was the only bookstore catalogue that specialized in Asian American writings, which were largely overlooked or deemed insignificant. The bookstore began to receive orders from libraries and individuals across the country and worldwide. The San Francisco Chinatown Library expanded its Asian American collection through the bookstore. EB was invited to display and sell its books at locations such as Visalia, in California's lower Central Valley, at events to promote friendship between the United States and China.

EB played a major role in the distribution of books and literature from the PRC. Many customers and institutions came to rely on EB as the source for Chinese books and their English translations. These titles included classics such as *Romance of Three Kingdoms*, *Outlaws of the Marsh*, *Dream of Red Mansions*, and *Journey to the West*. They also included educational titles from China on topics such as Taiji, martial arts, and Chinese medicine. There were books and magazines on political theory, agriculture, and the performing arts.

1972. Clerk in Everybody's Bookstore during its earlier days with magazines, pamphlets, and books focusing on China and the Great Proletarian Cultural Revolution, which ended two years later in 1974. Also, large assortment of Mao buttons and other Chinese revolution pins. (Steve Louie photograph)

Most prevalent from China were books explaining the merits of the Great Proletarian Cultural Revolution, about which very little was known in the United States. Many copies of *China Reconstructs* and *Peking Review* magazines and books about the Cultural Revolution were sold.

In a year the bookstore required more space to serve customer interests and begin mail-order shipping. When Inprintmatic Printing ceased operations EB expanded into that area, gaining twelve hundred square feet of floor space. The expansion was an expression of phenomenal growth of EB's customer base. The growing sales forced ACC to consider the politics of what to do with the bookstore profits. Should they be used for community programs? Or was distributing information important enough to justify using the profits to expand the bookstore's stock to further broaden or strengthen its customer base? ACC decided that strengthening the bookstore was an important political decision.

EB grew out of a movement that was intensely interested in Chinese politics. China was a leader in revolutionary politics, and its support of national liberation movements throughout the world motivated further interest in books related to its role in the world. The bookstore's Kearny Street block had become known as the left-wing progressive area. It hosted at least five active community organizations that established a political pole vastly different from that of the conservative Chinese Six Companies and Chinese Anti-Communist League. Kearny Street was beginning to chip away at the Cold War–era stranglehold the conservatives held over the community. When EB first opened, the right-wing press announced that the Red Guard Party based on Jackson Street in 1969 was now rejuvenated in the form of ACC and EB. The Red Guard, a political party composed of Chinatown street youth, had lost its space on Jackson Street due to right-wing pressures, including police raids, window vandalism,

1971. Long view of Kearny Street block. From far left, the Kearny Street Workshop (under the mural), the Chinese Progressive Association basement entrance, the International Hotel entrance, the ACC basement entrance, Leways, Tino's Barbershop, and Everybody's Bookstore. (Steve Louie photograph)

and eviction facilitated by negative press coverage. In 1971 these tactics were applied to the newly formed organizations on Kearny Street, including ACC and EB. Preventive measures were taken, such as boarding up the windows each evening with plywood.

The Chinese community was entering a new period. Two decades of antagonistic relations between the United States and China had made it difficult for Chinese Americans to have direct contact with family members in China. Sending remittances to family there was forbidden by the Trading with the Enemy Act of 1917. This situation was most difficult for the elderly bachelors, who often were not bachelors at all but had been forced by Chinese exclusion and the Cold War to live apart from their families. Now the community mood was much different, with many residents calling for normalization of relations between the United States and China. Previously businesses had been forbidden to sell items marked "Made in China." Now Chinese American commercial interests were yearning for changes in trade relations. Hong Kong– and Taiwanese-born students were also seeking to enhance their understanding of China.

These years of denial of the rights to contact, travel in, and trade with China and the yearning to correct the injustice became the basis for the U.S.-China friendship movement. Not only Chinese Americans were involved. Many non-Chinese took interest in China, its rehabilitation from being

the "sick man of Asia" and its subsequent establishment of socialism. In the early 1970s, U.S.-China friendship associations organized large-scale October 1 National Day events in several major U.S. cities to foster friendship between the two countries.

Beginning in 1970 EB personnel made weekly trips to pick up air cargo shipments of magazines and newspapers from Hong Kong and Macao. Hundreds of copies of *Ta Kung Pao*, *Wen Wei Bao*, *Macao Daily*, and *70s Magazine* were sold at EB. Most of these were Chinese-language publications that featured articles about China relations and politics. *70s Magazine* was different in that it served a younger overseas Chinese audience with articles on the Diaoyutai movement, modern China, Chinese culture, and overseas Chinese issues. EB was the main seller of these periodicals; brisk sales increased traffic flow and recognition of the store.

President Richard Nixon's visit to meet Mao Zedong in Beijing and the establishment of friendly relations between the United States and China further legitimized interest in books about China. No longer was it considered taboo to purchase or read materials that were favorable or even neutral toward China. EB, along with a number of Chinatown publications, including *Chinese Pacific Weekly*, *San Francisco Journal*, and *Chinese Voice*, represented the new cultural current that challenged the hold of the conservative right-wing establishment. Ever since World War II the Kuomintang

(KMT) and the Chinese Anti-Communist League had monitored the content of books and newspapers sold in the Chinese community. Boycott and intimidation were sometimes used against newspapers and bookstores that were not in line with the established conservative viewpoint. During the 1950s vendors of the progressive *China Daily News*, based in New York City, were physically assaulted by KMT-paid goons. In San Francisco Chinatown both *Chinese Pacific Weekly* and *Chinese World* were threatened by the KMT because their articles were considered oppositional. This atmosphere of intimidation was now changing, and EB took part in opening up the new cultural and political climate.

The bookstore functioned at two levels. It attempted to move from amateurish to professional bookselling, and it tried to establish itself as a political entity to propagate the Asian American movement. Some staff were paid; others were volunteers, often local college students who wanted more contact with the community. A manager of the English section and later a Chinese-section manager were added to run day-to-day operations. Some staff discussions involved the technicalities of running a business, but an ongoing point of contention was the store's political direction, including its very mission and whether the selling of less political titles (e.g., those on martial arts, culture, and language learning) should be continued. The store had been reaching out to the Asian American movement and to the "average" person on the street, but it would eventually move toward becoming more "politically correct."

The organization that oversaw bookstore direction was Wei Min She (WMS), "Organization for the People." WMS was a collective that emerged shortly after ACC. As ACC members and a group called Gung Hoc She began to meet regarding consolidation of community work, ACC members included some former UC Berkeley AAPA members, SF State College students, Merritt Community College students, and Chinatown residents. Gung Hoc She comprised foreign-born UC Berkeley and Stanford University students interested in community work and China politics.

WMS emerged as an anti-imperialist organization based in the Chinese American community. Its members were involved in various areas of community work, including labor organizing, community health care, student organizing, housing, ACC operations, U.S.-China friendship, publication of the *Wei Min Bao* newspaper, and EB. Work areas elected representatives to a leadership steering committee that discussed general policy decisions and coordinated them for further discussion at the committee level. WMS members attended several meetings a day in addition to performing their political work area tasks. Many non-WMS members also worked volunteer bookstore shifts that allowed them to participate on a limited level. Alan Chin, chairman of Chinatown–North Beach Youth Council, was one such person.

In 1975 the U.S. left as a whole was in debate over party building and establishing a single political direction. WMS politically aligned with one of a number of national organizations that sought to build the next vanguard political party. Similar discussions were taking place throughout the Asian American movement. This new direction took its toll on the grassroots organizational work and narrowed EB's customer base. Political disagreement among the bookstore staff resulted in resignations and ousters. The narrowing did not occur overnight; many customers continued to request a broad range of titles, including new works on Asian American history and books from China. Still, less attention went to the broader base of customers and more to establishing the correct political line.

Further, the 1977 eviction of all commercial and residential tenants from the International Hotel had devastating financial and political ramifications. EB had been paying $200 per month rent at 840 Kearny Street and paid $2,000 per month at its new location at 17 Brenham Place (now Walter U. Lum Place). The new landlord was tai chi chuan master Guo Lien-ying, who was a customer of EB and favored normalization of relations with China. Master Guo was representative of the realignments in Chinatown politics. Even though he was a member of the KMT and a former Taiwanese congressman, he was open to renting to EB. The new location was on the site of a former mortuary adjacent to Master Guo's studio. There were two stories and a basement where bodies of the deceased had been prepared for burial. To meet the higher rent, EB sublet the upper living quarters

1973. Priscilla Eng-Wong assisting customer. Note the copy of *Taishu Newspaper*, a Japanese American political newspaper. Attached to the back wall are revolutionary posters from throughout the third world. (Steve Louie photograph)

to an immigrant family. The bookstore itself was located on the main floor of the former casket display area.

The International Hotel evictions also made political organizing more difficult in the Chinatown-Manilatown community. The ACC had a smaller space in the lobby of the new EB. The sitting area for the elderly Chinese men was much smaller, though it did open out toward Portsmouth Square Park. This was very different from the previous space provided for community residents to organize labor disputes, youth programs, and food distribution. The only positive to the new location was that customers from out of town were now able to park their cars in the Portsmouth Square garage and walk directly into the bookstore.

In 1977 EB took a political position critical of the Chinese leadership and the post-Mao governmental policies leading toward the restoration of capitalism in China. The changes in China after Mao's death and the arrest of the Gang of Four leadership led WMS, ACC, and EB to de-emphasize China as the ideal. This was a difficult decision because it alienated customers who held more nationalist allegiances toward China. It also meant the breakdown of relations with many in the U.S.-China friendship movement. The bookstore continued to operate, but its direction was even more ambiguous, its base smaller, and its community future uncertain. Many of its staffers moved on to other jobs and other forms of political activity.

Everybody's Bookstore closed in 1980. The Guo family donated the building to Chinese for Affirmative Action, which has continued at this location to advance causes of social justice. In 1978 others influenced by EB began Eastwind Books & Arts, Inc. According to one former EB staffer, Eastwind filled the void created by the "new" direction of EB, which by this time was de-emphasizing the sale of broadbased books about China and Asian America and was concentrating more on political doctrine. Eastwind Books & Arts opened a Chinese-language bookstore on Stockton Street and later an Asian American bookstore on Vallejo Street in San Francisco. In 1982 Eastwind opened a store on the site of the former Yenan Bookstore in Berkeley. The Berkeley store was sold in 1996 by its new Hong Kong owners but continues today as the independently operated Eastwind Books of Berkeley, of which this author is a part owner.

Everybody's Bookstore was in operation when no other space tended to Asian American literature. It provided infor-

1971. International Hotel manager Joe Diones, who managed the property and collected rent from all the residential and commercial tenants. (Photograph courtesy of Steve Louie)

mation about revolutionary China when there were no other outlets. It was an integral part of the U.S.-China friendship and normalization movement when the taboo on this topic was being openly challenged. It provided the education resource space that its founders had hoped for. It provided books for researchers, scholars, students, and thinkers to help develop further understanding about the world. It provided important support to the International Hotel tenants in defending Manilatown against developers who had their sights on Chinatown as well. The bookstore contributed immensely to improving the life of the Chinese American community.

NOTES

1. The term "third world" was used to denote the colonized or formerly colonized countries of Asia, Africa, and Latin America. Third world people in the United States are descendants of residents of those countries. They have shared a common third world experience of colonization, discrimination, and segregation.
2. See Jeanie Dere, "A Wei Min Sister Remembers," this volume, p. 64.

Scenes from the Baodiao Movement in the United States

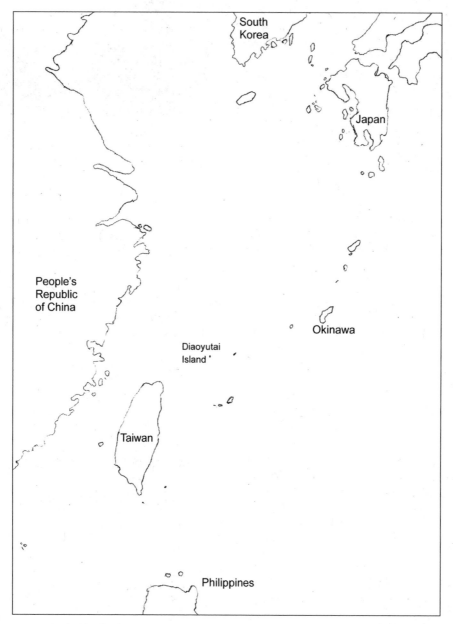

Diaoyutai Islands, also known as the Senkaku Islands, a group of uninhabited islands within seven square kilometers (1,700 acres). Their ownership is disputed. (After *Atlas of Maps of China* [*Zhongguo dituce*], Beijing: China Map Publishing Co. [*Zhongguo ditu chubanshe*], 2002[1999]. Courtesy Anna Naruta.)

Some 600 Chinese-American students picketed the Japanese Consulate and Japan Air Lines offices in New York. The protest is over ownership of Tiao Yu Tai where oil was discovered recently. (Sunday News photo)

New York Baodiao protest. (Sunday News photo, *East/West*, February 10, 1971. Courtesy Him Mark Lai.)

Tracking Baodiao
Diaspora, Sovereignty, and Chinese American Resistance
Chih-ming Wang

Images relating to the political activism around Diaoyutai (the Baodiao movement) are found in "Scenes from the Baodiao Movement in the United States," this volume, page 128, and Jeanie Dere, "A Wei Min Sister Remembers," this volume, page 64.

On June 10, 2008, the Taiwanese fishing boat *Lianhehao* was rammed and sunk by a Japanese patrol ship in the disputed waters of the Diaoyutai Islands, known in Japanese as the Senkaku Islands. The captain and two crew members were imprisoned immediately but soon returned to Taiwan after a series of protests and diplomatic negotiations. The incident made few waves in Japan but caused a heated debate in Taiwan. Newly elected president Ma Yinjiu was even asked by the parliament to reassert his determination to protect the Diaoyutai "at the cost of war." The demand was clearly hyperbolic; however, this incident invoked complex memories of the Protecting Diaoyutai movement (referred to hereafter as the Baodiao movement), in which Ma had been an active participant while studying at Harvard Law School in the 1970s.[1] In this essay I argue that the Baodiao movement in 1971, while initiated as diasporic student activism regarding a disputed territory, in fact had important connections with the Asian American movement and served as a third worldist critique of the capitalism and imperialism plaguing the Chinese people on both sides of the Pacific. It shows the neglected importance of student migration to the history of Chinese American resistance and gestures to a transnational reconfiguration of Asian America.

Thus, while Ma's experience of studying abroad seems to provide only insignificant biographical information, it touches on the trans/national character of the Baodiao movement, which is of concern to Chinese American history. In addition, the controversy concerning his holding of a green card adds an intriguing Asian American spin to Baodiao as a transpacific student movement that is often lost to the Asian American memory.[2] Had Ma stayed in the United States after graduation, he would have likely become a Chinese American professional, possibly a lawyer or a professor of law. In fact, one would be surprised to know how many Chinese American elites were once active Baodiao participants, that some of them were radical, and that most of them have since become cosmopolitan, with multiple ties to Hong Kong, Taiwan, and China.[3] Thus, that Ma Yinjiu is perceived as a representative Baodiao activist indicates that the Baodiao history and politics we are told is only the partial truth. The Baodiao movement was entangled in a complicated history that brings together Asian America and Asia in the nexus of imperialist wars, nationalist aspirations, and nascent identity formations.

Diaoyutai may be an insignificant rock in terms of world geography, yet it was—and still is—a volatile border space that is penetrated by contending nationalist ambitions and attached to unstable identities and cultural imaginaries.[4] It not only invokes complex memories of China-Taiwan-Japan relations coded in a history of colonial aggression, but also urges us to reconsider shifting U.S.-Asia relations and the Asian American politics of the Cold War era. By revisiting the Baodiao movement in the early 1970s as a critical juncture in the history of Chinese American resistance, this essay argues that diasporic identifications and demands for national sovereignty were critical concerns of Asian American activism. It also contends that Asia and America are not independent political entities, each with its own uncontaminated history, but mutually constitutive conditions, though discrepantly infiltrated spaces, as represented in the transpacific crossings of Chinese students and intellectuals. While the Diaoyutai Islands clearly do not belong to the United States, the territorial dispute was initiated by the U.S. decision to return them to Japan in 1969; while Baodiao appears on the surface to be a story of Chinese nationalism, it took place in the United States in the contexts of the revolutionary 1960s, when civil rights and anti-imperialist movements were powerful intellectual forces that inspired both U.S.-born Asian Americans and foreign-born Chinese students. To track Baodiao in the edges of America and Asia thus is also an attempt to reconsider the politics of Asian American transnationality today.

TRACKING BAODIAO:
A HISTORY OF BIFURCATION

Geographically Diaoyutai refers to a cluster of eight uninhabitable isles located from longitude 123°25′ to 124°45′ east and from latitude 25°40′ to 26°00′ north, at the eastern edge of the East China Sea, between Taiwan, Okinawa, and the Chinese mainland. The largest isle, named Diaoyu Dao, or Diaoyutai, has an area of only five square kilometers. These islets were little known until the reported discovery of natural resources beneath their seabed in 1968. The discovery excited economic interests of countries including Japan, Korea, the Republic of China (Taiwan), and the United States, which were interested in conducting a joint exploration of the area.[5] The possibility of claiming an extended economic zone on the continental shelf from these isles, coupled with the entangled historical relations of Japan, China, and the United States, made Diaoyutai a significant and very volatile border space.[6]

Diaoyutai became controversial when Japan acted to "legitimize" its sovereignty claim in May 1969 by installing cement poles on Diaoyutai and patrolling the nearby waters. Six months later, the Nixon-Sato Joint Declaration proclaimed that the Diaoyutai Islands, which were considered part of the Ryukyu Islands, occupied by the United States since 1945,[7] would be returned to Japan in 1972, a decision that favored Japan's claim. In response to Japan's proactive moves, supported by the United States, four civilians from Taiwan sailed to Diaoyutai and planted an ROC flag there in September 1970. It was quickly taken down and reportedly torn apart by Japanese police. On September 16, two fishing boats from Yilan, Taiwan, were driven away by the Japanese Self-Defense Force while fishing in waters near the Diaoyutai Islands. About the same time, the U.S. Department of State announced that based on the principle of "residual sovereignty," the United States would return these islands to Japan, as agreed in the Nixon-Sato negotiation, although the United States also maintained that territorial disputes were to be settled by the parties involved. Regardless of the eruption of Baodiao protests in Taiwan, Hong Kong, and North America in early 1971, the U.S. decision was put into effect by the Ryukyu Reversion Agreement in June 1971.

The story of the Baodiao movement is one of bifurcation, although it is usually recounted in a linear fashion and within a nationalistic frame.[8] The story begins with the territorial dispute outlined above, then zooms in to a series of protests, government responses, and left-leaning radicalizations, and finally ends with the movement's transition from innocent patriotism to a campaign for future unification. It is often understood as a story of failure.

The Baodiao movement started in mid-December 1970 at Princeton University, where a group of Chinese students, led by James Lee and Shen Ping, organized the first Baodiao Action Committee and publicized the dispute in a pamphlet called "What You Need to Know about Tiao Yu Tai." The pamphlet was sent to other university campuses via personal contacts and existing networks that had been established through such student publications as the *Big Wind* (*Dafeng*) and the *Science Monthly* (*Kexue yuekan*). The New York Baodiao Action Committee, which included a hundred or so East Coast participants, was quickly formed after the Princeton

meeting, and a decision was made to hold demonstrations and issue a manifesto to express the students' position and concerns. The Baodiao manifesto—declared in the New York demonstration on January 30, 1971—consists of four basic tenets:

1. Opposition to the revival of Japanese militarism
2. Determination to safeguard Chinese sovereignty over the Diaoyutai Islands
3. Opposition to the American support of Japan's claim
4. Opposition to any joint development in the area before Chinese sovereignty over these islands is recognized

The manifesto set the early keynote of the Baodiao movement, which focused more on the American and Japanese governments as targets of protest and avoided criticism of the Kuomintang (KMT) in Taiwan, although not every Baodiao participant was a supporter of the KMT government. In the meantime, Baodiao action committees emerged on university campuses across the United States, and the decision to hold public demonstrations was supported by Chinese students in the Midwest and on the West Coast. At the same time, students in Taiwan and Hong Kong responded to the cause with their own activism.

The first public demonstrations broke out in January 1971 in seven major cities: New York, Washington, Chicago, San Francisco, Los Angeles, Seattle, and Honolulu. According to James Lee, about five hundred Chinese students in San Francisco and about three hundred in Los Angeles participated in the first demonstrations on January 29. In New York more than one thousand students, intellectuals, and professionals from thirty colleges in seventeen areas along the East Coast marched from Hammarskjold Plaza, across from the United Nations, to the Japanese consulate general at Forty-Second Street near Second Avenue.[9] Interestingly, no national flags were displayed in the demonstrations; slogans and songs were also carefully chosen so as to present a uniform voice opposing Japanese militarism and upholding the "Chinese people" as the sole subject of identification. In fact, before the demonstrations, student activists had debated amongst themselves and agreed that the movement's position should be "more nationalist than political," to protect patriotic solidarity from being splintered by competing ideological positions reflecting the different opinions on the KMT regime. The New York demonstration consisted mostly of Chinese students from Hong Kong and Taiwan despite the unexpected presence of I Wor Kuen, a leftist Asian American youth organization based in New York Chinatown.

In contrast, the demonstration in San Francisco had a more diverse constituency and took a more radical stance. The date of that demonstration, January 29, was deliberately selected to resonate with the student movement of December 9, 1935, in Beijing, which was launched by the Communists to protest Japanese aggression. The date revealed the left-leaning tendencies of the San Francisco Baodiao activists. The strong presence of Cantonese-speaking Chinese Americans from

San Francisco Chinatown, which was undertaking struggles against KMT-affiliated establishments, also gave the demonstration a more critical orientation. The Berkeley Baodiao Action Committee in fact delivered its own manifesto and called for support from Chinatown and the Chinese American community. Unlike those in other cities, the protestors in San Francisco marched to the ROC consulate general to express their grievances against the government's inability to defend Diaoyutai. Wang Yongzhong noticed that the San Francisco demonstration also challenged the establishments supported by the KMT and enhanced the political consciousness of overseas Chinese.[10] Indeed, the Berkeley Baodiao group's publication, the *War Report* (*Zhan bao*), expressed criticisms of Chinatown institutions, such as the Chinese Consolidated Benevolent Association and *Youth China Morning News* (*Shaonian zhongguo chenbao*). *East/West: The Chinese-American Journal*, a San Francisco Chinatown–based weekly, suggested that the Chinatown establishments were an impediment to the Baodiao movement because the Chinatown community was largely controlled by an older generation that had close ties with the KMT.[11] Baodiao patriotism unavoidably hit on the vexing questions of national allegiance and political loyalty, with Taiwan, China, and the United States forming a complicated triangle of diaspora politics.

While the January demonstrations caught the KMT's attention, the KMT did little to secure the Diaoyutai Islands. Instead it sent envoys to the United States, hoping to placate the students, who had been feeling frustrated by the KMT. Worrying about Communist infiltration into the movement, the KMT resorted to political persuasion and scare tactics to suppress the movement, which only antagonized the students. Therefore, the second demonstrations were held in San Francisco and Washington, D.C., on April 9 and 10, 1971, two months before the signing of the Ryukyu Reversion Agreement. They marked the apex of the movement, but they were also the last sparks of such activism.

More than two thousand Chinese students and professors swarmed to Washington, D.C., to participate in arguably the largest demonstration ever held by Chinese in the United States.[12] These protestors marched to the U.S. Department of State, the ROC consulate, and the Japanese embassy. But in each place, their demands were bluntly rejected, leaving the students helpless, upset, and enraged. The San Francisco demonstration, moreover, was sabotaged by KMT-related personnel, who ran into the mass meeting to disrupt the speeches, tear down audio equipment and cameras, and strike the speakers. Before the rally, the KMT harassed pro-Baodiao students and dissuaded them from attending the protest; it also labeled the Berkeley activists, Liu Daren, Guo Songfen, and Cao Zhanmei, as "Maoist bandits" and forbade them from returning to Taiwan.[13] These sabotages represented the KMT government's political conservatism and its tremendous fear of the "Red menace," the legacy of the Chinese civil war and Cold War ideology. *East/West* later covered this story on the front page, suggesting that

the Baodiao movement had fractured along political lines. The reporters relayed ROC Consul Zhou Tong's comments that the Berkeley Baodiao group was "manipulated by a few ambitious people who had seized this patriotic movement to create anti-government sentiment" and that the Bay Area Chinese community should not be swayed.[14] This patriotic movement consequently ended with a smear campaign that generated in the overseas student community despair about and contempt for the KMT. Out of this frustration a question emerged: "What is the alternative?"

It is generally agreed that after the second demonstrations, the Baodiao movement hit its nadir and was soon transformed into a unification campaign. The students' attempts to pressure the KMT government to secure the Diaoyutai Islands failed, thus encouraging some activists to turn to the PRC in hopes of blocking Japan. Risking their careers and status, several Baodiao activists visited China in 1972 and 1973.[15] They were received warmly by Prime Minister Zhou Enlai and returned to the United States with reports on China's conditions and progress. They held a series of lectures and organized discussion groups on different university campuses, gradually transforming the movement into study groups on contemporary China to advocate both the PRC's legitimacy as the representative government of China and the agenda of future unification. This access to contemporary China had important effects on the generation of Baodiao students and intellectuals. Some students, such as Liu Daren and Guo Songfen, gave up pursuing their PhDs and went to work for the Chinese delegation at the UN; a few students even abandoned their lives and careers in the United States and returned to China to "serve the people."[16]

In the meantime, ping-pong diplomacy had broken the ice between China and the United States and led to Richard Nixon's historic visit in 1972; the U.S. Senate also abolished the Taiwan Resolution, which had been used to authorize U.S. military protection of Taiwan since the Korean War. As the PRC reasserted its presence in the international society, the KMT was presented with a legitimacy crisis and the fate of international isolation, especially after the termination of U.S.-Taiwan diplomatic relations in 1979. Uniform patriotism could not prevent the Baodiao movement from splintering into conflicting ideological positions and national imaginaries.

For many students Baodiao also represented a moment of discovery. The discovery of a "new" China not only initiated a radical break from the KMT historiography but also engendered critical inquiries about Taiwan's subjectivity and sovereignty. After 1972 it became apparent that the crux of the matter was not to which country Diaoyutai belonged but how and why it had become a disputed territory. The KMT's inability to protect the Diaoyutai Islands not only produced its legitimacy crisis in Taiwan and the international community but also revealed the perilous Cold War conditions that arrested Taiwan. As a U.S. protectorate, the KMT regime was in no position to challenge U.S. decisions, and its authoritarian rule and anti-Communist ideology had only adverse effects on the people of Taiwan and China.

The students' exposure to the Civil Rights and antiwar movements of the 1960s and 1970s, furthermore, challenged their belief in the capitalist values and the integrity of American democracy. Chinese American historian Shih-shan Tsai even suggests that "it was the Americanization of foreign-born Chinese students that inspired them to take to the streets."[17] Guo Jizhou conceives of the Baodiao movement as the emergence of radical consciousness; its objective was not obtaining political power but reflecting political consciousness and the intellectuals' class identification.[18] Hence Baodiao's turn to the left was not merely the result of the KMT's political incompetence and the students' nationalist identification with the PRC. More importantly, it was a conscious internationalist attempt at overcoming the Cold War determinations. It is thus more productive to situate the movement in the 1960s revolutionary contexts that had in effect informed the politics surrounding Baodiao.

WAGING WAR AGAINST IMPERIALISM: *ZHAN BAO*

The linear narrative provided above hinges on leftist radicalization as the turning point of the Baodiao movement, which renders clear the PRC-ROC opposition, the contradictory desires for unification and independence in Taiwan and the diaspora, and the ideological struggles of the Cold War, juxtaposed with the "hot wars" in Vietnam and the United States along racial and geopolitical lines. While the immediate goal of Baodiao remained nationalistic, the politics articulated via Baodiao actually referenced a more internationalist agenda. The Baodiao movement not only responded to the demands of sovereignty embedded in the memories of inter-Asia and transpacific conflicts but also reflected and reacted to the ideological environment of the time and place. *Zhan bao*, published by the Berkeley Baodiao group in 1971, represented a third world anti-imperialist critique that enabled the transpacific rearticulation of Chinese America.

The first issue of *Zhan bao* appeared after the first Baodiao demonstrations and declared an oppositional stance against the general consensus on the nonpartisan patriotic position. The *Zhan bao* collective strongly believed that the movement should prioritize politics over nationalism because the Diaoyutai dispute was the result of Japanese militarism, not of irreconcilable national hatred. Nationalism, they believed, could not resolve the dispute, and intellectuals should not advocate national discrimination. Rather, it was in the mutual interests of both China and Japan to halt the revival of Japanese militarism.[19] This is a perceptive analysis, fully conscious of the danger of narrow nationalism that borders on racism. It also shows that the Berkeley group understood the importance of building the movement on a larger political basis. The first issue of *Zhan bao* includes a speech by Japanese Americans that condemns Japan for "acts of international robbery against other Asian people" and the United States for "criminal action in Southeast Asia."[20] It also reprints a speech by Franz Schurmann, a UC Berkeley professor of history, that speaks of the Diaoyutai incident as an act of militarism and economic imperialism, again linking it with U.S. aggression in Southeast Asia. In addition to updates on the movement, it includes critical commentaries on liberalism, Taiwan independence campaigns, and KMT White Terror tactics in Taiwan and Chinese America. In his speech on the May Fourth Movement, Guo Songfen claims that Chinese students and intellectuals must unite with Chinese, Japanese, and American people in struggles against imperialism. He also urges them to overcome their "political impotence" and join the movement.[21]

The second—and last—issue of *Zhan bao* appeared after the April demonstrations. The editorial argues that the Diaoyutai incident is but "the tip of an iceberg," encouraging Chinese students to look beneath the surface of the territorial dispute. It also claims that a historical turning point has arrived and the students must act as a political collectivity to "declare war against all the vicious and dark forces. . . . Let the overseas students' 'era of war' start from now! Against all the unreasonable establishments, we declare war! Against all the practices and policies that violate the interests of Chinese people, we declare war! Against all the lackeys hiding in the dark corners, we declare war! Against all the taboos, hypocritical faces, self-deprecating mentalities, idols hung on the walls, and abstract 'truth' stored in the ivory tower, we declare war!"[22]

This position is both militant and revolutionary. Such a stance is further expressed in the proposal to organize a student court of justice—an unmediated diasporic public sphere open to all Chinese people at home and abroad to engage in ideological debates and political criticism—so as to break through the KMT domination in Taiwan and the overseas communities. The student court was intended to denounce unethical international treaties and world systems, irresponsible regimes, and imperialism in all forms; to create a global network for distributing accurate information; and to construct a "knowledge front" across the Pacific to defend the rights of Chinese people. In the name of "truth, people, and history," the *Zhan bao* collective found the language for struggle and realized that struggle must begin with self-criticism by examining diasporic intellectuals, for their pursuits of knowledge and individual successes had detached them from the nation that nurtured them. The war, ironically, was waged against Chinese students and intellectuals themselves.

The emblematic piece in the second issue is an article written by Guo Songfen entitled "Defeat the Bloc of Comprador Doctorates."[23] Using the pen name Luo Longmai, he ruthlessly criticizes overseas students, likening them to "pimps" of U.S. hegemony for allowing Taiwan to exist as a semicolonial state. He begins the article with an allegorical image of Taiwan as a belle raped by U.S. military, economic, and cultural forces, and the KMT as the shamefaced parent who sold her daughter into sexual exploitation in exchange for economic prosperity, political stability, and national security. In this extended metaphor of transpacific political economy, the overseas students are compradors, for they transported the American influences to Taiwan and gained for themselves invaluable cultural capital as a result. In doing so, they have served the interests of America rather than their own people and country.

With this stunning analogy Guo launches into an analysis of how, historically, foreign finance and cultural capital had been introduced to China to curb the growth of national industries; how that had only benefited a small sector of the national bourgeoisie; and how such compradorism is specifically tied to the U.S. military presence in East Asia. Thus, Baodiao's demand for independence not only challenged the legitimacy of the KMT rule but also surfaced America's Cold War violence against Asian people. Paraphrasing Charles de Gaulle's words, Guo asserts that "World War II did not end in Asia," because U.S. economic and military powers still hovered above Asia to grab resources and to expand market shares through military maneuvers. With anger and regret, Guo writes, "In the Vietnam War, Taiwan had not only served as a base of US military supply . . . but also functioned as a brothel for US military personnel."[24] This analysis of Taiwan as a semicolonial state dependent on U.S. hegemony is representative of the third world consciousness that was radicalizing youths all over the world.

This perspective, furthermore, enabled Guo and his *Zhan bao* comrades to challenge the belief in the "neutrality of knowledge" that many overseas students had maintained. Guo argues: "'Objectivity' and 'neutrality' are the pretexts of 'do-not-sing-the-opposite-tune.' [Under these doctrines,] social science becomes a troop of knowledge reserve and loses its function of guidance and criticism. . . . For third world countries and developing nations, including the oppressed minorities in the United States, especially the blacks and Asians, the social science they need is not the social science that describes and explains the status quo, but one that criticizes and resists the status quo."[25]

For Guo the "objectivity" upheld by American social science in the 1950s and 1960s was in every way a bourgeois, subjective state of mind. Unlike the revolutionary blacks and other Asians who were challenging and transforming established forms of knowledge through the ethnic studies movement, Chinese students in the United States were still mesmerized by such beliefs and tried to import them wholesale to Taiwan as gospels of truth. U.S. cultural colonization of Taiwan was thus facilitated and fortified by this historic bloc of comprador doctorates, who willingly enslaved themselves to perpetuate U.S. dominance. Guo's critical reflection on the subjectivity of diasporic intellectuals indicates that the "study abroad" movement had set many Chinese on a trajectory of Americanization. By studying abroad, Chinese students had become "Americanized" and lost touch with their own national roots. And by becoming loyal disciples of America, they had forfeited their intellectual responsibilities in order to pursue individualistic success and had become transpacific bridges for U.S. military and cultural expansion. They had come to embody the uneven, hierarchal relations of Asia and America.

Zhan bao did not only wage war on imperialist lackeys and existing establishments. More crucially, it articulated an epistemic break in reassessing the conditions of Taiwan. Specifically, it kicked the intellectuals out of their comfortable corners of nationalism and compelled them to confront the specter of America that was haunting them every step of the way along the transpacific ladder towards bourgeois prosperity. What *Zhan bao* revealed, to many people's horror, is that overseas students are actually Americanized Asians who wholeheartedly embrace America and its interests as their own, with or without American passports. This critical self-analysis is terrifying and disturbing because it not only indicates the successful U.S. "colonization of the mind" but also points to existing semicolonial conditions in which Chinese intellectual subjectivity is produced. The chilling fact is not that America is our enemy. It is that the United States has been deeply embedded within ourselves, that America is *us*.[26]

CONCLUSION: TOWARD ASIA/AMERICA

Although the Baodiao movement is generally regarded as a form of diasporic Chinese student activism, it is important to remember that Asian Americans also participated in it, albeit taking a minor role. Likewise, before and after the Baodiao movement many Baodiao activists worked in the Chinese American community and joined the Asian American movement. Wei Min She, an Asian American anti-imperialist organization active in San Francisco Chinatown from 1971 to 1975, consisted of both Asian American youths and foreign students from Hong Kong, Singapore, and Malaysia. The Berkeley Baodiao group connected up with Wei Min She, which helped them print the two issues of *Zhan bao*. I Wor Kuen and the Red Guard Party both participated in the Baodiao rallies in New York and San Francisco. As early as 1969 the Red Guards had already worked with Chinese students in the Bay Area to jointly hold a May Fourth commemoration and campaign for renaming Portsmouth Square Sun Yat-sen Park.[27] The AAA (Asian Americans for Action), a civil rights group led by Yuri Kochiyama, also expressed support for the Chinese claim of the Diaoyutai Islands, although it was concerned about the racism and jingoism rampant in the New York rally. The Basement Workshop organized by Chinese students in New York, which published *Bridge* magazine in 1971, also invited non-Chinese Asian American activists to join its panel discussion on Chinese student activism.[28] Asian American Studies scholars, such as Peter Kwong at Hunter College and Gordon Chang at Stanford University, were also Baodiao activists; Chang himself returned to China as a member of the Baodiao group. From this perspective, Baodiao was more than Chinese student activism, because it was conscious of the Asian/American divide and wanted to overcome it by addressing national issues from an internationalist perspective.

Zhan bao's internationalist critique of American imperialism enables us to resituate the Baodiao movement in the contexts of both third world politics and the Asian American movement. Its alliance with third world Asian and American minority issues indicates that the Diaoyutai dispute was not just a provincial Taiwanese concern; its emphasis on national sovereignty actually cut to the core of the anti-imperialist campaign located squarely in the blurred boundaries between Asia and America. In effect it was these struggles that created Asian America as a transpacific political space. To remember Baodiao in the context of the global anti-imperialist campaign suggests an imagination of "Asia/America" as a critical nexus of diaspora politics and Asian American cultural nationalism, in which the politics of alliance and solidarity had informed and been affected by multicultural claims of identity and ultraright nationalism.[29] My emphasis on the Baodiao left's critical reflection on diasporic intellectual subjectivity, moreover, articulates Asia/America as a both transnational and national space of conjunctures, flows, and contradictions of identities, ideas, and feelings, which intersected with the formation of a panethnic Asian American community. It also demonstrates that Asia/America actually was shaped by contending historical forces, was created as nodes of alliances and solidarity, and at times intervened in the transpacific movement of memories and knowledge.

If the 1960s constituted a radical break from the world of capitalism with a firm refusal of imperialism, the Baodiao movement, in its own bifurcated nationalist trajectory, manufactured a lucid rupture in the consciousness of the overseas students. They painfully realized that the victory over Japan in 1945 could not guarantee the end of national humiliation and that the security provided by the United States did not provide assurance of national sovereignty. The Baodiao students and intellectuals struggled not only against foreign invasion but also for the ideal of national independence, which has to be aligned with other third world and minority struggles. In their quest for territorial integrity and national independence, the Baodiao intellectuals turned Chinese America into a critical diaspora that seeks liberation from both the KMT's extraterritorial control and the imperial unconscious of America, while remaining loyal to a Chinese and Taiwanese national imaginary.[30] Their transpacific engagements in both professional and sociopolitical fields also changed the landscape of Chinese America, as marked by the shifting relations of the United States to Taiwan and China. Although the Diaoyutai Islands today continue to be disputed territory, the Baodiao movement of early 1971 remains an important chapter in the history of Chinese American resistance that allows us to envision a critical collectivity against irrevocable bifurcations and a transnational movement that is dead serious about the nation.

ACKNOWLEDGEMENTS

This essay was originally presented at the 2005 Chinese American Studies Conference in San Francisco (the proceedings of which are published as a special 2007 volume of *Chinese America: History & Perspectives—The Journal of the Chinese Historical Society of America*). I cordially thank Professor Russell Jeung for inviting me to submit it to the CHSA journal. I also thank Professor Te-hsing Shan for his perceptive comments and for introducing me to Peter Wang's book, and Jeff Cuvilier for his assistance in polishing this essay.

NOTES

1. Ma Yinjiu became interested in the Baodiao movement in Taiwan. The movement in North America had already waned by the time he arrived in the United States in 1974. However, he did join a pro-KMT Baodiao group called Aimeng (Free Chinese Association of the United States) and wrote a dissertation on the Diaoyutai dispute from the viewpoint of international maritime laws.
2. During the 2008 Taiwanese presidential election the opposing party attacked Ma Yinjiu and his family for being greencard holders. This became a controversial issue because Taiwanese government officials are not allowed to hold multiple passports. Whereas Ma argued that his green card, for which he had applied when studying in the United States, had been annulled, the opposing party used it to question his loyalty to Taiwan.
3. The Baodiao activists included renowned Chinese American elites Changlin Tian, late president of UC Berkeley; S. B. Wu, former lieutenant governor of Delaware; and Yang Zhengning, Nobel Prize winner in physics, just to name a few.
4. Mirana May Szeto describes Diaoyutai as a "petit objet a" of Chinese nationalism. She writes: "It is a little piece of the undeniably *real* materiality of the colonial and national experience that persists in the national memory, symbolic orders and cultural imaginaries of Chinese people. It is a leftover bit of the *REAL* traumatic experience of colonial invasion and occupation. Moreover, the national and cultural subject's form of attachment to the *petit objet a* defines and organizes the subject's relation to its nation and culture." Szeto, *The Radical Itch: Rethinking Nationalism in Contemporary Chinese Societies* (PhD dissertation, UCLA, 2004), 166.
5. See Victor Li, "China and Off-Shore Oil: The Tiao-yu Tai Dispute," *Stanford Journal of International Studies* 10 (1975): 143–62.
6. See Victor Li, "Sovereignty at Sea: China and the Law of the Sea Conference," *Stanford Journal of International Studies* 15 (1979): 232.
7. The Ryukyu Islands, referred to in Japanese as Ryukyu-retto or Nansei-shoto (the southwest archipelago), are located southwest of Japan in the western Pacific. The chain stretches about 650 miles (1,050 kilometers) between Taiwan and Japan, separating the East China Sea from the Philippine Sea. The Ryukyus are composed of three principal groups: from north to south, the Amami Islands (part of Kagoshima prefecture),

the Okinawa Islands, and the Sakishima Islands (both part of Okinawa prefecture). Okinawa is the largest and most important island of the Ryukyus. The islands were the site of an ancient independent kingdom that had its capital at Shuri on Okinawa. The kingdom was invaded by the Japanese prince of Satsuma in the seventeenth century and incorporated into the Japanese empire in 1879, but the islands were generally neglected by Japan.

During World War II the Ryukyus were the scene of fierce fighting between U.S. and Japanese forces, with the United States winning control of the islands in 1945. The Ryukyus became a key post of the U.S. Pacific defense perimeter. Though it returned the Ryukyus to Japan in May 1972, the United States retained its military bases there. Since then the campaign to "demilitarize" Okinawa has been a significant issue for Okinawans and the Japanese left; it has also informed the Okinawan identity. See Ronald Y. Nakasone, ed., *Okinawa Diaspora* (Honolulu: University of Hawai'i Press, 2002), especially Nomura Koya's piece, 112–19; and Atsushi Toriyama, "Okinawa's 'Postwar': Some Observations on the Formation of American Military Bases in the Aftermath of Terrestrial Warfare," *Inter-Asia Cultural Studies* 4, no. 3 (2003): 400–418. For the history of the Okinawa problem in Japan-U.S. relations, see Robert D. Eldridge, *The Origins of the Bilateral Okinawa Problem* (New York: Garland, 2001).

8. See Zhang Zhongxun, "Liumei xuesheng baodiao yundong yanjiu" (paper presented at fifth annual conference on the history of Chinese maritime development, Academia Sinica, February 24–25, 1992), and Pei Ran, "Baodiao yundong shuo congtou," *Taiwan yu shijie* [Taiwan and the World] 32 (June 1986): 14–27. Also see Lin Guojong et al., eds., *Chunlei sheng sheng: baodiao yundong sanshi zhounian wenxian xuanji* [Spring thunders: the anthology of the thirtieth anniversary of the Baodiao movement] (Taibei: Renjian, 2001), and the debates between Shui Binghe and Hua Zixu: Shui Binghe, "Huigu 'Diaoyun,'" *Zhishi fenzi* [The Chinese Intellectuals] (Spring 1986): 56–61; Hua Zixu, "Qiru chunmeng liaowuhen?—diaoyun yu tongyun de lingyimian," *Jiushiniandai* [The Nineties] (May 1995): 88–91; Shui Binghe, "Diaoyun yu liusi—jianda Hua Zixu jun," *Jiushiniandai* (June 1995): 106–9; Hua Zixu, "Huohong niandai de guangguailuli—zailun diaoyun," *Jiushiniandai* (July 1995): 101–3; and "Sanlun diaoyun—jieshuyu," *Jiushiniandai* (September 1995): 102–3.

9. James Lee, "The Story of the Tiao Yu Tai Movement," *Bridge* 1, no. 3 (1971): 6.

10. Wang Yongzhong, "Meiyou yingxiong de sueyue" [Years without a hero], *Fengyun de niandai: Baodiao yundong yu liuxue shengya zi huiyi* [The turbulent years: the Baodiao movement and remembrances of studying abroad], ed. Shao Yu-ming (Taibei: Lianjing, 1991), 7.

11. "Tiao Yu Tai Arouses US Chinese Students," *East/West* 5, no. 6 (February 2, 1971): 1.

12. James Lee, "The Story of the Tiao Yu Tai Movement," *Bridge* 1, no. 3 (1971): 7.

13. Ren Xiaoqi, *You ai wu hui: baodiao fengyun yu aimeng the gushi* [Love without regret: the Baodiao movement and the story of the Free Chinese Association of the United States] (Taibei: Fengyun shidai, 1997), 75.

14. "Diaoyutai yundong cheng fenlie xianxiang" [The movement to protect Diaoyutai appears disintegrating], *East/West* 5, no. 15 (April 14, 1971): 1, 18.

15. In 1971 a group of Baodiao student leaders—Li Woyan, Chen Zhili, Chen Hengci, Wang Zhengfang, and Wang Chunsh-

eng—visited China and met with Prime Minister Zhou Enlai. More groups visited China between 1972 and 1975. Wang Zhengfang, also known as Peter Wang, has written about his meeting with Zhou Enlai and his Baodiao experience. See Wang, *Wo zhe ren hua duo* [I am a talkative person] (Taibei: Jiuge, 2008), 81–142. Also see Chu Hongjun, "Sanshiwu nian qian huaren jingying de baodiao meng" [The Baodiao dream of Chinese elites thirty-five years ago], *Zhishi he shehui luntan* [Forum on knowledge and society], April 28, 2008, *http://www.fokas.com.tw/news/newslist.php?id=1869* (accessed July 20, 2008).

16. To many students' dismay later, however, the PRC, despite its assertions of territorial sovereignty, in fact shelved the Diaoyutai dispute in 1978 to prevent a regional conflict with Japan.

17. Shih-shan Henry Tsai, *The Chinese Experience in America* (Bloomington: Indiana University Press, 1986), 175.

18. See Guo Jizhou, *Qishi niandai Taiwan zuoyi yundong* [Taiwan left-wing movement in the 1970s] (Taibei: Xiachao, 1999), 17–42.

19. *Zhan bao* (February 15, 1971): 15–16.

20. Ibid., 50.

21. Ibid., 58.

22. *Zhan bao* (May 1971): 26.

23. Liu Daren, twenty-five years later, revealed that the article was written by Guo Songfen, his dearest comrade and fellow novelist. Sadly, Guo passed away in 2005 at the age of sixty-seven. See Liu, *Wode Zhongguo* [My China] (Taibei: Huangguan, 2000), 78.

24. Luo Longmai, "Dadao boshi maiban jieji" [Defeat the bloc of comprador doctorates], *Zhan Bao* (May 1971): 43.

25. Ibid., 46.

26. Kuan-hsing Chen also made a similar point. See Chen, "Missile Internationalism," *Orientations: Mapping Studies in the Asian Diaspora*, ed. Kandice Chuh and Karen Shimakawa (Durham: Duke University Press, 2001), 172–86, and "America in East Asia: The Club 51 Syndrome," *New Left Review* 12 (November–December 2001): 73–87.

27. See Alex Hing, interview by Steve Yip, in *Legacy to Liberation*, ed. Fred Ho, Carolyn Antonio, Diane Fujino, and Steve Yip (San Francisco: AK Press, 2000), 286–89.

28. The panel discussion had the rather provocative title "Chinese Student: Political Eunuch." It featured such speakers as Frank Ching and Peter Chow, both involved in the editorial work of *Bridge*; Peter Kwong; and Wei-Ming Tu, who was later known for his "Cultural China" thesis. Rose Pak, Korean American, and Um Soung, Cambodian, were the two non-Chinese Asian American activists at the panel. Pak was one of the managing editors of *Bridge*. The panel discussion was published in the inaugural issue of *Bridge* in 1971.

29. The concept of "Asia/America" is borrowed from David Palumbo-Liu, who argues that "Asia/America resides *in transit*, as a point of reference on the horizon that is part of *both* a 'minority' identity and a 'majority' identity." See Palumbo-Liu, *Asian/American: Historical Crossings of a Racial Frontier* (Stanford, Calif.: Stanford University Press, 1999), 5.

30. Ling-chi Wang coined the term "structure of dual domination" to describe how Chinese America is affected by both the pressure to assimilate in the United States and extraterritorial control from the ROC and later the PRC. See Wang, "The Structure of Dual Domination: Toward a Paradigm for the Study of the Chinese Diaspora in the US," *Amerasia* 21, nos. 1 and 2 (1995): 149–69.

Maurice H. Chuck and the *San Francisco Journal*

Promoting U.S.-China Friendship and Asian American Issues

Xiong Guohua

TRANSLATION BY DIANA HONG
INTRODUCTORY NOTE BY HIM MARK LAI

Extracts from "Yige ren chuangban liao Shidai Bao" 《一個人創辦〈時代報〉》 *[Single-handedly founded San Francisco Journal], chapter 6 of Xiong Guohua,* Meiji Huaren Huang Yunji zhuanqi: Meiguo meng *[An American dream: The life and times of Huang Yunji (Maurice H. Chuck), Chinese American] (Guangzhou: Huacheng Chubanshe, 2002)* 熊國華：《美籍華人黃運基傳奇： 美國夢》 （廣州：花城出版社，2002年）

Huang Yunji (Maurice H. Chuck) was born in 1932 in Doumen in Guangdong's Pearl River Delta. His father emigrated to California, leaving his family in the village. The year the Sino-Japanese War began, his wife passed away, leaving young Huang Yunji and his sister in the care of their uncle, who was a poor peasant. Huang Yunji's father returned to China after the war and in 1948 brought his sixteen-year-old son to California.[1]

Due to the Chinese Exclusion Act, which from 1882 to 1943 allowed only certain categories of Chinese immigrants to enter the United States, Huang Yunji's father had entered the country by assuming the identity of a Chinese American surnamed Chuck. Thus in America Huang Yunji became Chuck Joong Mun 卓忠民, or Maurice H. Chuck, son of an American citizen.[2]

Shortly after young Chuck landed, he became a frequent visitor to the Oasis Bookstore 綠原書店, which sold Chinese literature, including many works of a progressive nature. The proprietor allowed Chuck, who had had only four years of formal education in China, to browse in the store. New friends he met there induced introduced him to join the Chinese American Democratic Youth League 三藩市民主青年團, a progressive cultural youth group. These contacts inspired Chuck to become interested in progressive Chinese culture, especially in literature. Chuck soon also began his long association with Chinese American journalism, working as Chinese typesetter at the *Chinese Pacific Weekly* 太平洋週報 and then *Chung Sai Yat Po* 中西日報. Through these contacts and self-study Chuck expanded his knowledge of Chinese history and culture and improved his literary writing style. He also began to submit his writings to publications such as *China Daily News* 美洲華僑日報 of New York.[3]

Soon after he was inducted into the army in 1953, army intelligence discovered his writings, which were sympathetic to the PRC and expressed opposition to the Korean conflict. In 1955 he was given an undesirable discharge, which was upgraded to an honorable discharge only after several years of legal proceedings on his behalf by the American Civil Liberties Union. Worse was to come.[4] During the early 1960s the government intimidated Maurice Chuck's father into confessing his false claim of American citizenship and then indicted his son for falsely claiming U.S. citizenship when applying for a citizenship certificate while serving in the army at Fort Lewis, Washington, in 1954. The key government witness was Maurice Chuck's hapless father, whom the government forced to testify against his own son. Chuck was found guilty and given a three-month jail sentence.[5] However, in spite of all these adverse events, Chuck held on to this political beliefs.

By the late 1960s the political atmosphere in the United States was changing, spurred by the Civil Rights movement. In 1967 Chuck received a big opportunity when *East/West* 東西報, the bilingual Chinese American weekly, hired him as chief editor. His writings supported the increasing calls for a more rational U.S. policy toward the PRC. In early 1971 he became one of the founders of the U.S.-China Peoples Friendship Association in San Francisco. In 1972, after successive editorships at *Chinese World* 世界日報 and *Chinese Voice*, Chuck founded the weekly *San Francisco Journal* 時代報 during the same week U.S. President Nixon was on his historic visit to the PRC. The paper went on to become a daily in 1983, but lacking the deep financial resources available to the Hong Kong–based *Sing Tao Daily* 星島日報 and the Taiwan-backed *World Journal* 世界日報, the *San Francisco Journal* found it difficult to compete effectively with them for subscribers and advertisers, and in the end it had to cease publication.

Chuck's literary writings to date consist of several collections of essays and commentaries as well as three works of fiction, all published in China. He was one of the founders of the Chinese Literature and Art Association in America 美國華文文藝界協會 in March 1994 and served as chairman of the group for three consecutive terms from 1998 through 2003. In spring 1995 he was the principal financial backer of the bimonthly *The Literati* (*Meihua Wenhuaren Bao* 美華文化人報), which began publication in February 1995. In

June 1998 its Chinese name was changed to *Meihua Wenxue* 美華文學.[6] —HML

The founding of the new China gave Huang Yunji (Maurice H. Chuck) hope but also made him homesick for his motherland. When he was working as a typesetter for newspapers he witnessed how, by his own hands, words were turned into essays and essays into newspapers that reached thousands of readers. A dream was born: he wanted to be a reporter, an editor, and better yet, to publish his own newspaper. He had so much to say; writing articles and publishing a newspaper seemed to be the best way to transmit his thoughts. To realize this "American dream," Chuck strove diligently, step by step.

After his release from prison in the mid-1960s, Chuck's political infamy prevented him from finding work in San Francisco. He moved to the suburban town of Mountain View with his wife and daughter and toiled for a number of years on a chrysanthemum farm. Having saved up a small sum of hard-earned money, he made a tour of American cities and returned to write a series of articles for *East/West*, a new weekly newspaper in San Francisco's Chinatown. His topics ranged from American politics and the Civil Rights movement to economic issues. The editor of *East/West* appreciated his writings and always arranged their immediate publication. There was no monetary reward for contributing these articles, but Chuck's love of journalism and literary expression, the opportunity to communicate his views on world and American affairs, and the need of an outlet for the feelings buried in his heart urged him on. He continued writing tirelessly and derived great pleasure from such discourse.

Finally heaven was moved: Chuck was offered a job as editor at *East/West* with a monthly salary of $300. Chuck took his first job as editor earnestly and very seriously. *East/West* was the first Chinese newspaper printed on an offset press. While meeting stringent editorial deadlines, Chuck learned typing, cutting and pasting, darkroom techniques, and the principles of offset-printing technology.

In 1968, Chuck landed an editor's position at *Chinese World*, a Chinese-language daily, and he continued to contribute articles to other Chinese newspapers. The following year, noted San Francisco journalist John Ong 翁紹裘 invited Chuck to join him in cofounding *Chinese Voice*, a new Chinese weekly. Assuming the positions of editor in chief and general manager, Chuck began emerging as a journalist in his own right.

Chuck started the *San Francisco Journal* in a small office in San Francisco Chinatown. A desk, a telephone, and a $200 Double Dove Chinese typewriter were its only assets. But Chuck soon gained the support of his friends Jimmy Leung 梁源洲 and Henry Mah 馬開湛, who became the *Journal's* earliest shareholders.

Imagine a day in the new entrepreneur's life running his one-man operation as publisher, editor, reporter, typist, proofreader, manager, agent, gofer, and custodian all at once. In fact, he was the *San Francisco Journal* itself!

Chuck's unwavering passion as a journalist and his perseverance in realizing an ideal drew out the tremendous potential in him. The early *San Francisco Journal* was a twenty-four-page Chinese-English bilingual weekly. The volume of work involved was enormous. Chuck would gather the news, write his articles, lay out the pages, and then send the camera-ready pages to the print shop. He would later pick up the fresh-off-the-press papers and deliver them to newsstands. No one paid him any salary, and the risk of bankruptcy constantly loomed over his head. In addition to handling the heavy workload at the *Journal*, he had to work several hours a day at a restaurant he and his wife co-owned with their friend Harry Yuen. What he earned from the restaurant he used to cover the cost of publishing the *Journal*. Often when fatigue overcame him after a few days with very little sleep, he would take a nap to recuperate, then immerse himself again in the newspaper that he so loved.

Whether by historical fortuity or by intent, February 23, 1972, the date of the inaugural issue of the *San Francisco Journal*, fell in the same week that President Nixon made his historical journey to China. The headline read, "Icebreaking Journey: President Nixon Visits China!"

THE *SAN FRANCISCO JOURNAL*: A BIG, HAPPY FAMILY

The *San Francisco Journal* was the only Chinese-language publication in San Francisco that devoted a large amount of space to news from mainland China. Advocating friendly relations between China and the United States and opposing U.S. involvement in the Vietnam War, the paper quickly became a thorn in the Kuomintang's side. Shortly after it began publication, Chuck received an envelope that contained a bullet and a note scribbled in red ink: "WANTED: YOUR LIFE!" This would have scared some people, but Chuck believed what he was doing was just. He refused to submit to the threat and continued to publish his newspaper. He despised the Kuomintang operatives' underhanded tactics. The more they tried to thwart his work, the more determined he became, and he worked even harder to produce a better newspaper. This is the essence of Chuck.

As the *San Francisco Journal* established a distinct voice in San Francisco's Chinese community, conscientious and fair-minded volunteers started to rally around Chuck and join his cause. Initially Chuck did everything himself with occasional help from friends. Soon six or seven people offered their assistance. At one point, the volunteer *Journal* staff numbered over fifty. Among them were immigrants from mainland China, Taiwan, and Hong Kong, along with American-born Chinese, Japanese, Koreans, Filipinos, Caucasians, and African Americans. It was amazing that in a wealth-conscious

The *San Francisco Journal*'s all-volunteer staff included Curtis Choy (front row, second from left); Russell Lowe (far right); Diana Hong (second row, second from left); Maurice Chuck (far right); Mabel Ng (third row); and Kathy Fong (behind Maurice Chuck). (Courtesy Him Mark Lai)

Maurice Chuck 黃運基 (Huang Yunji) or Chuck Joong Mun (卓忠民), editor of the *San Francisco Journal*. (Courtesy Him Mark Lai)

society where workers are compensated by hourly wages, so many talented people of different colors, speaking different languages, were willing to devote themselves to the *Journal*'s work without monetary reward for so long. Only after eight years did the *San Francisco Journal*'s financial situation improve sufficiently for it to pay its staff.

The help and participation of fervent supporters allowed the paper to grow steadily, and it evolved from a Chinese-English bilingual weekly into separate Chinese and English editions. The Chinese weekly later became a semiweekly. In 1983, the *Journal* turned daily, publishing sixteen broadsheet pages six days a week. The *Journal* was now a full-blown news organization with its own fully equipped and staffed printing facilities and office space for—at the height of its operations—sixty editors, reporters, typesetters, photographers, graphic artists, and business and administrative staff. Yet in its extraordinary early days, some Chinese newspaper vendors were afraid to sell the *Journal* because of Kuomintang threats; Chinese immigrant volunteers went into the streets to sell and promote it. Chuck will forever be grateful to these supporters. Without them, the *Journal* would have met with an early end.

While Chuck was still working alone in a tiny rented space in a Chinatown office building, the room next door housed Chinese for Affirmative Action, another one-person operation, in this case a young woman named Katheryn Fong 方惠蓮. The two neighbors often ran into each other in the hallway, and after some time they introduced themselves.

"May I ask what your organization does, Miss Fong?" Chuck said.

"Please call me Kathy. We are a non-profit civil rights advocacy organization dedicated to promoting equal rights

and opportunities for Chinese in America. Our work is supported by the membership and volunteers." After a brief pause she asked, "What about you, Mr. Chuck?"

"Just Maurice, please." He smiled. "I publish a newspaper called *San Francisco Journal*. It promotes friendship and formal diplomatic relations between the United States and China. It covers news on mainland China and speaks for the Chinese in America."

"Great, another advocate of rights for the Chinese. It looks like we have a lot in common. Why is there no one else working in your office?"

"Aren't you quite alone yourself?"

Bursting into laughter, the two shook hands and became fast friends. Every time Fong went out to buy coffee for herself, she would bring back a cup for Chuck as well. Sometimes when Chuck was swamped with work, Fong would lend a hand. Chuck reciprocated by helping Fong with new ideas and translations of press releases into Chinese. The two neighbors became each other's great supporters.

Born in the United States, Fong had witnessed firsthand the discrimination that the Chinese experienced and felt the injustice most intimately. She immersed herself in promoting equal rights and equitable status for Chinese in America. She was versed in English and well connected in her work. When the *San Francisco Journal* became separate Chinese and English weeklies, Chuck invited Fong to become the English-language managing editor. Fong happily agreed. She was totally devoted, her work outstanding. She also brought on board her American-born Chinese, Japanese, Korean, and Filipino friends. The *Journal*'s volunteer staff continued to grow, with a good mix of ages and backgrounds—professionals, students, journalists, lawyers, writers, artists, engineers, broadcasters, college professors, business owners, civil rights advocates, community organizers, service workers.

From among the *Journal's* former reporters emerged an elected supervisor of the city and county of San Francisco, Mabel Teng 鄧式美, whose family—originally from Zhaoxin in Guangdong province—emigrated to the United States from Hong Kong when she was seventeen. Upon graduating from college in Massachusetts with a degree in genetics, Teng began her professional career at Harvard Medical School, working on the development of a diphtheria vaccine. But an event a few years later led her to seek public office.

In 1982, Vincent Chin 陳果仁, a young Chinese American engineer, was killed by two unemployed white men in Detroit who called him a "Jap" and accused him of stealing jobs from Americans. The incident shocked and outraged Asian Americans all over the country. Teng, having already relocated to San Francisco and established a great rapport with the Chinese community through grassroots civil rights work, was outraged, and she proposed to Chuck that she fly to Detroit as a *Journal* correspondent to investigate and report the truth of what had transpired.

Returning to San Francisco, Teng not only wrote detailed reports on the results of her investigation for the *Journal* but rallied the Asian community organizations and formed Asian Americans for Justice to fight for justice for Vincent Chin. As chair of the fundraising committee, she tirelessly raised money and organized support activities. Despite seven years of hard work by the Asian American community, injustice prevailed: The court rendered Vincent Chin's killers a token sentence of a $3,750 fine. The injustice prompted Teng to rethink her course of action. She decided to put herself in the mainstream legislative infrastructure, working to eliminate loopholes in the law and fighting for justice and equality for Chinese and other ethnic minorities through legislation. She believed that by motivating and uniting the citizenry, this goal could in time be realized.

Teng arrived at this conviction as a result of another incident. In 1981, U.S. Senator Alan Simpson had proposed an immigration law amendment to eliminate the fifth family preference (for siblings of U.S. citizens). Mabel Teng organized the Committee for 5th Preference and journeyed to Washington, D.C., with other community representatives to lobby against the amendment. Their efforts were triumphant. In 1982, the Simpson bill was defeated in Congress.

Seeing the power of concerted community effort and the benefits brought to communities through political action strengthened her determination to seek public office.[7] But being Chinese, especially a Chinese woman, running for political office was no easy endeavor! She had quite a few obstacles to overcome. The first was the bias among many Chinese for males over females in leadership positions. Most community bigwigs were men. To gain the confidence and recommendation of the Chinese community was a real challenge for a woman. Second, as a result of American society's historical bias against the Chinese, there had still, in 1977, been no Chinese elected officials in the history of San Francisco. Only two Chinese men had been appointed city supervisors by the mayor, and just one of these, Gordon Lau, had succeeded in keeping his seat in a subsequent election. Third, even mainstream America was biased against women in politics. If the candidate were from a background other than a political dynasty or less than prestigious, she would usually be snubbed and slighted. Fourth, a political campaign required a great deal of money. A candidate must be rich or backed by wealthy sponsors; Teng was an ordinary citizen from the Chinese community.

Perhaps precisely because she came from the grass roots, she was connected to the Chinese community by a thousand threads. Teng was also broadly tied to other communities through years of advocacy work and coalition building. What she had to offer was a truthful heart and her dedication. During her campaign, Teng canvassed the streets and alleys of the Chinese neighborhoods. Knocking on the doors of thirty thousand families, she urged them to register to vote, to cast their votes on election day, and to use their votes to benefit the Chinese community.

Teng won! On November 8, 1994, she was elected supervisor of the city and county of San Francisco, becoming the first Chinese American woman elected to this office in the city's history. And after taking office, she worked diligently to keep her campaign promises.

In 1995, through her efforts, the Lilli Ann Company, a longtime garment maker, was saved from closing its doors; San Francisco's garment industry was saved. Tens of thousands of Chinese workers escaped the fate of unemployment. Through legislation, she helped improve the conditions in Chinatown and propel its economic boom. She actively supported the Affirmative Action Act that protected the rights of women and ethnic-minority citizens. She fiercely fought the anti-Chinese California Civil Rights Initiative filed by "angry white males." She called for political activism among Chinese Americans to counter the anti-immigration current. Building upon the work of her forerunners in these civil rights struggles and working in concert with other community activists, her efforts yielded many positive results. San Francisco now has three Asian American city supervisors; the first Chinese American police chief, Fred Lau 劉百安; the first Chinese American chief administrative officer, William L. Lee 李偉量; the first female Chinese central police station captain, Heather Fong 方宇文; and the first female Asian American California Superior Court judges, Lillian Sing 郭麗蓮, then Julie Tang鄧孟詩. Today the white population no longer dominates the multiethnic city of San Francisco.

Another volunteer English-language editor of the early bilingual *San Francisco Journal*, Min Yee 余民星, was a former editor for *Newsweek* magazine. When Chuck realized that Yee was otherwise unemployed and without any income, he passed his own monthly paycheck from his teaching post at

San Francisco State University to Yee until the latter secured a new paying job.

Writer Lao Nan 老南—a native of Taishan county, Guangdong province—came to San Francisco in 1978. On arrival, he knew very few people and even less English. He could not find a job or meet anyone in the literary field. He felt as lost as a wild goose left behind by its migrating flock. Then an elderly immigrant told him about the *Journal*. Lao Nan bought a copy and immediately found comfort; he felt he had somehow touched ground and seen the light at the end of a tunnel.

One day his landlady's son-in-law came to pay her a visit. Lao Nan was introduced to him and they started chatting. Lao Nan mentioned the *Journal* and how it resonated in Chinese hearts. The son-in-law's eyes brightened; he happened to be a part-time editor at the *Journal*. He said if Lao Nan would like to contribute his writings to the *Journal*, he could help him do so. Lao Nan produced his poem "Homeland," which was published in the *Journal*'s literary section in November 1980. Lao Nan would write and submit many more poems to the *Journal*, and as he ruminated on this part of his life, he would always say with feeling, "The *San Francisco Journal* really made an impact on many of us; it gave us, the immigrant writers, a place to publish our work and keep our spirit high. Mr. Huang [Chuck] was indeed instrumental in promoting Chinese-language literature in America. He has brought together and nurtured a whole generation of writers."

During the *Journal*'s volunteer days, ten to twenty people got together regularly after their daytime jobs to work on it, racing earnestly against the clock. Each of them might have his or her own life experience, social background, ethnic traditions, language, and skin color, but all worked at the *Journal* of their own will, receiving no pay. There was a strong camaraderie among the volunteers, especially when burning the midnight oil together. Chuck's wife, Liang Jian 梁堅, would cook up some delicious snacks for everybody. They would chat, enjoying the food and a brief respite. They shared each other's problems and happiness. It was like a big, happy family.

REPORTS FROM THE FRONT LINE: DENG XIAOPING 鄧小平 IN ACTION

Chuck covered Deng Xiaoping's earthshaking activities on three different occasions for the *San Francisco Journal*.

The first time was in April 1974 during the Sixth Special Session of the United Nations General Assembly. The PRC delegation, headed by Deng Xiaoping, with Vice Foreign Minister Qian Guanhua 喬冠華 and China's permanent representative to the UN, Huang Hua 黃華, as deputy leaders, attended this special session. This was the first time that Chuck saw Deng in person. Condemned during the Cultural Revolution as the number two "capitalist roader" in

the country, Deng had just resumed his work in reshaping China's national economy, and he delivered an address on behalf of the government of the PRC, putting forth the theory of the "three worlds." Chuck's report, entitled "Deng Xiaoping's Speech at the UN General Assembly Special Session," recapped Deng's key points.

The state of the world today should be characterized as "havoc under heaven" rather than "peace under heaven." Havoc is caused by the aggressive rivalry between the United States and the Soviet Union, the world's two superpowers. And today's world is divided into three parts.

The first world comprises the United States and the Soviet Union. Irreconcilable contradictions exist between these two powers. Compromise and alignment between them are local, temporary, and relative, while rivalry is total, perpetual, and absolute. The third world consists of developing countries in Asia, Africa, Latin America, and other regions. The third world is the driving force of world history and the primary force against colonialism, imperialism, and especially the superpowers. In between the first and the third worlds is the second world. Second world countries strongly oppose hegemony and strong-arm politics. The United States and the Soviet Union are today's biggest international exploiters, oppressors and the cause of new global warfare. The third world has long suffered the brutal exploitation and oppression of colonialism and imperialism. The Soviet Union has become very "creative" in neo-imperialist economic pillages that far surpass its past exploits. The so-called economic cooperative and international division of labor may sound noble, but in reality they are disguises for securing high profit by oppressive tactics.

The third world strongly demands changes to these conditions. This special session of the UN General Assembly is a world forum for the third world united front to lay out for the people of the world the true nature of the issues as a first step in its struggle against exploitation and oppression. Therefore, the issues surrounding raw material and development are really about the developing countries protecting their national sovereignty, developing their national economies, and resisting imperialism, hegemony, pillage, and external control.

In his address Deng explicitly declared China a third world country that was not and never would be a superpower. Especially noteworthy was the following statement: "If China should one day change color and became a superpower, the people of the world should call her a social-imperialist; they should expose it, oppose it, and join with the Chinese people in defeating it." This statement certainly deserves our heedful reflection.[8]

Deng's speech expounded Chairman Mao Zedong's theory of the "differentiation of the three worlds," a key strategy in China's foreign policy in the 1970s. Deng's speech won the broad support of the third world countries in the United Nations and greatly impacted international politics.

This farewell statement by Maurice Chuck from the San Francisco Journal's *closing issue also appears in* Selected Works of Maurice H. Chuck *(San Francisco: Chinese Journal Corporation, July 1996), 2:254.*

After careful consideration and full deliberations, the Board of Directors and Shareholders of Chinese Journal Corporation reached the decision to cease publication of *San Francisco Journal* effective November 15, 1986.

This is a difficult and painful decision.

As readers who care about our community and the *San Francisco Journal* all know, the *Journal* started out fifteen years ago as a Chinese-English bilingual weekly newspaper staffed entirely by volunteers. Our only "asset" was a Chinese typewriter. It has grown out of nothing to having something of value to us and to our community, from a very small to a larger organization, from a weekly to a semiweekly newspaper, and in 1983, the *Journal* turned daily. Our operation also branched out to printing, translation, Chinese typesetting, phototypesetting, graphic design and mailing services. I must say the *San Francisco Journal* has truly lived up to an old Chinese saying, we have indeed "built" the *Journal* "with our bare hands." The *Journal*'s current assets are 2,000 times the worth when it first started.

Our financial health is now better than ever. The *Journal*'s influence in our community and in American society is gaining headway. Then why do we decide to cease publication now of all times?

It is our duty to tell the readers and friends who have loved and supported us all these years the truth.

Two years ago, we had said that in order to meet new challenges, we needed to resolve two basic issues: capital and manpower. Without fundamentally solving these two problems, everything else is pure talk. For the past few years, the *Journal* operated on a basically balanced budget. On one hand we were pleased, and on the other we were worried, but we worried a little more than we were pleased. The reason was simple. Even though we did not suffer any loss, staying stagnant was not where we should be. Many new Chinese newspapers sprang up in the Chinese community in recent years, and most of them came with inexhaustible funds and powerful overseas backing. Competition is ferocious. The *San Francisco Journal*, a newspaper founded by local Chinese Americans, has no such financial patronage. The *Journal* has always relied on the support of individual readers and friends in the community who are comparatively very limited in resources; only their love and care have sustained us through the years. We have tried our best, yet we have only reached the present level of success. To tell the truth, we are not satisfied with what we have been able to accomplish.

Our current financial situation and human resources would not allow us to make the *Journal* a much better newspaper and become more competitive. To raise more funds, traditional ways include developing new sources of income and cutting costs. Thus on one hand, we tried to improve the efficiency of our work in order to reduce labor cost. On the other hand, we attempted some business projects in the hope of bringing in income to fund the newspaper. We succeeded in cutting costs, but ran into walls with our business ventures. We found that doing business with

---

The second time Chuck covered Deng Xiaoping was in October 1974 in Beijing. On the invitation of China's foreign ministry, Chuck led a delegation of Chinese Americans to participate in the celebration of the twenty-fifth anniversary of the founding of the PRC. The group toured China for over a month after the festivities in Beijing.

"There were four journalists in our delegation," recalled Chuck. "Besides myself, there were Judy Yung 楊碧芳, editor for *East/West*, English edition; Herbert Lee 李漢齡, editor of *San Francisco Weekly* 舊金山週報; and Myland Fong 方大川, editor of *Wei Min Bao* 為民報, English edition. Other members included a seventy-year-old worker from Washington, a restaurant owner from Maryland, a farm owner from Arizona, three dancers from Chinese Folk Dance Association, and housewives. Among them were young people born and raised in the United States; others were senior citizens and middle-aged immigrants who had left their native land for many years. We differed greatly in our interests, political views, and education levels, but

we also had many things in common—we were all United States citizens of Chinese descent, and it was the first time that we were visiting the People's Republic of China. Like the American people at large, we all had strong desires to better understand the new China."

Chuck saw the esteemed Chinese premier Zhou Enlai 周恩來 for the first time at a National Day banquet held at the People's Great Hall. Premier Zhou looked rather thin as he had been unwell. He gave a short speech at the beginning of the banquet, toasted everyone, and left before the event ended.

On October 2 in the People's Great Hall, Deng received Chuck and other overseas Chinese who had come to Beijing for the National Day celebration. They were joined by Liao Chengzhi 廖承志 and other Chinese national leaders. During this meeting, Deng discussed the progress in China's industrial and agricultural construction in the past twenty-five years, the people's living standards, the Taiwan question, and the Chinese government's overseas Chinese policy.

Mainland China to generate income for the newspaper was no possible undertaking for us! Those who could really turn a profit doing so are big bosses with solid financial and power bases, and abundant funds at their disposal. They are a different breed from our modest friends who have for decades dedicated their hearts and minds in the US-China friendship movement but are a little less sophisticated in business savvy.

As we are unable to resolve the monetary problems, the prospect of the *Journal's* future looks gloomy. If we cannot move forward, we will be left behind. Advancing is beyond our means, yet retreating is against our wish. All these years, we have expended all the profits from our printing, translation, phototypesetting, Chinese typing, graphic design and mailing businesses in the publication of the *Journal*. Simply maintaining the current mode of operation is no small task. Is it worth it to continue spending all the income in this manner while there is little prospect of a breakthrough? Our conclusion: not really.

Individual friends have commented that the *Journal* has risen from nothing, and it has made important contributions in promoting the rights of the Chinese in America, in advancing the normalization of US-China relations and the peaceful unification of China. The *Journal's* opinions are well respected and influential in the United States, in China and in the Chinese community. At a time when the relations between the United States and China are progressing positively, when China has opened her doors and the Four Modernizations drive projects a bright future, to stop publishing the *Journal* is a great pity and a terrible loss!

We agree with our friends wholeheartedly.

Personally, the *Journal*, like a "favorite son," is an integral part of me. In the past fifteen years, I have tasted life's every flavor: sweet, sour, bitter and spicy hot. The *Journal* is like the blood in my veins endlessly circulating my body. Poignant scenes of the *Journal* volunteers working tirelessly day and night with me for over eight years frequently played back in my mind. In every demonstration to fight for the rights of Chinese in America or promote normalization of US-China relations, we were not merely journalists amid marchers from every walk of life, we were active participants as well. Now that the *Journal* will no longer publish, I feel as if the hot blood in me has stopped to flow. It is painful and suffocating.

Yet, we must face the cruel reality. Trying to make the *Journal* a more competitive, more influential newspaper with our current means would yield only one result: we will drain our wits and energy, and in the end, all financial and human resources as well.

So we say, it is not really worth it. But though we will no longer publish a daily newspaper, it does not mean that we will abandon our responsibilities and our participation in the community. We will continue to care and support issues and activities relevant to the welfare of our community.

The *Journal's* printing, translation, phototypesetting, Chinese typesetting and mailing services are still open for business. We will make realistic adjustments and continue to devote ourselves in meaningful cultural and educational works, only in different ways.

Last but not least, I wish to take this opportunity to express my deepest gratitude to all of you for your love and support of the *San Francisco Journal* in the years past.

Chuck wrote about this memorable meeting in a lengthy article titled "Deng Xiaoping on the Future of China and Overseas Chinese Policy."

The third time Chuck covered Deng was in 1979 from January 28 to February 5. Deng was visiting the United States shortly after the two countries had established formal diplomatic relations. Chuck filed reports from Washington, D.C., on Deng's activities.

According to Deng, his objectives for this visit were "to better understand the United States, to learn everything that is advanced in America, and to exchange views with American statesmen, especially President Jimmy Carter, on issues of bilateral concern. . . . Through direct contact and dialogue with American leaders and the American people, we hope to further understanding, friendly cooperation in science and technology, as well as economic and cultural exchanges between China and the United States."[9]

The first day of Deng's visit fell nicely on New Year's Day in the Chinese calendar. That day jubilant Chinese all over the United States really felt the meaning of the Chinese saying "Send away the old and usher in the new." Deng's "project charisma" on his U.S. trip exceeded expectations. Wherever he went, the American public was captivated by his charm and welcomed him warmly. Chuck wrote. "Welcome to the United States, Vice Premier Deng" and "Press Comments on Deng Xiaoping's Visit," in which he extolled Deng's visit as "marking the end of an old era and the beginning of the new,"[10] forcefully moving the two countries' cooperative relationship forward.

When President Ronald Reagan began his state visit in China on April 24, 1984, Chuck joined the U.S. press corps covering the six-day visit. While President Reagan and the American delegation gained a better understanding of their host country, Chuck was pleased and greatly encouraged by the changes and progress China had made since instituting long overdue reforms and opening its doors. In November of that year, Chuck accompanied San Francisco Mayor Dianne Feinstein (now a U.S. senator representing California) on her trip to Beijing, Xian, and Shanghai. He served as her official interpreter as well as correspondent for the *San Francisco Journal*.

FAREWELL, *SAN FRANCISCO JOURNAL*!

From its inaugural issue on February 23, 1972, to its last issue on November 15, 1986, the *San Francisco Journal* reached out to its readers for fifteen years.

To Chuck personally, the *San Francisco Journal* was the realization of a dream from his youth, as well as an expression of his values and ideals. For fifteen years, he devoted his time, energy, financial resources—his total being—to the *Journal*. Building something from nothing had been a challenging venture. The first years were very difficult indeed. Even though there were no paid staff, the *Journal* operated in the red, and Chuck had to support the newspaper with income from his business. He and his wife—partnering initially with Harry Yuen 袁樹榮, a friend from the Chinese American Democratic Youth League—opened Dragon Fountain 龍泉茶室, a Chinese *dim sum* restaurant. A few years later, Chuck started the Emperor 帝皇 Restaurant with good friends S. S. Ngai 魏需遜 and Peter Chi 池洪湖. Rising early and retiring late at night, Chuck used his entire income to defray the *Journal*'s deficit. At a critical moment, he even mortgaged his own house for some cash to ease the *Journal*'s financial crunch.

In 1975, the *Journal* won a contract from the City and County of San Francisco to translate election materials such as the voter information pamphlet into Chinese. Chuck and the volunteer staff delivered a highly praised Chinese election handbook for the monolingual Chinese voters of San Francisco. The entire fee of $25,000 from the contract was put into the operation of the *Journal*. Since then, the *Journal* has won the annual bids to translate San Francisco's election materials. As chief translator and editor of these projects and at the recommendation of San Francisco's registrar of voters, Chuck was sworn in as official translator of the City and County of San Francisco in 1977 by California Supreme Court Judge Harry Low 劉百昌. In 1996, he was certified as translator for the City and County of San Francisco and the County of Alameda by California Superior Court Judge Lillian K. Sing. Some years, the *Journal* also translated voter handbooks for the State of California, the State of Hawaii, and the County of Alameda.

With the investment of more funds in 1976, the *Journal* purchased a three-unit Goss web press and moved into a 4,500-square-foot facility. The *Journal* moved again in 1980 into a larger facility with 6,500 square feet and added two units to the Goss. In 1987, the company finally owned the building that had housed the *Journal* since 1980.

If you were to ask Chuck how much heart and time he invested in the *San Francisco Journal*, he would be at a loss to give an answer. For fifteen years, he "lived" the *Journal*. When the *Journal* turned daily, he was responsible for the front page. Every day, he would first select the news items from the English wires and articles submitted by staff reporters and outside sources. He would then translate the English pieces into Chinese and lay out the page. He also needed to write the headlines, subheads, and a daily editorial. When all the pages were ready, the paper went to press. The printed paper would then be delivered to newsstands, bookstores, and the post office. His day started around 4 A.M. along with the morning shift, and when the paper came off the press at 10 A.M., work started again for the following day's issue.

If you were to ask Chuck to name his happiest day in the *Journal*'s fifteen-year history, he would tell you, "January 1, 1979, absolutely!" This was, of course, the day the United States and China normalized their relations. After Jimmy Carter assumed office as the thirty-ninth U.S. president in January 1977, negotiations between the United States and the Soviet Union in the Strategic Arms Limitation Talks (SALT II) came to a standstill while the Soviet Union intensified its expansionist streak. U.S.-Soviet relations took a downturn. President Carter decided to accomplish the normalization of U.S.-China relations on his watch. "Our policy toward the People's Republic [of China] is guided by the Shanghai Communiqué, and the objective is normalization of relations," he assured Huang Zhen, chief of the liaison office of the PRC to the United States, shortly after taking office.[11]

Six months later, President Carter sent Secretary of State Cyrus Vance to China to resume the talks. Deng told Vance, "To solve this problem [of U.S.-Taiwan relations], three simple things can be done: abrogate the treaties, withdraw the troops and sever diplomatic relations. To accommodate reality, we can allow unofficial contact between Taiwan and the United States. As far as the unification of Taiwan with China is concerned, please leave the matter to the Chinese. We believe we are capable of resolving this problem on our own."[12]

But Carter still wanted to achieve some measure of detente with the Soviet Union in the hope that progress could be made in SALT. He intended to observe the Soviet situation for a little longer and therefore did not immediately accept the three conditions put forth by Deng. By 1978, with the Soviet Union continuing its expansion into different parts of the world, China decided to accelerate its economic development and actively extended its diplomatic exchanges with other countries. Carter determined that it was time to speed up the normalization of U.S.-China relations.

In May 1978, Carter sent White House National Security Adviser Zbigniew Brzezinski to China and authorized Chief of U.S. Liaison Office in China Leonard Woodcock to conduct detailed normalization negotiations with the Chinese. Negotiations started in Beijing the following July. China was represented by Foreign Minister Huang Hua. During a period when Huang was hospitalized, Han Nianlong stepped up to take his place. Both sides reached the following agreement after nearly six months of intensive negotiations:

1. The United States of America recognizes the government of the People's Republic of China as the sole legal government of China. Within this context, the people of the United States will maintain cultural, commercial, and other unofficial relations with the people of Taiwan.
2. At the normalization of U.S.-China relations, the United States will immediately sever formal relations with Taiwan and will withdraw all military personnel and installations from Taiwan before April 1, 1979. The U.S. government will notify the Taiwan government of the abrogation of the Mutual Defense Treaty.
3. The United States of America and the People's Republic of China have agreed to recognize each other and to establish diplomatic relations as of January 1, 1979. The United States of America and the People's Republic of China will exchange ambassadors and establish embassies on March 1, 1979.

A joint communiqué on the establishment of diplomatic relations between the PRC and the United States was released on December 16, 1978, in Beijing and in Washington, D.C.

President Carter made the formal announcement in Washington, D.C., on the eve of normalization of U.S.-China relations. Chuck and the *Journal* staff captured the president's announcement off the TV screen with a camera and worked through the night, changing three pages of the paper to include a feature story recapping a century of U.S.-China relations. January 1, 1979, fell on a Sunday. All Chinese newspapers took the day off except the *San Francisco Journal*. The *Journal* headlined this momentous event on its front page. It was also the first Chinese-language newspaper in the United States to report this monumental news. The circulation of the *Journal* reached its peak, with readers in every state in the country.

The *Journal*'s influence bloomed and peaked with the normalization of U.S.-China relations. However, after normalization, as other Chinese and English publications began to carry news on China, the *Journal*'s unique status as the sole reporter of such news no longer existed. This was certainly good news for the readers, but it also meant that the *Journal* was losing its edge. After China opened its doors in the 1980s, and especially when an increased number of Chinese immigrants settled in the United States, news enterprises from Taiwan and Hong Kong became optimistic about the U.S. market; funds started to pour in for new establishments. Competition among Chinese language newspapers was fierce. The *San Francisco Journal* started out humbly without the backing of financial moguls and remained an independent Chinese American newspaper. In terms of printing equipment, sources of content, reporting and editorial expediency, and cash flow, the *Journal* remained at a disadvantage to the competition with no long-term solution in sight.

By 1986, Chuck had to consider ceasing publication of the *Journal*. Friends and readers were shocked when they heard the news. How they wished that it were not true! Some *Journal* editors tearfully pleaded with Chuck, "We'll take a smaller salary, or none at all, but please don't close down the *Journal*!" In fact, no one had a heavier and more tormented heart than Chuck. He had given birth to the *Journal*; his ideals, his heart and soul, his life, were all infused in it. The *Journal* was his baby and a part of his life. Holding back tears, he penned the announcement of the *Journal*'s decision to discontinue publication. One can imagine how he must have felt at such a moment.

After careful consideration and full deliberation, the board of directors and shareholders of the Chinese Journal Corporation reached the decision to cease publication of the *San Francisco Journal* effective November 15, 1986.

In historical context, the *San Francisco Journal*'s contributions were unique, timely, and significant in many ways:

- The *San Francisco Journal* was the only Chinese-language newspaper that devoted a large amount of space to news on China. It featured China's economic construction, education and culture, providing a long overdue link between the overseas Chinese and their land of ancestry. It provided a window for the American people to better understand China.
- The *Journal* advocated peace and was one of the few newspapers that openly opposed the United States' military involvement in Vietnam.
- One of the *Journal*'s goals was to promote full diplomatic relations between the United States and China. Its work contributed positively to advancing friendly exchanges between the two peoples and the peaceful unification of China.
- The *Journal* opposed racial discrimination and all anti-Chinese actions and currents. Its opinions were a strong, positive voice in promoting equal rights for the Chinese in America. It was also one of the very few truly community-based, professional news organizations in the United States.
- One of the *Journal*'s mottoes was truth and justice in reporting and in practice. It dared to challenge forces that obstructed change and progress by communicating the progressive, proactive new reality. It was a fertile field for its readers and staff to tell their stories, to express their ideals, to offer analytical views, and to issue challenges to injustice. The volunteers and staff that passed through

THE san francisco JOURNAL

927 kearny st. S.F., Ca. 94133 / a perspective on the news: local, national, the third world, asian america

20¢

(USPS 417-010)

Vol. 4 No. 45 July 30, 1980

The Last Journal

The San Francisco JOURNAL-English Edition ceases publication with this issue after nearly five years of operations.

Over the years, we have operated with the hard work of an all-volunteer staff whose goal was to produce an Asian American newspaper which focused on issues in the Asian American community...issues which were ignored by the mainstream media...issues which reflected the struggles and progress of the Asian American community.

We, at the JOURNAL would like to take this opportunity to thank all of you who worked with us as either a contributor or reader to help sustain the JOURNAL for nearly five years.

During that time, we covered various struggles which will be remembered as landmarks in Asian American history: the battle for the International Hotel, US-China normalization, efforts for Japanese American redress, justice for Chol Soo Lee, nurses Narciso and Perez, Iva Toguri, and other political prisoners, the Bakke Decision, and the Charlie Chan controversy.

The JOURNAL reported on the housing problems of the San Francisco Asian communities with the Nihonmachi eviction, the Ping Yuen renters' strike, and the efforts to build low-cost housing for seniors.

The JOURNAL investigated labor and educational issues which affected the Asian American community such as workers' strikes, massive cutbacks in childcare, mental health, and public education.

We went to press conferences, demonstrations, fundraising dinners, community meetings, hearings, and other events to report what we thought was important and vital to the Asian American community.

We photographed street fairs, benefits, performing arts, and people in the community and reviewed the best and worst of Asian American art, drama and literature.

We published the JOURNAL for 195 issues with the purpose

continued on page 16

San Francisco Journal, July 30, 1980. (CHSA, 2008.4. Gift of Kathy Fong.)

the *San Francisco Journal* continued their activism in their respective fields, promoting justice in America.

- The *Journal* promoted Chinese culture and traditional Chinese virtues with extensive coverage and special features on local cultural activities, cultural exchanges between China and the United States, and a rich culture and literary section.

- It was also a source of vital bilingual information for Chinese in America on such matters as voting rights, equal opportunities in employment, education, and public services.

- The *Journal* united a great number of Chinese-language writers, reporters, and editors who are still active in San Francisco's Chinese community today. The *Journal* provided a space for the publication of their works and their thoughts. Liu Huangtian and Lao Nan, acclaimed poets and authors; Liu Kaiping 劉開平, news director of *World Journal*; noted correspondent and editor Ou Weiye 區維業 of *Sing Tao Daily*; and Meng Changlin 孟長麟, former associate editor in chief of *Chinese Times* 金山時報, were all on the editorial staff of the *San Francisco Journal* daily in the 1980s.

For Maurice Chuck, the *San Francisco Journal* will always be a shining milestone in his life journey.

NOTES

1. Xiong Guohua, *Meiji Huaren Huang Yunji zhuanqi: Meiguo meng* [An American dream: the life and times of Huang Yunji (Maurice H. Chuck), Chinese American] (Guangzhou: Huacheng Chubanshe, 2002), 24–29.
2. Ibid., 36–38, 58.
3. Ibid., 76–82.
4. Ibid., 92–98.
5. Ibid., 102–12.
6. "Meiguo Huawen Wenyijie Xiehui jianjie" [Brief introduction to Association of Overseas Chinese Language Literature], *http://ocl.shu.edu.tw/org_news/db/data/american.htm* (accessed September 27, 2008).
7. *Literati* (April 1, 1966): 2.
8. Huang Yunji, "Deng Xiaoping's Address at the Special Session of the United Nations General Assembly," in *Selected Works of Maurice H. Chuck* (San Francisco: Chinese Journal Corporation, April 1966), 1:40.
9. Huang Yunji, "Welcome to the United States, Vice Premier Deng Xiaoping," in *Selected Works of Maurice H. Chuck* (San Francisco: Chinese Journal Corporation, July 1996), vol. 2.
10. Huang Yunji, "Press Comments on Deng Xiaoping's Visit to the United States," ibid., 50.
11. Li Changjiu and Shi Lujia, eds., *200 Years of US-China Relations* (Xinhua Press, 1984), 248.
12. *Foreign Affairs of Contemporary China*, 227.

The Making of the
Chinese American Symphony

Jon Jang

Composer Jon Jang was featured in Wei-hua Zhang, "Fred Ho and Jon Jang: Profiles of Two Chinese American Jazz Musicians," Chinese America: History & Perspectives—The Journal of the Chinese Historical Society of America (San Francisco: Chinese Historical Society of America), 1994.

When I attended an arts conference in Pittsburgh, Pennsylvania, during the summer of 2004, I bumped into Michael Morgan, a classmate of mine at the Oberlin Conservatory of Music during the late '70s. We did not know each other at the time because I was more recognized in the jazz clique (the "undesirables"), although I was a performance major studying Western European classical music. Michael had been the music director and conductor of the Oakland East Bay Symphony and the Sacramento Philharmonic Orchestra for many years. When I mentioned my interest in composing a Chinese American symphony, a lightbulb flashed in Michael's mind: This would be a perfect project for the Sacramento Philharmonic's California Compositions initiative, which celebrates the state's greatest achievers by commissioning new works of music in their honor. It could also be part of the Gold Mountain project, a tribute to the Chinese of California.

That meeting with Michael Morgan led to my collaboration with the Sacramento Philharmonic Orchestra and the Oakland East Bay Symphony with support from the Chinese Historical Society of America. They commissioned me to compose the *Chinese American Symphony*, a work that pays tribute to the Chinese laborers who built the first transcontinental railroad in the United States.

The Sacramento Philharmonic Orchestra premiered the *Chinese American Symphony* to an audience of over two thousand at the Sacramento Community Theatre on April 28, 2007. This happened to be the anniversary of the day in 1869 that the Chinese workers set the record for laying down ten miles of track in one day. The premiere coincided with a centennial celebration in Sacramento that honored both the Chinese railroad workers and respected Bay Area and local Chinese community leaders, such as Philip Choy, who were invited to speak.

The *Chinese American Symphony* is dedicated to Choy, a longtime visionary leader and historian. Philip Choy and oth-ers laid the early tracks of Chinese American history, just as the Chinese workers of the Central Pacific had laid the physical tracks of the railroad (faster than the Irish American workers of the Union Pacific). Philip Choy was reclaiming Chinese American history before the term existed, and despite the realities of both racism and anti-Communism in the McCarthy era, when it was taboo to utter a word about Chinese America or China. Choy also played a recurrent role in the development of the *Chinese American Symphony*, though that development began before I even knew his name.

FIRST DESTINATION: OBERLIN COLLEGE

During my undergraduate years (1975–78) at the Oberlin Conservatory of Music in Ohio, I learned about the town of Oberlin as an important destination for slaves who had escaped via the Underground Railroad. I was encouraged to take an African American music history course taught by my mentor, Dr. Wendell Logan.

At that time there were very few books about African American music. One book, *Blues People*, by Leroi Jones (aka Amiri Baraka), had a profound impact on me. I was struck by this passage: "The work song took on its own peculiar qualities in America for a number of reasons. First, although singing to accompany one's labor was quite common in West Africa, it is obvious that working one's own field in one's own land is quite different from forced labor in a foreign land."[1] After reading this passage, I thought, "If the Chinese sang work songs while building the railroad, they must have brought their work songs as well as folk songs from China but may have had to change them to fit the context of the American West."

Dr. Logan's incredible history course also introduced me to a recording of William Grant Still's *Afro-American Symphony* (1930). This symphony honored the blues and other African American folk forms that had been considered lowly expressions of the despised and primitive. This gave me the idea of someday composing a Chinese American symphony that honored Chinese folk music.

Like the Chinese as a race, Chinese music had historically been despised by Westerners. For example, the *San Francisco*

148

Bulletin had made comments such as the following: "The music seems to be a series of soft, whining tones, varying between bad, worse and intolerable."[2] Reading such criticisms brought back childhood memories, such as when a white teacher at my elementary school, scolding us for disrupting the class, made racist comparisons to a "Chinese fire drill" or "Chinese kindergarten," as though we were whiney and chaotic.

Music and books kept me out of the harmful darkness. I found a book by W. E. B. DuBois called *The Souls of Black Folk*. In his introduction Henry Louis Gates Jr. paraphrases part of DuBois' last chapter, "Of the Sorrow Songs," as follows: "It is through these songs, half despised, mistaken and misunderstood, and they represent the singular heritage of the nation and the greatest gift of the Negro people. These songs are the articulate message of the slave for the world."[3] And DuBois himself says, "Through all the sorrow of the Sorrow Songs there breathes a hope—a faith in the ultimate justice of things. The minor cadences of despair change often to triumph and calm confidence."[4]

I began my search for "Chinese sorrow songs" (a term that I coined, inspired by DuBois' writings) in the music library at Oberlin. I failed to find any. At that time books and recordings of Chinese music did not exist. Because the field of ethnomusicology had been marginalized, the study of Asian music had been confined to the music of Indonesia, Japan, and India. In the eyes and ears of the academic world and the public, the koto (Japanese zither) was always more familiar than its predecessor the *guzheng* (Chinese zither).

SECOND DESTINATION: SAN FRANCISCO

Feeling frustrated, I made a long-distance telephone call to my aunt Helen Jang, who had married my father's youngest brother and lives in San Francisco, close to Chinatown. Auntie Helen said, "Maybe Philip Choy, your Uncle Phil, can help you. He knows a lot about the history of Chinese of America. He is not your real uncle by blood. But Uncle Phil is part of the family because he is married to my sister Sarah."

I made another long-distance call to ask Uncle Phil about Chinese folk music recordings. He did not know of any, although he did recall lullabies sung by his mother. To ease my disappointment, Uncle Phil gave me a reprint of a poem written by a Chinese immigrant expressing his sorrow on Angel Island.

When I next visited San Francisco, I haphazardly plunged into Chinatown. Walking around the maze of alleyways, I followed the beautiful melodies emanating from Cantonese opera clubs, not knowing what was going to happen in my life. Walking on Stockton Street toward Broadway, I saw a fruit-stand vendor standing on the corner singing joyful Chinese songs as bright as the tangerines and oranges he sold. This planted the idea that my musical language could be about making Chinese folk songs sound American, just as I, an American-born Chinese, look Chinese but sound American.

In 1990 Sarah and Phil Choy sent me a copy of the Chinese Historical Society of America's *Tenth Anniversary Commemorative Booklet (1963–73)*.[5] One article caught my eye: a story about the Chinese laborers getting snubbed at the national centennial celebration of the golden spike at Promontory Point in Utah.[6] Sixteen years later, the Chinese Historical Society of America gave me an article written by Kent Wong in *East/West* that shared the same observations.[7]

With the exception of Charles Crocker's offhanded recognition of the Chinese, whom he called the "despised race," the original ceremony had ignored the contributions of the Chinese to building the first transcontinental railroad. History repeated itself one hundred years later. Kent Wong wrote:

> The main speaker, Federal Transportation Secretary John A. Volpe asked, "Who else but Americans could drill ten tunnels in mountains 30 feet deep in snow? Who else but Americans could chisel through miles of solid granite? Who else but Americans could have laid ten miles of track in 12 hours?"
> The irony of Volpe's speech was that these "Americans" were in fact, foreign-born Chinese barred for years from becoming citizens.
> Philip Choy told the audience of politicians including four U.S. Senators, seven Congressmen, and historical society buffs, that "many of the historical facts presented at the program were false, distorted and inaccurate. A white supremacy attitude persists and prevents many from recognizing the validity of the Chinese role in the construction of the transcontinental railroad."[8]

After reading this article I became angry but proud that Uncle Phil had taken a strong stand and spoken out. And I channeled my anger into something positive and creative.

LAYING DOWN THE FIRST TRACK OF THE *CHINESE AMERICAN SYMPHONY*

As a composer, I used Volpe's exclusion of the contributions of Chinese laborers in his speech to add another layer to the meaning of the *Chinese American Symphony*. The work opens with the sound of a percussion instrument called the anvil representing the golden spike. But when the anvil is struck, one cannot determine the racial identity of the striker. Is it an Irish American worker? Is it a Chinese worker? This places the responsibility on the listener to make a choice. When we hear the "Danny Boy" reference performed on the pennywhistle early in the symphony, we can immediately make the Irish connection. But even today the Chinese Americans have no anthem like "Danny Boy," which has been considered the unofficial Irish American anthem.

As a child I learned to sing songs about building the railroad, such as "I've Been Working on the Railroad," "Casey Jones" (Irish reference), "Paddy Builds the Railroad" (Irish), and "John Henry" (African American). Volpe's exclusion of the Chinese contribution made me realize that no children's songs or folk songs existed to valorize the Chinese building the railroad.

THE *ERHU*:
SYMBOL OF THE CHINESE WORKER

During the summer of 2006 in Beijing, I witnessed Chinese workers building high-rise buildings and hotels 24/7. I remembered reading about Charles Crocker, the member of the Big Four who hired Chinese workers in 1865 because the Irish workers were making little progress after two years. The other members of the Big Four—Leland Stanford, Mark Hopkins, and Collis P. Huntington—were highly skeptical of the Chinese because of their diminutive size. Justifying his decision, Crocker made the cogent point that the Chinese railroad laborers possessed as strong a work ethic as their ancestors who built the Great Wall in China.

At this point it became very clear to me that I would design the *Chinese American Symphony* to be performed in one nonstop movement that was close to 24 minutes in length to reflect the frantic and relentless pace of labor of the Chinese workers, which was typical in constructing monumental works such as the Great Wall, the transcontinental railroad, and high-rise buildings in Beijing for the 2008 Olympic Games. The music reflects the strong Chinese work ethic that existed then and continues now. Like Duke Ellington and Billy Strayhorn's classic "train theme" work, *Track 360*, it came full circle, 360 degrees.

The *Chinese American Symphony* depicts the American West, the Irish workers and railroad barons, harsh and dangerous working conditions, and the iron horse. The anvil, a percussion instrument used in operas, represents the golden spike. The dazzling virtuosity of Jiebing Chen's *erhu* (Chinese two-string fiddle) becomes the hero, symbolizing the unconquerable Chinese worker, whose strength reaches mythic proportions despite his small stature. As is evident in one of Chen's showcase works, *Galloping Horse*, the horse in Chinese culture is a powerful symbol of boundless spirit and energy. Toward the end of the *Chinese American Symphony* I incorporated this spirit and energy. When the *erhu* plays a four-note figure and accelerates to rapid speed, the instrument sounds like the iron horse.

PROGRAMMATIC ASPECTS OF
THE SYMPHONY

When my daughter Mika was ten years old, she had never experienced snow. In January 2006 we planned a family vacation: a train ride from Emeryville to Truckee. I did not realize that we were traveling through the high Sierra and American River, areas where the Chinese had performed the most dangerous work. From time to time a recording gave us a history lesson about the Chinese of California. It even stated that the Chinese workers ate a healthier diet than the Irish Americans, partially explaining why the Chinese were better workers! The long train ride also gave me an opportunity to read a new book, *Chinese American Voices: From the Gold Rush to the Present*, edited by Judy Yung, Gordon H. Chang, and Him Mark Lai. The book states:

> In the 1860s the Central Pacific Railroad, facing the rugged terrain of California's Sierra Nevada and the scarcity of reliable labor, made little progress on the western end of the railroad line, until they hired Chinese workers. These workers proved so capable and effective that some 12,000 to 14,000 Chinese, four of every five men hired by the Central Pacific, were soon put to work in all phases of construction leveling roadbeds, boring tunnels, blasting mountainsides, and laying tracks. The work was hard as well as dangerous. To carve a roadbed out of the granite promontory of Cape Horn, towering 1,400 feet above the American River, Chinese laborers lowered themselves from the top of the cliff in wicker baskets to drill holes and light explosives, pulling themselves up before, hopefully, the gun powder exploded beneath them. Working through two severe winters in the High Sierras, the Chinese lived in caverns carved out below the snow level and were often victims of snow slides and avalanches.[9]

While I was reading the first few pages of this book, I heard musical sounds in my mind. For example, to create music describing the dangerous working conditions in the high Sierra during the two severe winters, I composed quick descending-to-ascending chromatic figures in all of the woodwind parts to depict the fierce cold wind, and the strings' descending figure to symbolize the avalanches, snowslides, and fallen Chinese workers. (See illustration of music from page 27 of the score.)

END OF THE ROAD:
WHO DROVE THE GOLDEN SPIKE?

The symphony ends with a pastoral musical setting featuring a simple Chinese folk melody performed by the *erhu*. A single flute, oboe, and clarinet each echo a call of pathos to the departing *erhu* as a sweet whisper of a flower. The violas, cellos, and basses become deciduous trees that shed their leaves as the harp glides away. As the memory of the unconquerable Chinese worker fades away, the *erhu* becomes the lily that can endure the winter of our discontent made glori-

Facing page: In 2006 Jon Jang was commissioned by the Sacramento Philharmonic Orchestra and the Oakland East Bay Symphony to compose the *Chinese American Symphony*, a work that pays tribute to the Chinese laborers who built the first transcontinental railroad in the United States. The symphony also received support from the Chinese Historical Society of America and is dedicated to one of its longtime leaders, Philip Choy.

The image is one page of music from the *Chinese American Symphony*.

At the top of the page are the woodwind parts (flutes, oboes, clarinets, bassoons, etc.). At the bottom are the string parts (violins, violas, cellos, contrabasses). Quick descending-to-ascending chromatic figures in the woodwind parts depict the fierce, cold winds of winter in the high Sierra. The strings' descending figures symbolize avalanches, snowslides, and fallen Chinese workers.

(Score of Jon Jang's *Chinese American Symphony*, page 27. CHSA, 2008.2. Gift of Jon Jang in honor of Philip P. Choy. Reproduced by permission of the composer.)

ous summer by our sun. We are left with just three sounds of the golden spike to express the ephemeral sense of life. As it opened, the *Chinese American Symphony* closes with the sound of the golden spike (anvil). Let America remember not only the golden spike but the Chinese worker who drove it!

NOTES

1. Leroi Jones, "African Slaves/American Slaves: Their Music," chap. 3 in *Blues People* (New York: William Morrow, 1963), 19.

2. *San Francisco Bulletin*, Oct. 6, 1856, cited in Ronald Riddle, *Flying Dragons, Flowing Streams: Music in the Life of San Francisco's Chinese* (Westport, Conn., and London: Greenwood Press, 1983), pt. 1, "Chinese Theatre: The Early Years (1852–1869)," 22.

3. Henry Louis Gates Jr., introduction to *The Souls of Black Folk*, by W. E. B. DuBois (New York: Bantam, 1989), xxi.

4. W. E. B. DuBois, *The Souls of Black Folk* (Chicago: A. C. McClurg, 1903), 186.

5. This special edition of the *CHSA Bulletin* was published in January 1973.

6. Dale Champion, "The Forgotten Men at Gold Spike Ceremony," reprinted ibid., 14–16.

7. Kent Wong, "Gold Spike Rites Snub Chinese Rail Workers," *East/West*, May 14, 1969.

8. Ibid.

9. *Chinese American Voices: From the Gold Rush to the Present*, ed. Judy Yung, Gordon H. Chang, and Him Mark Lai (Berkeley and Los Angeles: University of California Press, 2006), 3.

Chinese role in railroad remembered

By H. M. LAI

Under fair, sunny skies on Adler St., which was decorated specially for this occasion with potted green shrubbery, the Chinese Historical Society of America held a ceremony in front of its headquarters in commemoration of the role played by the Chinese pioneers who worked on the Central Pacific Railroad, completed 100 years ago on May 10, 1869.

Among those paying tribute to the Chinese workers from the speaker's platform were the Chinese consul-general, the president of the Chinese Six Companies, as well as other local and national dignitaries. An original water-color painting by Prof. Mui Yue-tin, depicting the Chinese at work during the construction of the railroad was presented to the society by Col. John Young on behalf of the artist.

The high point on the program came when 99-year-old Mrs. Chinn

Please turn to Page 4

Centennial plaque

AT CHINESE Historical Society's ceremonies unveiling plaque to honor Chinese laborers who worked on the Central Pacific Railroad are: H. K. Wong, Philip Choy, Chinese Consul Chou Tung-hua, Supervisor Peter Tamaras, Mrs. Lee Shee Wing Chinn and Thomas Chinn. (Kem Lee photo)

Above: A Kem Lee photo documents the unveiling of the transcontinental railroad centennial commemorative plaques in San Francisco Chinatown on May 4, 1969, "to honor Chinese laborers who worked on the Central Pacific Railroad." (*East/West*, May 7, 1969; Philip P. Choy Collection, CHSA.) Pictured are (left to right) H. K. Wong, Philip P. Choy (standing behind plaque), Chinese Consul Chou-Tung-hua, Supervisor Peter Tamaras, Mrs. Lee Shee Wing Chinn, and Thomas Chinn. The *CHSA Bulletin* identifies Mrs. Chinn, who unveiled the centennial plaques, as the ninety-eight-year-old daughter of '49er Lee Man Bien. The full front page of this issue of *East/West* includes coverage of the Red Guards taking over a rally the same day at Portsmouth Square and is featured in "Taking to the Streets: Scenes from 1968 to 1972" (this volume, page 107). "A 'Landmark': History of Chinese Californians by Chinese Californians, 1969" (Anna Naruta, this volume, page 56) shows the *Bulletin's* report of the centennial ceremonies in San Francisco and gives further context to the society's activities that year.

Bulletin

FOR MAY & JUNE, 1969   VOL. IV., NOs. 5 & 6

Chinese Historical Society of America

MONTHLY MEETING

JUNE 20, 1969 — 7:30 p.m.

At 1001 Pine St., San Francisco

SPECIAL NOTICE—Please note the change in meeting place for this month. The Pine Terrace Lounge and Recreation Room was secured so that following the meeting, a social can be held. Refreshments will be served, and friends are cordially invited to both meeting and social.

President Philip Choy is endeavoring to secure a special tape that he wants the audience to hear. It concerns Promontory.

BUSY APRIL AND MAY . . .

Many things have happened during April and May, and because of this, the Executive Board decided that the regular May meeting would be replaced by a special Executive Board meeting on May 4, open to members also. A full report will be made at the June 20 meeting on this.

The May Bulletin was also withheld,

RAILROAD CENTENNIAL BRONZE MARKER

This Commemorative Plaque, one of two identical bronze markers, was unveiled at local centennial observance on May 4th at Society headquarters.

The Society conceived the idea, and solicited the financial support of the San Francisco Chinese community. Local unveiling was to give the community an opportunity to see the plaques, as well as to observe the centennial with an appropriate ceremony.

One of the plaques was placed at the national historical site headquarters at Promontory, Utah, where the Central Pacific joined the Union Pacific in 1869. The other plaque will be placed in Sacramento, California, the starting point of the Central Pacific. A new railroad museum, to house many of the railroad's former locomotives, is to be erected in the near future and this plaque will then be permanently affixed to this building. In the meantime, it may be seen at the Pioneer Hall Museum in Sacramento.

The wording on the plaque was composed by Thomas W. Chinn, with the translation and Chinese calligraphy by well-known calligrapher Mr. P. C. Lee. The design was arranged by Philip P. Choy.

A more complete story on the railroad centennial is contained in the several articles written on the following pages.

and its 4 pages added to a combined May-June issue of 8 pages, in order to more fully cover the activities for the period.

The centennial ceremonies in San Francisco Chinatown at CHSA, then at 17 Adler Place (now called Jack Kerouac Alley): "At Adler Place handsomely decorated for the occasion, the Chinese Historical Society [of America] previewed plaques honoring Chinese rail work- ers which will be permanently placed in Sacramento and Promontory Point, Utah." (Kem Lee photograph, *East/West*, May 7, 1969; Philip P. Choy Collection, CHSA)

Facing page: "To commemorate the centennial of the first trans-continental railroad in America, and to pay tribute to the Chinese workers of the Central Pacific Railroad whose indomitable courage made it possible" (*CHSA Bulletin*, May & June 1969). With wording by CHSA cofounder Thomas W. Chinn, translation and calligraphy by P. C. Lee, and design by Philip P. Choy, the plaque bears the legend "May 10, 1869–May 10, 1969 / Plaque placed by the Chinese Historical Society of America / Plaque donated by San Francisco Chinese Community."

History caught in rut

Gold Spike rites snub Chinese rail workers

by Ken Wong

OGDEN, Utah — Philip Choy, president of the Chinese Historical Society of America, and Thomas W. Chinn, executive director of the society, were burnt at the Golden Spike Centennial ceremonies last Saturday. They were burnt not by the blazing desert sun but by the National Gold Spike Centennial Commission ignoring the 12,000 Chinese who helped build the Central Pacific.

A hundred years ago, Chinese laborers helped conquer the Sierra Nevadas to link the Central Pacific with eastern tracks. They were forgotten men when the last spike was pounded at Promontory Point in 1869. Last weekend a century later, history repeated itself. The Chinese were out in left field once again.

WHO ELSE?

Only once during the three hour program were the Chinese mentioned and this was in passing, along with the roles played by the Indians, Irish, Mormons, and Negroes.

Great Leap Backward

Locomotives met again for spike ceremony at Promontory Summit

rived Choy found the society's spot on the program deleted with no prior explanation. The plaque dedi-

"Burnt by the national Gold Spike Centennial Commission ignoring the 12,000 Chinese who helped build the Central Pacific" (*East/West*, May 14, 1969; Philip P. Choy Collection, CHSA)

About the Contributors

Jeanie Dere was born in 1950 in San Francisco Chinatown at the Chinese Hospital and has spent her whole life in the San Francisco Bay Area. This volume publishes her autobiographical article, "A Wei Min Sister Remembers."

Harvey Dong graduated from UC Berkeley with a BA degree in 1972 and a PhD in ethnic studies in 2002. He was active in the Third World Liberation Front Strike at UC Berkeley and was also a member of the Asian American Political Alliance. He helped found the Asian Community Center in San Francisco Chinatown, the Chinatown Cooperative Garment Factory, and Everybody's Bookstore, and was active in immigrant labor organizing. He currently teaches Asian American Studies as a lecturer at UC Berkeley.

Diana Hong worked at Chinese for Affirmative Action before joining the *San Francisco Journal* as an editor and later general manager.

Composer **Jon Jang** has followed his own path of creating music that has become "two flowers on a stem," a metaphor expressing the symbiotic relationship of his cultural identity and musical aesthetics as an American-born Chinese. For two decades, Jang's works have chronicled and brought to life the Chinese immigration experience in the United States. His compositions include *Chinese American Symphony*; *Unbound Chinatown—A Tribute to Alice Fong Yu*; *Paper Son, Paper Songs*; *Island: the Immigrant Suite no. 2* for the Kronos Quartet and Cantonese Opera singers; and the score for the dramatic adaptation of Maxine Hong Kingston's *The Woman Warrior*. Jon and James Newton composed and performed *When Sorrow Turns to Joy—a Musical Tribute to Paul Robeson* to commemorate the anniversary of the World Peace Conference in 1949, and performed this work at the April 2004 Banlieues Bleues Festival in Paris. Jon Jang has been a visiting fellow at Stanford University and a lecturer at UC Berkeley and UC Irvine.

Him Mark Lai—*see About the Editorial Committee*

Ruthanne Lum McCunn—*see About the Editorial Committee*

Anna Naruta—*see About the Editorial Committee*

Roz Payne was born in 1940 in Paterson, New Jersey. She has a long family history of progressive activism. Her mother, Edith Berkman, was a union organizer during the 1932 textile strikes in Lawrence, Massachusetts. Called the "Red Flame," she was arrested a few times and spent two years in detention while the government tried to deport her to Poland, where she had been born. Roz Payne's father, James Cristiano, in 1932 ran for New Jersey State Senate on the same ticket with Norman Thomas, a founder of the precursor to the ACLU and later collaborator with Detroit labor leader Walter Ruether. Roz Payne attended Los Angeles High School and UCLA and in 1968 received her Masters in Art Education from CCNY. She notes, "The photo Yellow Peril Supports Black Power" (reproduced in this volume) is "my favorite photo of the thousands I have shot. I was always concerned with race and equality. In 1967, I was living in New York City, teaching school, when I was invited to attend the first meeting of the film group Newsreel. I loved working with film and began shooting events, covering many antiwar demonstrations, the Black Panthers, demonstrations in Chicago during the 1968 convention, the Young Lords, women's actions, and more. Newsreel started a chapter in San Francisco. I was visiting when the trial of Huey P. Newton opened in Oakland, and Newsreel filmed the demonstrations." Roz Payne lives in Vermont and teaches history at Burlington College. She has a daughter named Sierra and a granddaughter, Delia. More of Roz Payne's work is found at *www.newsreel.us*.

Chih-ming Wang graduated with a PhD in literature from UC Santa Cruz in 2006 and is an assistant research fellow at the Institute of European and American Studies, Academia Sinica, Taiwan. His research interests include Asian American literature, transnational cultural studies, diaspora activism, sports studies, and disciplinary history. He has published articles in *American Quarterly* and *Inter-Asia Cultural Studies* and is currently revising a book manuscript titled "Transpacific Articulations: Study Abroad and the Making of Asia/America."

Leland Wong's art has been part of the Bay area's Asian American community for more than thirty-seven years. Born in 1952, he grew up in San Francisco Chinatown, surrounded by art goods and curios sold in his family's business on Grant Avenue. The longstanding interest in art of his father, Fueng Wah Wong, greatly influenced Leland Wong, so that by the age of fourteen, he already sought to become an artist. Actively involved with printmaking and photography since high school, Wong first began designing posters and handbills for street fairs and local Chinese community events. These emerging interests led to his enrollment in San Francisco State University, where he earned a BFA in 1975. During the 1970s he also became involved with the Kearny Street Workshop, a Chinatown/Manilatown community art group, where he produced posters and conducted workshops in screen printing and photography. Wong designed his first Nihonmachi Street Fair poster at Kearny Street in 1974, inaugurating a highly popular series that has continued for nearly three decades, while simultaneously working on projects with various community service organizations. He remains active in the community as an artist, screen printer, and photographer. Leland Wong's prints and photography have been widely published and exhibited in both national and regional venues. Among them are the Corcoran Gallery (Washington, D.C.), San Francisco Museum of Modern Art, Oakland Museum of California, the de Young Museum, Children's Art Museum (Oakland), National Japanese American Historical Society, Asian Resource Gallery, Chinatown Community Arts Gallery, SOMARTS Gallery, and Chinese Culture Center.

William Wong is author of *Yellow Journalist: Dispatches from Asian America* (Temple University Press, 2001) and *Images of America: Oakland's Chinatown* (Arcadia Publishing Co., 2004), as well as coauthor of *Images of America: Angel Island* (Arcadia Publishing Co., 2007). He was a journalist for the *Wall Street Journal* and the *Oakland Tribune*; has written for other newspapers, including *East/West* and *Asian Week*; and was a regional commentator (1995–96) for the *News Hour* with Jim Lehrer on PBS.

Yolanda Garfias Woo, ethnographer, artist, and educator, is a San Francisco native. She is most widely known as the person who brought the Day of the Dead back northward to the United States. She started creating memorial altars (*ofrendas*) after the passing of her father and in 1961 began a series of public altars. Since her first major exhibition (de Young Museum, 1973), her work has been exhibited throughout Europe and North America, including at major Bay Area museums and the Smithsonian. With the painter Gary Woo, her husband and lifelong partner, she began exploring the Chinese influence on Mexican culture in a 1998 exhibit at the Encantada Gallery of Fine Art in San Francisco. In her most recent publication, *A Meeting of Two Souls: A Tribute to Gary Woo, a Painter's Painter* (San Francisco: CHSA with Oakland Museum of California and City Lights Foundation, 2008), she writes about the deep connections between Chinese and Mexican traditional cultures, connections demonstrated in the *ofrenda* for her husband.

Xiong Guohua was born in Xiangtan, Hunan province, in 1955 and received his master of arts degree from Xiangtan University in 1988. He is currently deputy head of the Chinese department of Guangdong College of Education and executive director of the Research Institute of Overseas Chinese Literature. He is active as a literary critic as well as the author of a number of award-winning poems.

Ellen Yeung, an instructor in the ESL Department of City College of San Francisco, is a published translator in Chinese American history, Chinese American literature, and modern Chinese literature.

About the Editorial Committee

Colleen Fong is professor of ethnic studies at California State University, East Bay. She received her doctorate in sociology from the University of Oregon in 1989. Her teaching and research interests lie in the contemporary and historical dimensions of family, gender, immigration, and interracial relationships. Her publications include "In Search of the Right Spouse: Interracial Marriage Among Chinese and Japanese Americans," *Amerasia Journal* 21 (1995–96) (coauthored with Judy Yung, and subsequently reprinted elsewhere), and reviews, in the *Journal of American Ethnic History*, of *Cultural Compass: Ethnographic Explorations of Asian America*, edited by Martin F. Manalansan IV (2001), and *On Gold Mountain: The One-Hundred-Year Odyssey of My Chinese-American Family*, by Lisa See (1998). She is completing an article-length manuscript with the working title "Establishing and Maintaining Chinese Immigrant Laborers' Families in the Shadow of Exclusion: The Gin Chow and Jin Fong Families of Santa Barbara County, California." Contact Colleen Fong at *colleen.fong@csueastbay.edu*.

Russell Jeung is an associate professor of Asian American Studies at San Francisco State University. He has authored *Faithful Generations: Race and New Asian American Churches* (New Brunswick, N.J.: Rutgers University Press, 2004) and several articles on Asian Americans and religion. He also is a community organizer in East Oakland, California, where he lives with his wife, Joan, and son, Matthew.

Him Mark Lai is adjunct professor of Asian American Studies at San Francisco State University and past Chinese Historical Society of America president. In 1969 he team-taught the first college-level course in the United States on Chinese American history at San Francisco State College (now San Francisco State University). He has compiled two bibliographies of Chinese-language materials on the Chinese in America and written books and essays on Chinese American history. Major works include *Island: Poetry and History of Chinese Immigrants on Angel Island, 1910–1940* (coauthored with Genny Lim and Judy Yung; San Francisco: HOC DOI, 1980); *Cong Huaqiao dao Huaren [From Overseas Chinese to Chinese American]* (Hong Kong, 1992); *Becoming Chinese American: A History of Communities and Institutions* (Walnut Creek, Calif.: Altamira Press, 2004); *Chinese American Voices from the Gold Rush to the Present* (coauthored with Judy Yung and Gordon H. Chang, Berkeley and Los Angeles: University of California Press, 2006); and articles on the history and society of Chinese in the United States in *Harvard Encyclopedia of American Ethnic Groups* (Cambridge, 1980) and the *Encyclopedia of Chinese Overseas* (Singapore, 1998). Contact Him Mark Lai at *hmlai@aol.com*.

Russell C. Leong, a recipient of the American Book Award and the PEN Josephine Miles Literature Award, is an adjunct professor of English and Asian American Studies at UCLA and the editor of UCLA's *Amerasia Journal*.

Laurene Wu McClain is a history professor at City College of San Francisco and a practicing attorney. She is the coauthor, with Charles J. McClain, of "The Chinese Contribution to the Development of American Law" in *Entry Denied: Exclusion and the Chinese Community in America, 1882–1943*, and coeditor of *California Legal History Manuscripts in the Huntington Library*. She edited "Breaking Racial Barriers: Wo Kee Company—A Collaboration Between a Chinese Immigrant and White American in Nineteenth-Century America" and "A Chinese American Woman's Plight during the Cultural Revolution" by Wen Zhengde for the 2005 volume of *Chinese America: History & Perspectives*, and authored "From Victims to Victors: A Chinese Contribution to American Law—Yick Wo versus Hopkins" for the 2003 volume. Her work has been published in both China and the United States. Contact Laurene Wu McClain at *lmcclain@ccsf.edu*.

Ruthanne Lum McCunn has been publishing books on the experiences of Chinese on both sides of the Pacific since 1979. Her books—which include *God of Luck, Thousand Pieces of Gold, Wooden Fish Songs, Sole Survivor, The Moon Pearl*, and *Chinese American Portraits*—have won critical acclaim and have been translated into eight languages and adapted for the stage and film. Contact Ruthanne Lum McCunn at *ruthanne@mccunn.com*.

Archivist and researcher **Anna Naruta** earned a PhD from the University of California, Berkeley for her work synthesizing the history and archaeology of California's early Chinatowns. A set of documents found in this research—and published at *UptownChinatown.org*—shows the relationship in California history between redevelopment projects and drives to dislocate or expel Chinese and Chinese American community members. She contributed "Activating Legal Protections for Archaeological Remains of Historic Chinatown Sites: Lessons Learned from Oakland, California," to CHSA's 2007 journal. As director of archives for the Chinese Historical Society of America through 2008, Naruta served as CHSA's lead curator and project manager for the society's exhibits *Earthquake: The Chinatown Story* (2006), *To Enjoy and Defend Our American Citizenship* (2007), *Glamour & Grace: The History and Culture of Miss Chinatown USA*, and *Remembering 1882: Fighting for Civil Rights in the Shadow of the Chinese Exclusion Act*, a traveling exhibit and companion website of primary source documents, research, and video: *Remembering1882.org*. She and Felicia Lowe created for CHSA the video short *Him Mark Lai: The Master Archivist* (*HimMarkLai.org*). Curator and project manager for CHSA's booklet series, Anna Naruta was also lead curator for *The Chinese of California* (2008), a collaborative exhibition by the Bancroft Library, the California Historical Society, and the Chinese Historical Society of America (*CivilRightsSuite.org*). Contact: *annanaruta.com*.

CHINESE AMERICA: HISTORY & PERSPECTIVES—
THE JOURNAL OF THE CHINESE
HISTORICAL SOCIETY OF AMERICA

Published annually since 1987

CHSA thanks Editorial Committee members past and present for their service!

Him Mark Lai (1985–present)

Judy Yung (1985–94, 1995–96)

Ruthanne Lum McCunn (1985–present)

Marlon K. Hom (1988–2006)

Ted S. Wong (1988)

Laurene Wu McClain (1990–present)

Colleen Fong (1992, 2000–present)

Lilian Louie (1993–2000)

Vitus Leung (1996–2000)

Madeline Hsu (1997–2005)

Beth Wilson (2001–3)

Lorraine Dong (2006)

Russell Jeung (2006–present)

Anna Naruta (2007–present)

Russell Leong (2008–present)

From Him Mark Lai, "Twenty Years of Chinese America: History & Perspectives," 2007:1–2. Year listed represents year of commencement of committee service, for the following year's volume.

Guidelines for Manuscript Submission

Chinese America: History & Perspectives—The Journal of the Chinese Historical Society of America is published annually by CHSA.

The journal invites original contributions on all aspects of Chinese American history and culture. The editorial committee encourages prospective authors to contact us to discuss suitability of manuscripts before submission.

For an author's checklist for submissions, or for more information, see *chsa.org/publications*, or email *journal@chsa.org*.

Manuscripts should not exceed five thousand words in length, excluding endnotes and captions, and should be formatted according to the CHSA style sheet, a modified version of the *Chicago Manual of Style*. Submitting relevant images is highly encouraged.

Manuscripts are accepted in Windows or Mac-compatible file (.doc or .rtf) as an email attachment to *journal@chsa.org*. Images may be submitted as separate attachments.

A few specific pointers:

- Avoid footnotes. All notes should be placed at the end of the article as endnotes.
- Do not use double spaces. Use only single spaces between sentences.

Contributors will be sent a copyedited proof for review before publication. Upon publication, contributors receive five complimentary copies of the journal.

Chinese Historical Society of America

Established January 5, 1963

965 Clay St. • San Francisco, CA 94108 • (415) 391-1188

MEMBERSHIP FORM

Please print.

❑ Check here if you added extended address information on back.

NAME _____
(*please circle*): Mrs. Ms. Mr. Dr.

ADDRESS _____ CITY_____

STATE _____ ZIP_____ COUNTRY _____

PHONE NUMBER_____

❑ Renewal Membership   ❑ New Membership

Membership and donations are **tax-deductible** as provided by federal tax laws. Membership expires December 31. Persons who join after September 30 are automatically members until December 31 of the *following* year. Please make checks payable to CHSA and send with this form, or join online at chsa.org.

❑ Regular (*individual*). . . . .$50   ❑ Institution (*group*) $100

❑ Senior (*age 60+*) . . . .$30   ❑ International (*outside USA*) $60

❑ Student (*now enrolled*) . . . .$30   ❑ Contributing $100

❑ Family . . . .$60   ❑ Sponsor $250

❑ Patron . . . .$500   ❑ President's Circle . . . . . over $1000

❑ Donation . . . . $ _____

❑ I want to help with (*please circle*): Docent Tours • Programs • Field Trips • Publications • Special Events • Museum Operations •

Other (*please specify*) _____

❑ I want to give (*please circle*): a gift membership to • a donation in memory of • a donation in honor of:

NAME _____

ADDRESS _____ CITY_____

STATE _____ ZIP_____ COUNTRY _____

CHSA will send a card to the honored or remembered or his/her family informing them of your gift.

CHSA
PUBLICATIONS

SPRING 2009 CATALOG

**CHINESE
HISTORICAL
SOCIETY OF
AMERICA**
Museum & Learning Center
965 Clay Street
San Francisco, CA 94108

(415) 391-1188 | bookstore@chsa.org

chsa.org | CivilRightsSuite.org

http://youtube.com/CHSAmuseum

CHINESE HISTORICAL SOCIETY of AMERICA

Museum & Learning Center
965 Clay Street
San Francisco, CA 94108

(415) 391-1188 I bookstore@chsa.org
chsa.org I CivilRightsSuite.org
http://youtube.com/CHSAmuseum

CREDITS

cover, page 9: James Leong's *History of the Chinese in America*, 1952, egg tempera and casein on masonite panels, 60 x 210 inches, restored by the artist in 2000, Chinese Historical Society of America Collection, 1999.3, Gift of Ping Yuen Tenants Association; Reproduced courtesy James Leong; Photo courtesy Sharon Spain, Stanford Asian American Art Project

page 4: Gary Woo's *Untitled [A/15]*; Reproduced courtesy of Yolanda Garfias Woo

page 6: Remington's "Chinese Must Go" cap gun, an 1882 patent by Connecticut's Charles Coester; CHSA, Gift of Jeffery P. Chan

page 7: Miss Chinatown USA 1958 June Gong; Courtesy June Gong Chin, L2007.8

page 9: Benjamen Chinn's *Untitled [Washington Street below Stockton, Chinatown, San Francisco]*, 1947, silver gelatin print; Reproduced courtesy of the photographer

page 12: Laura and Him Mark Lai, 1962; Reproduced courtesy Him Mark Lai, L2007.65

page 14: "East on Market St. from Grant Ave. N.S.G. [Native Sons of the Golden] West Parade. Sept. 10/23," Jesse Brown Cook Scrapbooks Documenting San Francisco History and Law Enforcement, ca. 1895-1936, Volume 17: 56a, BANC PIC 1996.003--fALB, The Bancroft Library, University of California, Berkeley.

Our American Citizenship flag portraits: (from upper left corner) Walter U. Lum, Virginia C. Gee, Dr. Theodore Lee, Nancy Gee; (second row) Kenneth Fung, Judge Samuel Yee, Francis Louie, Bea Wong; (third row) Leong Kow, S. K. Lai, Justice Harry Low, Y. C. Hong; Courtesy Chinese American Citizens Alliance Grand Lodge

CHSA Booklet series Curator & Project Manager: Anna Naruta, PhD, Director of Archives and Exhibits, CHSA; Art Direction & Design © Jeff Mellin, Big Blue Ox.

CHSA Journal Design & Publishing Services: Side by Side Studios

CHSA Publications *Spring 2009 Catalog* Art Direction & Design © 2009 Jeff Mellin jeffmellin.com

© 2009 Chinese Historical Society of America. All rights reserved.

Established in San Francisco in 1963, CHSA is a 501(c)(3) non-profit operating under Federal Tax ID #94-6122446

TABLE OF CONTENTS

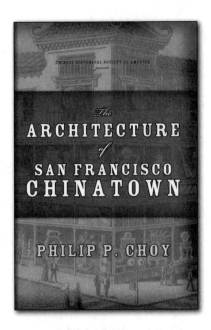

**San Francisco:
Chinese Historical
Society of America
2008
48 pages
color
5.5"x8.5"
saddle-stapled
ISBN: 978-1-885864-38-3
$7**

"Present-day visitors to
Chinatown see it only as
an unassimilated foreign
community where
cultural traditions are
preserved and where
the architectural forms
are mere transplants
from China. Transfixed
by cultural exotics,
few see that the social
history of the community
is intimately interwoven
with its architecture."

— PHILIP P. CHOY,

     *THE ARCHITECTURE OF SAN
     FRANCISCO CHINATOWN*

The Architecture of San Francisco Chinatown

BY PHILIP P. CHOY

**The seminal study by Phil Choy, with a new
selection of images from the CHSA Museum and
the Philip P. Choy Collection, and updated with
recent discoveries**

ABOUT THE AUTHOR

Philip P. Choy was born and raised in San Francisco
Chinatown. A retired architect, Choy is a renowned authority
on California and Chinese American history and historical
sites. He has served on the San Francisco Landmarks Board,
the San Francisco Museum and Historical Society Advisory
Committee, and the California State Historical Resources
Commission.

When the Angel Island Immigration Station – today a museum
– was slated for demolition, he served on the Chinese Cove
Historical Advisory Committee to develop the preservation of
the historic site and the poetry-inscribed walls of the detention
barracks. In 1993 he prepared the case report that placed the
Station on the National Registry of Historic Places.

With Him Mark Lai and Thomas W. Chinn, he co-edited *A
History of the Chinese in California – A Syllabus* (San Francisco:
Chinese Historical Society of America, 1969), a reference work
based on their identification and analysis of a wide range of
historic documents, and which was prepared in response
to popular and institutional demand for accurate historical
information. Philip P. Choy and Him Mark Lai then co-taught the
nation's first college-level course in Chinese American history.

He has created or consulted on numerous historical studies,
publications, traveling and permanent exhibits, and media
projects. With Him Mark Lai, Choy researched and produced
Outlines: History of the Chinese in America (first edition
1971); *Journeys Made...Journeys to Come: A Pictorial
History of the Chinese in America* (2001), and, as a KRON
six-part television series, the early masterwork documentary,
Gam Saan Haak – The Chinese of America (http://www.
youtube.com/user/CHSAmuseum). 2007 saw the first
publication of his new book-length study, *Canton Footprints:
Sacramento's Chinese Legacy.*

**San Francisco:
Chinese Historical Society
of America with
Oakland Museum of
California and
City Lights Foundation
2008
68 pages
color, 5.5"x8.5"
saddle-stapled
ISBN: 978-1-885864-39-0
$7**

"For me life begins with a line. Or a stroke of a brush/pen."

– GARY WOO

"Very few can pursue art so relentlessly. A painter's painter."

– AMALIA MESA-BAINS, PHD,
   CO-CHAIR, CSU MONTEREY
   BAY SCHOOL OF VISUAL AND
   PUBLIC ART
   MACARTHUR FELLOW

A Meeting of Two Souls: A Tribute to Gary Woo, A Painter's Painter

BY YOLANDA GARFIAS WOO

In this multifaceted work, traditional artist and ethnographer Yolanda Garfias Woo shares about the deep connections between Chinese and Mexican traditional cultures, shown in the ofrenda for her husband, the painter Gary Woo.

"I paint to live," wrote Gary Woo wrote in a vibrant, near-calligraphic script in a handmade book describing his directions in research into balance, turbulence, art, and the cosmos. His 1960 de Young Museum solo exhibition described by the *San Francisco Chronicle's* preeminent art critic Alfred Frankenstein as "a many-sided, ripe, and totally rewarding fusion of Eastern and Western ways in art," "fusion" here must be restored to its atomic-age meaning: adding considered, nearly-overpowering yet focused energy to the most basic, elemental particles – for Gary Woo, line and color – and releasing an entirely new state of being, tied to and yet beyond only human scale.

No wonder new generations are again recognizing Gary Woo's central place among the most groundbreaking exploratory abstract expressionist painters. No wonder artists and viewers alike are excited about the courses he's charted. We now have new directions to explore in developing technique and new pathways for seeing the infinite wonder of our relation in the world.

Herself an artist and educator, his wife and lifelong partner Yolanda Garfias Woo shares the multi-world perspectives of a deeply rooted Chinese American experience, and the new and innovative explorations made possible by deep study of traditional cultural forms and their enactment by the ancestors before us.

Following the 50-year retrospective of Gary Woo's work in 2004 with *A Meeting of Two Souls*, the Chinese Historical Society of America continues to join with scholars and culture-bearers to document and make accessible to the public these essential works, as part of CHSA's work creating broad-based conversations exploring the experiences of Chinese Americans and the Chinese legacy of the United States.

CHSA is joined by the Oakland Museum of California and City Lights Foundation in this publication on the occasion of this 2008-2009 celebration of the life and work of groundbreaking painter Gary Woo.

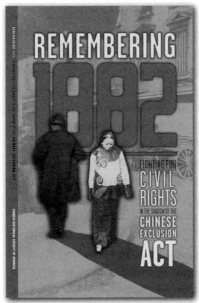

San Francisco:
Chinese Historical Society
of America
2007
36 pages
color, 5.5"x8.5"
saddle-stapled
ISBN: 978-1-885864-34-5
NAPABA edition
$5

"It is impossible to preserve the integrity of a government like ours if we deny to any class in our community the equal protection of the laws."

—   PATRICK J. HEALY AND
     NG POON CHEW, 1905,
     A STATEMENT FOR NON-
     EXCLUSION

Remembering 1882: Fighting for Civil Rights in the Shadow of the Chinese Exclusion Act

FEATURING "UP AGAINST THE LAW," THE GROUNDBREAKING HISTORY BY CONNIE YOUNG YU

In 1882 Congress passed the nations first major immigration legislation – a law to prevent people of Chinese descent from entering the United States. The law would tear apart families, cut the nation's Chinese American population in half, and remove from people of Chinese descent the right to become citizens.

Remembering 1882 explores the historical debate around the Chinese Exclusion Act from its origins through its full repeal in 1968, the civil rights struggle of Chinese Americans and allies, and the historic importance of *habeas corpus* in the Chinese American community.

CHSA's *Remembering 1882* booklet includes a legislative timeline of the Chinese Exclusion Act, outlining the challenges legalized against people of Chinese descent in the U.S., from the 1868 signing of the Burlingame Treaty to formally recognize "the inherent and inalienable right of man to change his home and allegiance," through the increasingly discriminatory laws of the 20th century to the final repeal of the Chinese Exclusion Act in 1968.

The *Remembering 1882* booklet is also available as a free download at the Remembering 1882 Online Reading Room. View videos, articles, historic texts, and photos at Remembering1882.org | CivilRightsSuite.org

ABOUT THE AUTHOR

Honored as a 2008 KQED Bay Area Local Hero, Connie Young Yu is a historian; member of the board of the Chinese Historical Society of America; invited discussant of the 2008 Society for Historical Archaeology's special journal issue on archaeology about Chinese Americans; and author of the remarkable account of the post-1882 explusions and alliances in San Jose's Heinlenville, the new Chinatown where

"We have yet to learn the lessons from history. Pandering xenophobia in the 19th century is repeated in our 21st century. Only the targeted group is different."

— PHILIP P. CHOY

the original Chinatown community members who had just suffered an arson and a German immigrant family who stood up against the exclusionist forces in their town together created a new multicultural community that yet survives as today's Japantown, one of only three remaining in the U.S. Like *Chinatown, San Jose, USA* (History San José, 2001), the *Remembering 1882* booklet shows Connie Young Yu's signature approach to history, a captivating lyricism in sharing stories supported by meticulous research and attention to evocative historical detail.

Connie Young Yu's "Up Against the Law" originally appeared in *Bulletin of Concerned Asian Scholars*, Vol. 4 No. 3, special issue editors Victor and Brett Nee, Connie Young Yu, and Shawn Hsu Wong, 1972. This new edition, with original title restored, premieres a new selection of images from the CHSA Museum.

Glamour & Grace: The History & Culture of Miss Chinatown USA

For a half century San Francisco has been captivated by the grace, glamour and exuberance of the Miss Chinatown pageant.

In the pageant tradition, contestants, family, and friends serve as ambassadors of Chinese American heritage and culture, drawing attention to San Francisco Chinatown and other home communities as they spread goodwill throughout the Bay Area and beyond. Join the Chinese Historical Society of America in an affectionate and fun-filled look at the glitz, substance and significance of this favorite community tradition.

This CHSA booklet features images contributed by former participants and supporters, and, through the generous donation of Karen Jue Iovino and Calvin Jue, the Harry Jew photographic collection of the CHSA Museum.

**San Francisco:
Chinese Historical Society
of America
2007
32 pages
color, 5.5"x8.5"
saddle-stapled
ISBN: 978-1-885864-33-8
$5**

"The Cold War was really a tough time. To this day, whenever I see the word 'Chinese', I always look to see if it's going to be negative. I still do. …The reason that my dad did the War Memorial [in St. Mary's Square] – my mom told me later – is because…. the Japanese went to the internment camps… the Chinese were preparing to fight Americans in the Cold War. Where would that put Chinese Americans?"

— **CONNIE YOUNG YU**

View photos, video, and history at GlamourandGrace.org

SELECTIONS FROM
ART Catalogs

OF THE CHINESE HISTORICAL SOCIETY OF AMERICA MUSEUM & LEARNING CENTER

Jade Snow Wong:
A Retrospective

BY MAXINE HONG KINGSTON, KATHLEEN HANNA, JADE SNOW WONG, AND FORREST L. MERRILL

Full color, collector's cloth edition with dust jacket and illustrated endpapers

**San Francisco: Chinese Historical Society of America, 2002
full color, hardbound, dustjacket
ISBN 10: 1-885864-14-0
$30**

The Art of Win Ng:
A Retrospective

BY ALLEN R. HICKS

with more than 60 color images.

**San Francisco: Chinese Historical Society of America, 2005
color, softcover
ISBN 10: 1-885-864-25-6
$5**

A Meeting of Two Souls: A Tribute to Gary Woo, A Painter's Painter
BY YOLANDA GARFIAS WOO (San Francisco: Chinese Historical Society of America with Oakland Museum of California and City Lights Foundation, 2008) See page 4

Dong Kingman in San Francisco

Includes:

"When I was Born in San Francisco" by Dong Kingman

"America's Dong Kingman—Dong Kingman's America" by Stanford University's Gordon Chang, and essays by painters James Leong, Keith Morrison, and SF MoMA Director Harry S. Parker III.

San Francisco: Chinese Historical Society of America, 2001
34 color plates, softcover
ISBN 10: 1-885864-36-1
$15

Benjamen Chinn at Home in San Francisco

Featuring selections of the artist's black and white photos, 1946-50, plus his 1952 cover of the Paris art world publication, *Aperture*. Photographic artist Benjamen Chinn studied under Ansel Adams, Edward Weston, Dorthea Lange, and, in Paris, the sculptor Giacometti.

Includes "My Friend and Teacher" by photographer Paul Caponigro.

San Francisco: Chinese Historical Society of America, 2003
saddle-stapled
ISBN 10: 1-885864-16-7
$5

James Leong's *History of the Chinese in America* (detail), 1952 mural, 60" x 210", Chinese Historical Society of America Collection, 1999.3

James Leong: Confronting My Roots

Featuring the painter's memoir of his time in the Beat scene of 1950s San Francisco; the local provincialism that led him to live and work the next three decades as an expat in Europe (to the great success of his career); the experience of listening, in Italy, to the reports of the 1989 Tiananmen Square protests and violent repression; and his subsequent return to the U.S. and the reincorporation of his roots.

San Francisco: Chinese Historical Society of America, 2006
saddle-stapled
ISBN 10: 1-885864-30-2
$5

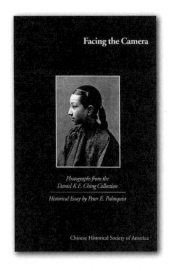

Facing the Camera: Photographs from the Daniel K. E. Ching Collection

BY PETER E. PALMQUIST

Featuring "In Splendid Detail", a thoroughly researched and inspired interpretative essay on the history of Chinese American photography in San Francisco and beyond, 1860s-onward.

**San Francisco: Chinese Historical Society of America: 2001
saddle-stapled
ISBN 10: 1-885864-13-2
$5**

Remembering C.C. Wang

Innovative work in the Chinese landscape and calligraphy traditions.

**San Francisco: Chinese Historical Society of America: 2005
20 pages
7 color plates
saddle-stapled
ISBN 10: 1-885864-28-0
$5**

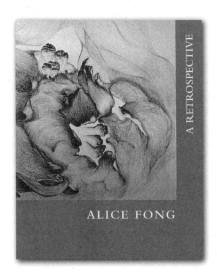

Alice Fong: A Retrospective

Traveling in Indonesia, Thailand, Turkey, China, Japan, Australia, and Paupa New Guinea (a photo of Alice with two Huli Wig Men is a favorite), influences from artists working in traditional cultures come across in her sensitive and exploratory works in an impressively successful number of media. An autobiographical essay enriches the artist's own works in this catalogue, rendered all the more vivid and touching with the accompaniment of family and historical photos from growing up as a Chinese American female in the early twentieth century.

**San Francisco: Chinese Historical Society of America: 2007
80 pages, full color
softcover
ISBN 10: 1-885864-32-9
$15**

San Francisco:
Chinese Historical Society
of America and the
Him Mark Lai Birthday Party
Planning Committee
2007
24 pages,
color, 5.5"x8.5"
saddle-stapled
ISBN: 978-1-885864-41-3
$3

Celebrating Him Mark Lai: The Dean of Chinese American Historians Birthday Party booklet

麥禮謙生日會紀念冊

FEATURING

讓歷史告訴未來 — 美國華人歷史學家麥禮謙
黃運基撰 〈時代報〉（中文）
"Bringing History Forward – Him Mark Lai, Dean
of Chinese American History" by Maurice Chuck,
San Francisco Journal editor (In Chinese)

"Him Mark Lai – A Tribute to the Dean of
Chinese American History"
L. Ling-chi Wang, professor emeritus, University
of California, Berkeley (In English)
王靈智撰
加州大學柏克萊（英文）

麥禮謙小傳
區維業撰 〈星島日報〉（中文，英文）
"A Brief Biography of Him Mark Lai"
by Weiye Ou, correspondent and editor of *Sing
Tao Daily* (In English and Chinese)
Translation by Piera Kwan

PLUS TESTIMONIALS FROM:

中国华侨历史学会（中文，英文）
National Society for the Study of Chinese
Overseas, Beijing, China (In English and Chinese)
Translation by Danian Lu
Nancy Pelosi, Speaker of the House, United
States House of Representatives (In English)
and a selection of Him Mark and Laura Lai's own photos

ABOUT HIM MARK LAI

Proclaimed by *The Chronicle of Higher Education* as "the Scholar who legitimized the study of Chinese America," Him Mark Lai has been at the core of many community institutions as well as a pivotal figure for the Chinese Historical Society of America.

Born in San Francisco in 1925 to immigrant parents, Him Mark Lai's trailblazing accomplishments are many and varied. In 1969 with Phil Choy he team-taught the first college-level course in the United States on Chinese American history at San Francisco State College (now San Francisco State University), before moving on to teach the first course at the University of California, Berkeley. He has compiled two bibliographies on Chinese language materials on the Chinese in America and wrote books and essays on Chinese American history. His major works include: *Island: Poetry and History of Chinese Immigrants on Angel Island, 1910–1940* (coauthor with Genny Lim and Judy Yung; San Francisco: HOC DOI, 1980); *Cong Huaqiao dao Huaren [From Overseas Chinese to Chinese American]* (in Chinese; Hong Kong, 1992), *Becoming Chinese American: A History of Communities and Institutions* (Walnut Creek, CA: Altamira Press, 2004); *Chinese American Voices from the Gold Rush to the Present* (coauthor with Judy Yung and Gordon H. Chang, Berkeley: University of California Press, 2006), as well as articles on the history and society of Chinese in the United States in *Harvard Encyclopedia of American Ethnic Groups* (Cambridge, 1980) and *The Encyclopedia of Chinese Overseas* (Singapore, 1998). He has consulted on the special collections of and in 2000 made a major

donation of his research files to the Ethnic Studies Library of UC Berkeley. He has served as an adjunct professor of Asian American Studies at San Francisco State University and past president of the Chinese Historical Society of America. An integral part of the Editorial Committee of the Society's journal since its inception in 1987, Him Mark Lai also currently has multiple books in prep and in press.

The *Celebrating Him Mark Lai* Birthday Party booklet is also available as a free online feature at HimMarkLai.org. Through the HimMarkLai.org project, the Chinese Historical Society of America aims to bring awareness and understanding of the depth of Him Mark Lai's contributions to Chinese American history and create an interface for people worldwide to be able to access, learn from, and work with Him Mark Lai's groundbreaking scholarship.

San Francisco: Chinese
Historical Society of America
1969
Softcover, includes
diagrams and maps
ISBN 10: 0-9614198-0-6
$10

A History of the Chinese in California: A Syllabus

BY THOMAS W. CHINN, HIM MARK LAI, AND PHILIP P. CHOY.

Created in the wake of the widespread student strikes of 1968, in response to popular and institutional demand for accurate historical information, the rigorous attention to accurate scholarship and primary sources has made this volume a reference work of unparalleled value to this day.

Coauthors Him Mark Lai and Philip P. Choy would then bring their signature method of identification and analysis of a wide range of historic documents to teaching the nation's first college-level courses in Chinese American history.

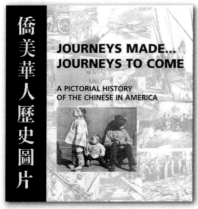

San Francisco: Chinese
Historical Society of America
2001
images, with guiding text in
English and Chinese.
Softcover
11x11¼"
illustrated
ISBN 10: 1-885864-12-4
$10

Journeys Made... Journeys to Come: A Pictorial History of the Chinese in America

This lavishly illustrated catalog is the History of the Chinese in California told in an artful combination of reproductions of historic photos and documents.

"Past historians have generally presented the history of the United States and its expansion purely from a Eurocentric perspective. The Chinese of America did not exist, or if they did, they were portrayed as a population unfit to become Americans. *Journeys Made...Journeys to Come* documents that the presence of Chinese in America was not due to the benevolence of the United States. Instead, it tells of the struggle and perseverance of thousands of Chinese who participated in the building of the American West against insurmountable odds. It is the story of generations of Chinese denied their inalienable rights. Their legacy is indelibly rooted in the landscape of the American West."

— PHILIP P. CHOY, JOURNEYS MADE, PREFACE

To Enjoy and Defend Our American Citizenship bookmark

A color bookmark featuring a quote from Y.C. Hong, with selected milestones on reverse

TO ENJOY AND DEFEND OUR AMERICAN CITIZENSHIP

In the 1880s, the federal government passes legislation that removes the equal protection under the law provided by the 14th Amendment to the Constitution. Racial discrimination and violent attacks intensify throughout the next decades, and community members face the challenge of organizing to fight for basic human rights.

Join CHSA in exploring the experiences of the Chinese American Citizens Alliance in their groundbreaking work alongside groups such as the NAACP to challenge discriminatory laws and create the support systems necessary for survival in a segregated United States.

OurAmericanCitizenship.org | CivilRightsSuite.org

ISBN: 978-1-885864-42-0
20¢ each
8 bookmarks for $1
100 for $10

San Francisco: Chinese Historical Society of America
2008
100 pages
illustrated
8.5"x11"
softcover
ISBN: 978-1-885864-35-2
$20

"The long history of Chinese immigrant and Chinese American workers organizing in guilds and labor unions – in California, from the Gold Rush to the building of the transcontinental railroad and onwards – has been obscured in the decades following the passage of the Chinese Exclusion Act of 1882. ... Today most labor historians are completely unaware of this major part of labor history's existence. This volume is part of correcting that record."

Chinese America: History & Perspectives – The Journal of the Chinese Historical Society of America

SPECIAL ISSUE: LABOR AND SAN FRANCISCO'S GARMENT INDUSTRY

ABOUT THE COVER PHOTO:

Lai Family portrait, 1946. Bing Lai and his wife, Dong Shee Lai (Dong Hing Mui), raised three sons and two daughters while working their whole careers as garment workers in Chinatown factories. Eldest child Him Mark Lai (standing behind parents) worked as a general helper from 1942 to 1946, and while the pay was meager – 25 cents per hour – his garment-shop earnings helped pay for his college education. Him Mark Lai's article "Chinese Guilds in the Apparel Industry of San Francisco" (this volume) describes his family's involvement in the Garment Workers' Guild, Gam Yee Hong, the roots of which trace back to the 1870s, according to oldtimers. Dong Shee Lai was one of the few female members accepted to apprenticeship in the guild. (Courtesy Him Mark Lai)

INCLUDES:

INTRODUCTION – LABOR AND SAN FRANCISCO'S GARMENT INDUSTRY

GUILDS, UNIONS AND GARMENT FACTORIES
Notes on Chinese in the Apparel Industry
Him Mark Lai and Russell Jeung

SCENES FROM THE GARMENT INDUSTRY BEYOND SAN FRANCISCO, LATE 1800s-EARLY 1900s
Beyond San Francisco

CHINESE LABOR UNIONS IN AMERICA [1896]
Walter N. Fong, with introductory note by Him Mark Lai

CHINESE GUILDS IN THE APPAREL INDUSTRY OF SAN FRANCISCO
Him Mark Lai

Signboard of the Garment Workers' Guild, Gam Yee Hong (Cantonese), or Jinyi Hang (Mandarin); CHSA, Gift of Park Hong Ng and Him Mark Lai

San Francisco:
Chinese Historical Society
of America
2009
illustrated
8.5"x11"
softcover
ISBN: 978-1-885864-40-6
$20

Chinese America: History & Perspectives – The Journal of the Chinese Historical Society of America

SPECIAL ISSUE: SEIZING THE MOMENT: TWENTIETH CENTURY CHINESE AMERICAN ACTIVISM

A complimentary copy of the year's journal is one benefit of becoming a member of CHSA. Sign up and join us for the launch in 2009!

ABOUT THE IMAGE:

Ruthanne Lum McCunn purchased this poster from San Francisco State College's Campus Book Store in 1968. A graduate student training to teach in inner city schools, Ruthanne was enrolled in a special program that held classes off campus in Sausalito. At the start of the Third World Student Strike, students and faculty in the program voted unanimously to halt methodology classes as a demonstration of solidarity with the strikers but to maintain student-teaching commitments.

Ruthanne and her husband, Don, were then living in the 1400 block of Sacramento Street in San Francisco. Unwittingly, they had rented in a "whites-only" building. When Ruthanne's Chinese relatives from Hong Kong came to stay, the building's Irish manager accused her and Don of signing the lease "under false pretenses" and ordered them to leave. Refusing, they taped this poster on their apartment's frosted-glass front door so that until their lease expired, renters and visitors in the building's hallway could not avoid seeing "Yellow Power." Ironically, the "whites-only" policy was that of the Chinese owner, who believed it would command higher rents. (Courtesy Ruthanne Lum McCunn)

A special volume on the fortieth anniversary of a wealth of activism in the San Francisco Bay Area and beyond

INCLUDES:

Introduction – Seizing the Moment: Twentieth Century Chinese American Activism
A special volume on the fortieth anniversary of a wealth of activism in the San Francisco Bay Area and beyond

Chinese Communists in the United States during the 1920s and 1930s, a memoir
Zhang Bao, translation and annotations by Him Mark Lai

Life and Times of Benjamin Fee
Him Mark Lai

Selections from *Collected Poems of Mu-yün [Ben Fee]*, with introductory note by the author
English translations by Ellen Yeung and Him Mark Lai

China Books and Periodicals: Extracts from the autobiography *China Born*
Henry Noyes

The Changing Roles Played by China Books and Periodicals
Him Mark Lai

***East/West*: The Chinese American Journal**
William Wong

A "Landmark": History of Chinese Californians by Chinese Californians, 1969
Anna Naruta

Yellow Power 1968
Ruthanne Lum McCunn

A Wei Min Sister Remembers
Jean Dere

Third World Liberation Comes to San Francisco State and University of California Berkeley
Harvey Dong

Taking to the Streets – Scenes from 1968-72

Art and Living Revolution
Gary Woo and AION Magazine
Yolanda Garfias Woo

A Bookstore for Everybody
Harvey Dong, with photos by Steve Louie

Scenes from the *Baodiao* Movement in the U.S.

Tracking *Baodiao*: Diaspora, Sovereignty, and Asia/America
Chih-ming Wang

Maurice H. Chuck and *The San Francisco Journal*: Promoting U.S.-China Friendship and Relevant Asian American Issues
[translated by Diana Hong from a chapter in *Xiong Guohua, An American dream: The life and times of Huang Yunji (Maurice H. Chuck), Chinese American]* With an introductory note by Him Mark Lai and photos courtesy Maurice Chuck

The Making of the *Chinese American Symphony*
Jon Jang

PLUS MORE AUTHENTIC DOCUMENTS AND PHOTOS SHARING THE STORIES OF THIS WIDESPREAD COMMUNITY ACTIVISM!

CHSA PUBLICATIONS ORDER FORM

Please indicate how many of each title you wish to order, and complete the payment and shipping form. Contact bookstore@chsa.org to inquire about quantity discounts.

CHSA BOOKLETS

___ THE ARCHITECTURE OF SAN FRANCISCO CHINATOWN by Philip P. Choy ($7)

___ A MEETING OF TWO SOULS: A TRIBUTE TO GARY WOO, A PAINTER'S PAINTER by Yolanda Garfias Woo (CHSA with Oakland Museum of California and City Lights Foundation) ($7)

___ REMEMBERING 1882: FIGHTING FOR CIVIL RIGHTS IN THE SHADOW OF THE CHINESE EXCLUSION ACT featuring "Up Against the Law" by Connie Young Yu ($5)

___ CELEBRATING HIM MARK LAI: THE DEAN OF CHINESE AMERICAN HISTORIANS 麥禮謙生日會紀念冊 (CHSA with the Him Mark Lai Birthday Party Planning Committee) ($3)

___ GLAMOUR & GRACE: THE HISTORY & CULTURE OF MISS CHINATOWN USA ($5)

ILLUSTRATED EXHIBIT CATALOG

___ JOURNEYS MADE...JOURNEYS TO COME: A PICTORIAL HISTORY OF THE CHINESE IN AMERICA ($10)

SELECTED ART CATALOGS

___ JADE SNOW WONG: A RETROSPECTIVE by Maxine Hong Kingston, Kathleen Hanna, Jade Snow Wong, and Forrest L. Merrill ($30, hardbound with dust jacket)

___ THE ART OF WIN NG: A RETROSPECTIVE by Allen R. Hicks ($5)

___ DONG KINGMAN IN SAN FRANCISCO with essays by Dong Kingman, Gordon Chang, James Leong, Keith Morrison, and Harry S. Parker III ($15)

___ BENJAMEN CHINN AT HOME IN SAN FRANCISCO with essay by photographer Paul Caponigro ($5)

CORE REFERENCE WORK

___ A HISTORY OF THE CHINESE IN CALIFORNIA: A SYLLABUS by Thomas W. Chinn, Him Mark Lai, and Philip P. Choy ($10)

___ JAMES LEONG: CONFRONTING MY ROOTS ($5)

___ A MEETING OF TWO SOULS: A TRIBUTE TO GARY WOO, A PAINTER'S PAINTER by Yolanda Garfias Woo (CHSA with Oakland Museum of California and City Lights Foundation) ($7)

___ FACING THE CAMERA: PHOTOGRAPHS FROM THE DANIEL K. E. CHING COLLECTION by Peter E. Palmquist ($5)

___ REMEMBERING C.C. WANG ($5)

___ ALICE FONG: A RETROSPECTIVE ($15)

CHINESE AMERICA: History & Perspectives
The Journal of the Chinese Historical Society of America

Published annually since 1987
Volumes 1987-1997 are 6"x9" perfectbound.
Volumes 1998-present are 8.5"x11" perfectbound.

TABLE OF CONTENTS BY ISSUE:
www.chsa.org/uploads/hp_journal/chsa_hp_article_listing.pdf
www.scribd.com/doc/3223000/CHSA-Journal-article-list-19872007

A complimentary copy of the year's journal is one benefit of becoming a member of CHSA!

Issues $10 each, except most recent three volumes:

___ 1987
(sold out) 1988
(sold out) 1989
(sold out) 1990
(sold out) 1991
(sold out) 1992
___ 1993
___ 1994
___ 1995
___ 1996
(sold out) 1997
___ 1998
___ 1999
___ 2000
___ 2001
(sold out) 2002

(sold out) 2003
___ 2004
___ 2005
___ 2006

(sold out) 2007
special issue:
Conference
proceedings ($20)

___ 2008
special issue:
"Labor and San
Francisco's
Garment
Industry" ($20)

___ 2009
special issue:
"Seizing the
Moment:
Twentieth Century
Chinese American
Activism" – a
special volume
on the fortieth
anniversary of a
wealth of activism
in the San
Francisco Bay
Area and beyond
(forthcoming in
2009; $20)

BOOKMARK

___ TO ENJOY AND DEFEND OUR AMERICAN CITIZENSHIP BOOKMARK (8 for $1, 100 for $10; inquire for further quantity discounts)

MEMBERSHIP

___ **YES! I WANT TO SUPPORT CHSA AS A MEMBER!** I'll also receive a complementary copy of the current year's journal at the launch event or at the mailing address I provide.

___ INDIVIDUAL $50

___ STUDENT/EDUCATOR $30
(inclose copy of current id)

___ SENIOR $30

___ FAMILY $60

___ CONTRIBUTING $100

___ SPONSOR $250

___ PATRON $500

___ PRESIDENT'S CIRCLE $1,000

___ Please double my contribution with my employer's matching program

---

SUBTOTAL $_____

___ CA residents add 8.5% sales tax on items except membership $_____

___ Standard shipping within US (media mail) $5 first item, $1 each additional item $_____

___ Expedited shipping within US (priority mail) $10 first item, $2 each additional item $_____

___ Shipping outside the US, add $15 $_____

TOTAL AMOUNT DUE $_____

We accept payment in the form of check or credit card. Make checks payable to "CHSA."

NAME:_____

STREET ADDRESS:_____

CITY:_____ **STATE:**_____ **ZIP:**_____

CREDIT CARD NUMBER:_____ ❏ VISA / ❏ MC **EXP. DATE:**_____

PHONE #: (____) _____-_____ CARDHOLDER SIGNATURE: _____

PLEASE SEND COMPLETED ORDER FORM BY
FAX: (415) 391-1150
EMAIL: bookstore@chsa.org
or MAIL: CHINESE HISTORICAL SOCIETY OF AMERICA
Museum & Learning Center
965 Clay Street, San Francisco, CA 94108

CHSA THANKS YOU for your support of broad-based and historically-grounded explorations of the experiences of Chinese Americans and the Chinese legacy of the United States!